Making Democracy Safe for Business

Businesses in the Middle East and North Africa have failed to bring sustainable development despite decades of investment from the private and public sectors. Yet we still know little about why the Arab Uprisings failed to usher in more transparent government that could break this enduring cycle of corruption and mismanagement. Examining post-transition politics in Egypt and Tunisia, Kubinec employs interviews and quantitative surveys to map out the corrupting influence of businesses on politics. He argues that businesses must respond to changes in how perks and privileges are distributed after political transitions, either by forming political coalitions or creating new informal connections to emerging politicians. Employing detailed case studies and original experiments, *Making Democracy Safe for Business* advances our empirical understanding of the study of the durability of corruption in general and the dismal results of the Arab Uprisings in particular.

Robert Kubinec is an assistant professor of political science at New York University Abu Dhabi. He was formerly a postdoctoral fellow at Princeton University and a diplomat with the US Consulate in Saudi Arabia. His writing has appeared in *The Washington Post, The Brookings Institution,* and *The Carnegie Endowment for International Peace.*

Making Democracy Safe for Business
Corporate Politics During the Arab Uprisings

ROBERT KUBINEC
New York University Abu Dhabi

Shaftesbury Road, Cambridge CB2 8EA, United Kingdom

One Liberty Plaza, 20th Floor, New York, NY 10006, USA

477 Williamstown Road, Port Melbourne, VIC 3207, Australia

314–321, 3rd Floor, Plot 3, Splendor Forum, Jasola District Centre, New Delhi – 110025, India

103 Penang Road, #05–06/07, Visioncrest Commercial, Singapore 238467

Cambridge University Press is part of Cambridge University Press & Assessment, a department of the University of Cambridge.

We share the University's mission to contribute to society through the pursuit of education, learning and research at the highest international levels of excellence.

www.cambridge.org
Information on this title: www.cambridge.org/9781009273527

DOI: 10.1017/9781009273541

© Robert Kubinec 2023

This publication is in copyright. Subject to statutory exception and to the provisions of relevant collective licensing agreements, no reproduction of any part may take place without the written permission of Cambridge University Press & Assessment.

First published 2023

A catalogue record for this publication is available from the British Library.

ISBN 978-1-009-27352-7 Hardback

Cambridge University Press & Assessment has no responsibility for the persistence or accuracy of URLs for external or third-party internet websites referred to in this publication and does not guarantee that any content on such websites is, or will remain, accurate or appropriate.

For Elyse

Contents

List of Figures		*page* ix
List of Tables		xi
Acknowledgments		xiii
Data Availability Statement		xv
	Introduction	1
	Militaries, Business, and Democracy	5
1	How Firms Respond to Regime Change	8
	1.1 Corruption in Developing Countries	11
	1.2 The Outcome: Business Political Engagement Following Transitions	14
	1.3 The Causes of Business Political Engagement	18
	1.4 Combined Causal Process	28
	1.5 Observable Implications of the Theory	30
	1.6 The Model in a Nutshell	34
	1.7 Alternative Explanations	38
	1.8 How to Test the Theory	39
2	Case Study: The Egyptian Military as the Gatekeeper	46
	2.1 Evidentiary Basis	48
	2.2 Historical Political Economy in Egypt	49
	2.3 The Arab Spring	55
	2.4 Democratic Elections	58
	2.5 Business Discontent	60
	2.6 Military Coup	62
	2.7 Strong Business Coalition	66
	2.8 Conclusion	75

viii   *Contents*

3   Case Study: Broad Rent-Seeking and the Collapse
     of Tunisia's Antidemocratic Coalition   77
     3.1 Historical Political Economy in Tunisia   78
     3.2 Regime Transition: The Arab Spring   83
     3.3 Democratic Elections   85
     3.4 Business Discontent   86
     3.5 Coalition Fracturing   90
     3.6 Plus Ça Change   101
     3.7 Conclusion: Tunisia's Democracy Remains under Threat   106

4   Experiments on Businesses and Political Connections   108
     4.1 A New Way to Obtain Data on Business Political Engagement   111
     4.2 Experiment on Business Political Engagement   118
     4.3 Observational Results on Business Political Engagement 121
     4.4 Descriptive Evidence Concerning the Military-Clientelist Complex   130
     4.5 Experimental Results   134
     4.6 Fading Influence Over Time   141
     4.7 Conclusion   143
     4.8 Methodological Appendix   144

5   Crony Capitalism in International Comparison   148
     5.1 Regional and International Perspective   148
     5.2 Comparing Business Political Engagement across Regions 151
     5.3 Military-Clientelist Complex in Comparative Complex   159
     5.4 Experimental Results   160
     5.5 Conclusion   167

6   Conclusion   169
     6.1 Corruption and Democracy   171
     6.2 Rents Are the Key to Power   172
     6.3 A Perfect Transition Will Never Happen   173

References   177
Index   195

Figures

1.1	Causal diagram for presence of capturing institution	*page* 10
1.2	Causal diagram for absence of capturing institution	10
1.3	Causal diagram for rents, firms, and brokers	25
2.1	Event map for Egypt case study	47
2.2	Egypt development statistics	52
2.3	Varieties of democracy values for Egypt	58
2.4	Average affect toward democracy among business employees and managers in Egypt, online survey in Summer 2018	62
2.5	Political activities of firms as reported by employees	69
3.1	Event map for Tunisia case study	78
3.2	Varieties of Democracy values for Tunisia	84
3.3	Average affect toward democracy among business employees and managers in Tunisia, online survey in Summer 2018	90
3.4	Similarity of voting records of Tunisian MPs, 2014–2016	103
3.5	Comparison of top three Tunisian conglomerate revenue growth versus individual firms	105
4.1	Proportion of respondents by firm sector and by country	115
4.2	Proportion of survey respondents by firm size and by country	115
4.3	Reported firm political activity by country	122
4.4	Political activities by answers to has government officials' exploitation of regulations increased since the Arab Spring?	123
4.5	Reported political activities for companies who saw bribes increase post-Arab Spring	124
4.6	Number of inspections from regulators by whether company engaged in political activity	125
4.7	Ties between military-linked firms and companies in Egypt and Tunisia	131
4.8	Count of Egyptian military personnel by sector	132

4.9	Proportion of time spent by Egyptian military on daily tasks	133
4.10	Estimates for rent treatments (appeal types) by dependent variable	136
4.11	Estimates for political actor treatments by dependent variable	137
4.12	Egyptian country-level intercepts across all three experimental outcomes	138
4.13	Appeal of institutions for companies with military connections	139
4.14	Interaction of military treatment and Islamic finance in Egypt Survey I	141
4.15	Estimates for head of state actor treatments by Egypt samples and dependent variable	142
4.16	Interaction of military treatment and Brotherhood support in Egypt Survey II	143
4.17	Survey proportions by firm size, 2017 Facebook surveys	146
4.18	Time to survey completion, 2017 Facebook surveys	147
5.1	World Bank development indicator statistics	149
5.2	Varieties of Democracy political indicators by country	150
5.3	Reported firm political activity in regional comparison	152
5.4	Political activities by answers to how much have bribes increased since the Arab Spring?	154
5.5	Difference in number of inspections from regulators for politically active versus politically inactive companies	154
5.6	Ties between military-linked firms and companies by country	162
5.7	Estimates for rent treatments (appeal types)	162
5.8	Estimates for political actor treatments	163
5.9	Rent treatments by firm type	164
5.10	Estimates for rent treatments by beliefs about corruption	165
5.11	Country-level intercepts across all three experimental outcomes	166

Tables

1.1	Mechanisms for narrow rent-seeking causal graph	*page* 11
2.1	Mechanisms for narrow rent-seeking causal graph	47
3.1	Mechanisms for broad rent-seeking causal graph	78
3.2	Interview transcription, 2016	88
3.3	Representative tweets from parliamentary plenary on economic reconciliation law	100
4.1	List of online surveys	114
4.2	Percentage of total annual sales as informal payment across survey types	117
4.3	Treatment profiles for conjoint survey experiment	120
4.4	Covariates predicting historical corporate political engagement	126
4.5	Proportion of respondents by age	146
5.1	Covariates predicting historical corporate political engagement	156

Acknowledgments

This book is first and foremost dedicated to my firstborn daughter, Elyse Noelle Kubinec, who passed away from leukemia while I was engaged in field research in Tunisia. Her life is intertwined with this book in a way I could not envision when I first began, and I look forward to one day being able to share it with her in the new heavens and the new earth.

My wife Karen supported me during the long and hard times of writing this book. In so many ways it represents a part of our journey together. My parents and my three siblings supported me in this endeavor at every stage. My other children, Amelie, Evelyn, and Nathan, each participated in their own unique way in this project.

My adviser David Waldner believed in the book from its earliest and very unpromising stages. His talent for research design and sharp insight into business politics helped me form my ideas from their inchoate beginnings to a theory with promise. His support as well during my personal tragedy helped me stay on track with the project and prepare me for turning the dissertation into a book. I am also grateful for the helpful comments and professional direction of my dissertation committee members, Daniel Gingerich, Sonal Pandya, and Jonathan Kropko. I thank the University of Virginia for invaluable financial assistance in completing my field research, including grants from the Quantitative Collaborative. I thank P. J. Hill and Sandra Joireman for sparking my interest in the politics of property rights as an undergraduate student.

I am indebted to the Middle East research community for helping me do field research and strengthen my grasp of regime politics in Egypt and Tunisia. Sharan Grewal and Kim Guiler provided crucial moral and intellectual support during field research, and Laryssa Chomiak at Le Centre d'Études Maghrébines (The Center for the Study of the Maghrib) à Tunis, helped me work my way into the intricacies of Tunisian politics. Hamza Mighri, my research assistant-turned-colleague, traveled with me across Tunisia interviewing businesses, and I owe him quite a debt for the book's research. Dhafer Malouche helped me both understand Tunisian politics and facilitated my research whenever he could. Dhia Hammami, a journalist at the time and now a scholar in his own right, gave me crucial insights into the political-economic relationships of Tunisian elites. The Tunisian NGO Al-Bawsalah gave me both detailed information about the parliament through in-person interviews and their robust data-sharing platforms. I thank L'Economiste Maghrebine for allowing me to digitize their corporate revenue data, and I thank the Project on Middle East Political Science for supporting my research with travel funding.

I should add those who lived with us in Tunisia, helping us navigate the complexities of expat life, including Emily and Ethan, Janet and Eric, Tyler and Gretchen, and William.

The process of developing my dissertation into a book took place at two institutions. First, the Niehaus Center for Globalization and Governance provided me with a one-year postdoctoral fellowship, a crucial time to revise the manuscript and push forward with my ideas. The critical yet supportive feedback of other fellows, including Dan Nielson, Lindsay Dolan, Jack Zhang, Marco Martini, Andrey Tomashevskiy, Haillie Lee, Shannon Carcelli, Quynh Nguyen, and In Song Kim, is deeply appreciated. The rest of the manuscript was written and researched at New York University Abu Dhabi. I am indebted to the political science department for their warm collegiality and sharp intellects, especially Joan Barcelo, Giuliana Pardelli, Aaron Kaufman, Peter van der Windt, and Andy Harris.

The participants in my book conference – held online in the midst of the COVID-19 pandemic – helped me push the manuscript to a much higher level, and I am deeply in debt to Jason Brownlee, Leo Arriola, Stan Markus, and Ishac Diwan for their professionalism, encouragement, and detailed revisions. I thank Tim Frye and Scott Williamson for reviewing the manuscript and providing helpful feedback.

Many others contributed to this manuscript in ways crucial to its final state. For additional research assistance, I thank Muhannad AlRamlawi and Mouad Kouttroub. Amal Mrissa translated and transcribed interviews with a high standard of professionalism.

Soli Deo gloria

Data Availability Statement

R code and de-identified data to reproduce results in this book are available from this public Github repository website: www.github.com/saudiwin/crony_book.

Introduction

On May 19, 2017, an incident occurred for the first time in the political history of the Middle East and North Africa: A corrupt businessman confessed on live television the exact manner in which he had taken advantage of state institutions to reap massive profits. Imed Trabelsi, the businessman in question, was a nephew of Tunisia's former dictator Zine Abedine Ben Ali, who had been ousted in 2011 after nation-wide protests. Following his departure, the country organized its first democratic elections since independence, inaugurating the first democratic transition in the region since the 1990s. Tunisian officials quickly prosecuted Trabelsi for corruption following Ben Ali's departure, and by the time he testified he had spent nearly six years in prison.

His motivation to testify arose out of a truth and reconciliation process initiated by the country's transitional justice committee (another first for the region). While the committee made no promises that his sentence would be commuted if he testified, Trabelsi leaped at the chance, likely in an effort to shift his image to a penitent worthy of forgiveness. His rambling two-hour testimony on a live broadcast[1] provided Tunisians an open window into how crony capitalists in their country exploited political connections for personal gain.

Imed Trabelsi's scheme, which apparently netted him millions of dollars that were promptly stashed in Swiss bank accounts, involved maintaining a de facto monopoly on the importation of certain consumables that were in high demand: bananas and alcohol. He described giving regular bribes over a period of years to specific customs officials who were responsible for approving the importation of bananas and alcohol, sometimes amounting to as much as ten thousand dollars for a single bribe. As a result, customs officials refused to let anyone have access to containers containing those goods unless Trabelsi agreed to their importation. In theory, Tunisia's trade policies governed the

---

[1] For the full video, see www.youtube.com/watch?v=8zvUK3HWHNc&t=68s

importation of these goods, but in practice there was only one person who would decide if Tunisians were going to eat bananas.

Trabelsi's prosecution, while a landmark event, unfortunately represented the high-water mark of Tunisia's efforts to hold politically connected businesspeople accountable. Other efforts to examine a broader range of deals under the prior dictatorship sputtered and finally died. Only a few months after Trabeli's confession, Tunisia's parliament passed a bill, euphemistically named the "economic reconciliation law," restricting the transitional justice committee's ability to bring to light further corrupt agreements. The vast majority of businesspeople with connections to the former regime remained largely untouched, fueling public protests in recent years as Tunisia's rural poor and unemployed youth saw little change stemming from their revolution. These protests culminated in suspension of the parliament by President Kais Saied in July 2021, ushering in a renewed era of authoritarianism reminiscent of the Ben Ali regime.

Egypt likewise experienced a popular movement for democracy in 2011 that emphasized an end to corruption and successfully forced out Hosni Mubarak, the ruling dictator, via the rallying cry, "the people want the downfall of the regime" and "bread, freedom, social justice." Yet the Egyptian public had its own riveting revelations in the fall of 2019 when Mohamed Ali, an Egyptian businessman who fled to Spain for asylum, posted detailed accounts on YouTube describing his corrupt dealings with President Abdel Fattah al-Sisi, including work building a lavish palace for the president along the Mediterranean.[2] While Egypt also saw high-profile corruption trials like the steel magnate Ahmed Ezz's conviction in 2012,[3] on the whole Egypt's system of corruption and crony capitalism remained intact following its democratic transition and subsequent takeover by the military in a 2013 coup. While Tunisians until recently enjoyed more democratic freedoms than their Egyptian counterparts, it has not become any easier for Egyptians to navigate the crony web of relationships governing many aspects of obtaining employment and starting businesses.

Prior to 2011, both of these countries for decades had been single-party dictatorships, and both countries scored abysmally in most indices of economic reform, quality of institutions and corruption. For example, in Transparency International's widely cited corruption scores from 2010, right before the revolution, on a scale of 10, where 1 meaning most corrupt and 10 meaning least corrupt, Egypt scored a 3.1 while Tunisia received a 4.3.[4] Both states struggled then and continue to struggle today with dense relationships between business and state officials that lead to improper enrichment on both sides.

This failure of democracy to remove corrupt businesspeople raises the question of how corrupt businesspeople can survive regime changes that should

---

[2] For more information, see www.youtube.com/watch?v=qPETFKD-Mlo.

[3] See www.bbc.com/news/world-middle-east-19830922.

[4] www.transparency.org/cpi2010/results

Introduction

threaten their livelihoods. The aim of this book is to explain how businesspeople reacted to the fall of these regimes and managed through political action to secure their interests in the turmoil that followed. Through analysis of survey data, in-depth case studies of both Egyptian and Tunisian politics, as well as on the ground interviews with businesspeople, I describe the calculus facing business following popular mobilization for regime change.

In short, the extent to which the new political leaders are able to control state privileges that businesses want determines the methods businesses use to engage politically. When new leaders are relatively strong, business political action becomes more partisan in support of the new regime; when leaders are weak, businesses will strategically cultivate allies across the political spectrum to maximize their corporate interests. These different business strategies can have a significant impact on these new regimes, either undermining them, as in the case of Tunisia, or strengthening them, as in Egypt.

The best way to understand this theory is to see it in operation in the political contexts of post-revolution Egypt and Tunisia. In the initial period following democratic transitions, businesspeople in both countries became involved in pro-authoritarian political parties, known as the Nidaa Tounes (Call of Tunis) party in Tunisia and the Tamarod (Rebellion) movement in Egypt. In the intervening years, these two antidemocratic coalitions diverged sharply. Tunisia's business leaders pursued their own interests in Tunisia's democratic regime, resulting in hidden backroom corruption, while Egypt's businesses were forced into a very public marriage with the military despite its negative consequences for their livelihoods.

These different business strategies became evident over time in the divergent political environments in the two countries. By 2017, at the time of Trabelsi's prosecution mentioned above, Tunisia's pro-authoritarian movement had captured a plurality in parliament but seemingly little else. Business elites feuded publicly over the allegiance of members of parliament they had financed, and the Nidaa Tounes party appeared little able to implement its plans for democratic retrenchment. The president, the ostensible leader of the party who harbored clear inclinations of becoming a strongman, remained relegated to a referee with scant ability to punish breakaway factions. By the end of 2017, Nidaa Tounes had lost its parliamentary majority and had to rule with its erstwhile enemy, the Islamist party al-Nahda.

In Egypt, by contrast, the Tamarod movement helped to overthrow Egypt's elected government and ultimately became multiple parties that subsequently won seats in Egypt's parliament under military rule. Following the military's coup in 2013 (Ketchley 2017), Egyptian businesspeople remained loyal and stable partners of a new authoritarianism, refusing to break away even as President al-Sisi, a former military general, embarked on a series of catastrophic economic decisions, spending billions of dollars on wasteful infrastructure projects and delaying Egypt's economic recovery following the Great Recession.

4   *Introduction*

For these reasons, while the overall level of business corruption remained unchanged in Egypt and Tunisia, there are important political differences stemming from the distinct ways that businesspeople adjusted to the transitions in both countries. In Tunisia, businesspeople were willing to make deals with all sides of the political spectrum, including democratic reformers, Islamist revolutionaries, and former members of the dictator's party, their natural allies. The horse-trading nature of Tunisia's democracy resulted in a chaotic parliament that accomplished little, though the interests of individual businesspeople were respected, and when threatened, legislation inevitably stalled. I call this type of backdoor lobbying and influencing *broad rent-seeking* because businesses were willing to work with anyone across the political spectrum, whoever might be willing to cut them a deal to regain their influence.

By contrast, Egyptian businesspeople were forced into engagement with the Egyptian military, or what I call *narrow rent-seeking*. The Egyptian military's influence over the economic and many government agencies, which increased exponentially following its coup in 2013, forced previously autonomous businesspeople to come to grips with a political actor who could punish them if they deviated from its goals. The Egyptian military has become the de facto and de jure ruler of both Egypt's formal and informal institutions, doling out government contracts and other goodies to those it values and driving others out of business.

This book examines how businesses practice these two types of political engagement to protect their interests. The research I will present on this question comes from months of on-the-ground interviews with politicians, business leaders, anti-corruption activists, and journalists in Egypt and Tunisia. I combine this field research with four surveys of businesspeople and military personnel in Egypt and Tunisia, which provide some of the first in-depth and quantitative information about how and to what extent businesspeople were involved in politics in both countries. To help substantiate the theory's explanatory power outside these two countries, I also examine four additional surveys of business political activities in Jordan, Morocco, Algeria, Ukraine, and Venezuela. With this data and fine-grained contextual information, I am able to examine precisely how businesspeople are affected by regime changes and also how they manage to gain influence following setbacks.

By comparing both Egypt and Tunisia in this book, I am able to make it clear that democracy itself is not a threat to crony capitalists and others who might fear more transparent and accountable government. While Tunisian governing institutions did go through a systemic shock, and this shock disrupted long-standing relationships between powerful companies and bureaucrats, it did not last. Businesspeople were able to weather the storm by re-establishing relationships with parties and in some cases running as candidates or starting their own parties. The opening of Tunisia's political system perversely created more possible allies for businesspeople willing to give campaign funds and other supports.

On the other hand, Egyptian businesspeople did play a role in the stability of President al-Sisi's regime, but that support was not necessary for them to restore their lost privileges and benefits. Rather, it was the military's long-standing influence and rapid expansion in post-coup control that left businesspeople with little choice in whom they could support. Counterintuitively, many businesspeople lost more under the military dictatorship than they likely would have if Egypt had remained a democracy, and are now left with little choice but to play handmaiden to President al-Sisi's authoritarian experiment.

MILITARIES, BUSINESS, AND DEMOCRACY

Identifying businesspeople as a possible antidemocratic rather than pro-democratic force departs from conventional wisdom in political science. A rising commercial class (the bourgeoisie) is often credited with pushing for representative government in early modern Europe, and the thesis that capitalism and democracy are intimately connected has persisted in the scholarly and popular literatures (Lipset 1959; Moore 1966; Almond 1991; Rueschemeyer, Stephens, and Stephens 1992). However, in many states where bureaucrats are compromised by personal relationships to particular firms, the idea of business as a force for political change is unrealistic. In order for business to push back against the state and guard against unjust expropriation, it must first become a group that is separate from the state. In many developing countries, those lines are blurred by the daily acts of exchange taking place between ostensibly private firms and ostensibly public officials (Haber, Razo, and Maurer 2003; Arriola 2012; Cammett et al. 2015; Markus 2015; Frye 2017; Albertus and Menaldo 2018; Malik, Atiyas, and Diwan 2020).

For this reason, this book emphasizes the political engagement of the business community as the outcome to be explained rather an outcome that is assumed. While we can assume that many crony capitalists stand to lose under a regime transition, political preferences alone do not explain business actions. Businesses must be involved in party-building and mobilization in order to have real influence in politics. It is even possible that, under some conditions, business can become a tool to bring down a new democratic regime. However, in order for crony capitalists to make the leap from a latent political force to a potent one, a powerful institutional actor must be able to impose some kind of order on the business community and help mobilize them around a consequential political goal like regime change. In crony capitalist systems, this order is only likely to arise if the institutional actor can subsume control over access to state provision of public and private goods for businesses like property rights enforcement, licenses to operate, and contracts.

The main institutional actor that I study in this book, and that I argue explains much of the divergence in business political engagement between Egypt and Tunisia, is the Egyptian military and in particular its economic network. The Egyptian military maintains a vast network of government-owned and quasi-private companies that exist across virtually all sectors of the Egyptian economy. While at one point this economic infrastructure served the military's purpose of providing for the country's defense, today it hews more closely to a basic profit-maximizing logic. Military-owned or affiliated companies in Egypt produce baby formula, administer private schools, build public housing, manage toll roads, and manufacture pharmaceuticals, and have increased their control over government contracting substantially since the 2013 coup (Marshall and Stacher 2012; Morsy 2014; Abul-Magd 2017; Sayigh 2019).

I term this network of military-affiliated businesses *the military-clientelist complex*. Because these firms and their primary suppliers and producers are all connected to the military, they also have a political allegiance they must uphold. For these reasons, the military pushed the business community in Egypt to rally around the goal of opposing democracy. In Tunisia, by contrast, no such institution existed that could command a wide range of support from businesspeople and penalize those who opposed. While antidemocratic sentiment morphed into a powerful wide-ranging movement in Egypt, in Tunisia the antidemocratic backlash resulted in a short-lived party that had brief electoral success but has been largely consumed with internal squabbles. In the one case, increasing control over networks of privilege by the military led to pressure on businesspeople to join their coalition, while in the second, businesspeople were able to play all sides in seeking to protect their companies' interests.

This apparent failure of the Tunisian business community to mobilize around a widely shared interest is puzzling in light of the similarities between the Tunisian and Egyptian business communities. It is not as though Tunisia was spared antidemocratic backlash from elites, but rather that these elites proved incapable of remaining united around a common platform. Collective action of a sort did occur in Tunisia, in no small part because the largest business clan threw its weight behind the emergence of a pro-authoritarian party. Yet without wider support from the business community and other elite actors, the movement never passed beyond its initial electoral success into a capable organized movement. Instead, business elites were content to advocate for their own particular firm interests and funded parties across the ideological spectrum, ironically helping to stabilize party competition.

The comparatively widespread support for the military regime among the Egyptian business community is even more remarkable considering the military's abysmal economic management and more recent brutal austerity policies. It would appear more natural to assume that a regime that had received significant business support in its early stages would also become a boon for business elites, but the military has pursued policies that have largely enriched its own cronyist network while throwing macroeconomic prudence to the wind (Sayigh 2019). More recently, the military has abruptly switched tracks and has successfully implemented economic reforms that have brought considerable pain to established businesses, especially a dramatic increase in the value-added tax

Militaries, Business, and Democracy 7

charged on business profits.[5] This direct taxation combined with continued high unemployment and low investment would appear to be a perfect cocktail for business defection, but that has not happened even five years after the military's coup. The bandwagoning equilibrium, supported by the military's domination of the state bureaucracy, makes it difficult for any one business, even a powerful one, to take the risky position of supporting any kind of opposition.

In summary, the outcome that this book explains is that of business political engagement. I provide a theory in this book that explains the reasons that businesspeople are forced into politics following regime transitions, and the ways that they decide what kind of political action to undertake. The main independent variable in this book is the institutional actor that can prompt differences in business participation. In this study, I focus on the military-clientelist complex as comprising the motive force for business participation, but it is possible that in other contexts another actor could play this role, such as state-owned banks that have control over capital allocation. Identifying further actors is an important area for additional research on post-transition business political action.

To test the theory, I employ case study-based process tracing and extensive online survey research of Egyptian and Tunisian businesspeople during the period from 2013 to 2018. This critical period, during which the nascent democracies either survived their initial challenges or collapsed, provides a compelling window into the political troubles and machinations of businesspeople. By providing both historical accounts of the political transitions with quantitative research into business preferences and actions, I can substantiate the theory at different points in time and using a variety of methods and sources.

In Chapter 1 of this book, I discuss my theory of business political orientation more in-depth, especially how it relates to the unique issues facing developing countries transitioning to democracy. In Chapters 2 and 3, I discuss the rise and subsequent impact of Egypt and Tunisia's pro-authoritarian parties and the prominent role played by businesspeople in each party. In Chapter 4, I discuss survey research conducted in Egypt and Tunisia that offers experimental evidence of the theory in operation and also expands the focus to other countries with issues of crony capitalism. In Chapter 5, I continue my examination of quantitative survey data with an exploration of how crony capitalism and the military-clientelistic complex compares across the region and even outside of it.

---

[5] See https://timep.org/reports-briefings/timep-brief-vat-law/.

1

How Firms Respond to Regime Change

In this chapter, I put forward an informal model explaining how businesspeople engage in politics during episodes of political transition. In brief, the theory argues that, absent some kind of external intervention, most businesses tend toward a type of political engagement called *broad* rent-seeking in which they seek to recruit allies from across the political spectrum. As a result, following political transition, businesses continue with this modus operandi, except that they must succeed in obtaining new allies in a changing political establishment, contributing to political corruption as they seek to influence reformers. On the other hand, a rare yet politically consequential outcome can occur after political transition if an institutional actor is able to quickly replace the prior dictator and monopolize the distribution of perks and privileges. This actor can subsequently obtain considerable support from the business community due to a phenomenon I describe as *narrow* rent-seeking: to please the gatekeeper, business must focus their energies on this one actor at the expense of others.

I focus in this theory on the *type* of business political engagement following regime transitions as it is not necessarily true that the *level* of engagement will vary. Following a regime transition, in countries where legal rights are not taken for granted, businesses must pursue strategies to ingratiate themselves with incoming elites. An institutional actor may be able to coerce or manipulate a greater number of companies into political action, but it is more likely to have an effect on how companies pursue politics rather than whether they do so (or as economists like to put it, the intensive rather than extensive margin). Regardless of the structure and aftermath of transitions, businesses in previously corrupt regimes need to respond to new political institutions and power holders. Failure to do so could expose them to the reformers' zeal against the corruption of the ancien régime or lead to a loss of privileges in favor of rivals jockeying for a limited supply of state privileges.

Though most of the research in this book comes out of the Middle East and North Africa, I believe this theory is more broadly applicable to countries with

1 How Firms Respond to Regime Change

endemic problems of corruption and crony capitalism. Most of our studies are either about corruption in normal periods of regimes or about the immediate aftermath of regime transition when prior crony relationships are exposed (Fisman 2001; Hinnebusch 2006; Heydemann 2007; Acemoğlu and Robinson 2008; Svolik 2012; Earle and Gehlbach 2015; Acemoğlu, Hassan, and Tahoun 2017; Szakonyi 2018). This theory addresses the role of business after the initial euphoria of regime transitions has ended and the strategies available as they seek to find a place in the new system, whether that system turns democratic or authoritarian (Loxton 2015; Grzymala-Busse 2020).

Further, this chapter makes it clear what is the main outcome of interest: how and when businesses engage in political action following regime collapses. Some of the data presented in the following chapters will examine implications of this argument, such as how the involvement of crony capitalists affects democratic transitions and authoritarian durability. While these are very important implications to discuss, they follow from the main argument rather than constitute the main aim. I believe that by understanding how elite actors behave, we can better understand very large outcomes like democratization and regime survival; though to do this well, it is important to separate these processes.

To illustrate this argument, I produced causal graphs showing the relevant variables and the outcome of business political engagement. By causal graph, I mean a network plot in which each node of the network is a variable in the theory, and the causal process moves sequentially from left to right to produce the outcome. I use the word causality here to refer to my expectation that if some of the values of these variables changed, then the outcome itself would change, even though we may not be able to observe these counterfactuals.

The outcome I want to explain, business political engagement, can take on two levels: *broad* and *narrow* rent-seeking. Given these two possible outcomes, there are two separate causal graphs due to some asymmetry in the causal argument. Figure 1.1 shows the causal graph that produces the outcome of narrow rent-seeking. Figure 1.2 has the causal graph that produces the outcome of broad rent-seeking. In the next few sections, I discuss the parts of these causal graphs in turn, starting with the outcome (terminal node) of the graph, and moving back to the independent variables.

I use the term causal graph to imply that this combination of variables with this combination of values for those variables will likely or probably result in the outcome (Pearl 2000). In other words, as is often the case in the social sciences, we do not assume deterministic relations between variables, but rather that relationships exist because the outcome becomes more likely when certain conditions hold. Including some uncertainty is important due to the complexity of predicting or explaining human nature and human social relations.

What both Figures 1.1 and 1.2 share in common is the bottom line of the causal process. Both causal sequences begin with the initial political shock of a regime change, which prompts the loss of a dictator, that is, the principal,

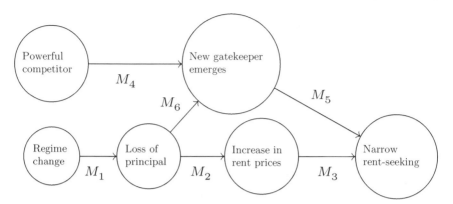

FIGURE 1.1 Causal diagram for presence of capturing institution

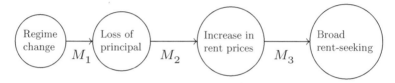

FIGURE 1.2 Causal diagram for absence of capturing institution

who has some level of control over bureaucracies and the distribution of rents and other state-sanctioned privileges. This loss of control leads to an increase in rent prices for businesses, such as to maintain monopoly privileges over lucrative domestic markets. The increase in rent payments prompts businesspeople to engage in business political engagement to protect their company from competitors and rogue bureaucrats.

In terms of differences in the arguments, Figure 1.1 has an additional branch in which a new gatekeeper emerges following the postregime chaos. A powerful competitor, or a political actor with substantial strength, becomes a gatekeeper by replacing whoever functioned as the principal of the state. It is this gatekeeper that proves to be decisive in whether or not businesses engage in narrow instead of broad rent-seeking. If a gatekeeper exists, the business must engage in narrow rent-seeking to protect their perks and privileges. If not, as shown in Figure 1.2, the business will engage in broad rent-seeking and seek to curry favor from a wide swath of the incoming political elite. For this reason, it is important to note that the primary difference between the two processes is the existence or not of a powerful competitor at the point that the regime change occurs.

The labels on the arrows between nodes in the graph (M_1 through M_5) represent causal mechanisms. These are processes through which the variables influence each other. Compared to the variables, mechanisms operate at a very low level, representing people's judgment of costs and benefits that ultimately push them to take action (Elster 1994; Waldner 2007; Mahoney 2012). In the

1.1 Corruption in Developing Countries

TABLE 1.1 *Mechanisms for narrow rent-seeking causal graph*

Mechanism	Definition
M_1	Costs of repression exceed the costs of tolerance.
M_2	Bureaucrats no longer accountable to a former dictator and the dictator's party.
M_3	Firms need to offset higher bribe costs and risks to existing privileges.
M_4	Greater institutional resources enable the gatekeeper to control rents via credible threats.
M_5	Gatekeepers make obtaining rents conditional on political allegiance.
M_6	Loss of ruler creates opportunity for other actors to seize control.

causal graph, the mechanisms are edges (arrows) because they do not represent distinct variables but rather processes through which variables have their influence. While the theory is primarily about the variables and the values they take, I also address the mechanisms to better understand exactly how the variables in question are related to each other.

I summarize the mechanisms in Table 1.1. As can be seen, the mechanisms relate to how businesspeople, politicians, and bureaucrats all evaluate the trade-offs of various actions based on the effect of the preceding variable. Because the actors in this narrative are all people, it is important to ultimately ground the theory in the individual calculations made over different alternatives that collectively sum up to aggregate political outcomes.

1.1 CORRUPTION IN DEVELOPING COUNTRIES

To understand how the causal argument unfolds, it is important to first consider that firms in developing countries with weak state institutions differ fundamentally from companies in wealthier countries with very strong state institutions. At a very basic level, firms in developing and developed countries share a similar profit-maximizing motive. But firms in countries with highly institutionalized markets are limited in terms of how they can seek profits; consequently, they maximize over their marginal revenue and marginal demand curves, which are largely set by consumer demand (Schumpeter 1976). These idealized economic models, while they have never been entirely true of firms even in free-market paragons like the United States, are nonetheless much more relevant to firm behavior where other avenues of maximizing profits, such as coercing customer behavior, are heavily restricted (North 1990).

By contrast, firms in regions like the Middle East are profit-maximizing organizations that have the potential to gain access to significant levels of government coercion in order to control the behavior of either their competitors or consumers (or both) (Cammett et al. 2015; Diwan, Keefer, and Schiffbauer 2015; Malik, Atiyas, and Diwan 2020). The common term for this kind of profit maximization is rent-seeking (Krueger 1974), which refers to a unique resource that a firm can obtain to provide it with a guaranteed source of return. Firms in the Middle East can generally obtain two forms of rent that help them to maintain revenue streams: protection from foreign competition and protection from domestic rivals (Rijkers, Freund, and Nucifora 2014; Cammett et al. 2015; Diwan, Keefer, and Schiffbauer 2015; Acemoğlu, Hassan, and Tahoun 2017). The first involves nontariff barriers that make it very difficult for foreign firms to meet the paperwork and bribery demands of government officials in these countries (Rijkers, Baghdadi, and Raballand 2015). Theoretically, Middle Eastern countries are open to investment and world markets; in practice, potential market entrants have much trouble either moving their goods through corrupt ports or obtaining the necessary permits to compete by setting up subsidiaries (Oliva 2000; Sayan 2009; Bhattacharya and Wolde 2010). Because of these internal and external barriers to investment and market competition, companies in the Middle East and North Africa tend to have lower overall productivity relative to their size and access to capital (Kinda, Plane, and Véganzonès-Varoudakis 2011).

The second rent that Middle Eastern firms have access to is the ability to use bureaucrats as a weapon against each other. This form of coercion is exercised by established firms that are concerned about domestic entrants. On the one hand, domestic entrants cannot be so easily excluded as foreign entrants. However, aspiring entrepreneurs can be defeated by forcing them to die by a thousand bureaucratic paper cuts, requiring competing firms to delay investment and expansion by an unending succession of licenses and permits (Djankov et al. 2002). These two primary forms of rent can, for those firms that have access to them, create substantial monopoly profits by capturing domestic markets (The World Bank 2014). Monopoly profits in turn provide a form of largesse that firm owners can share with government officials, either via direct enrichment (bribes) or by offering patronage, such as jobs, to those whom the state wants to co-opt or reward (Djankov et al. 2002). In addition to sharing profits, firms can remunerate government officials by acting as quasi-political organizations, ordering their employees to vote for government-backed candidates in elections or participating in election campaigns (Gandhi and Lust-Okar 2009; Blaydes 2011; Haddad 2011; Boubekeur 2013; Diwan and Haidar 2020).

This basic comparison between firms maximizing in the market and those maximizing via government rents might suggest at first that the two modes are distinct, but they are not necessarily better or worse as far as economic production is concerned. The main problem is how government rents are distributed. It would be possible, such as in the so-called developmental states, to distribute rents to those firms that were more productive or had the possibility of generating substantial innovation (Evans 1989; Soifer 2013). If that were the case, then the rents provided to firms would act as a form of investment that would over time yield profits for the society as a whole. As I discuss later in Chapter 2,

1.1 *Corruption in Developing Countries* 13

that was indeed the goal of many states in the Middle East when these forms of government control were implemented (Waterbury 1999).

Unfortunately, autocrats rarely remain so committed to maximizing social welfare (Levi 1989). Firms that stand to gain the most from these kinds of government-sanctioned privileges are those with the highest levels of political connections because autocrats seek allies to shore up their regime's support (Magaloni and Kricheli 2010; Markus and Charnysh 2017). Quite often, though, in Middle Eastern countries, political connections are more subtle than these direct relationships. It may involve business leaders with familial or tribal connections to government leaders. Certain regions or ethnic groups can receive greater attention than others (Monroe 2019). Properly speaking, political connections outside of advanced industrial countries are a latent variable that cannot be measured directly but rather by reference to social behaviors that indicate political connections (Kubinec 2019a). These behaviors may be as subtle as attending the birthday party of the ruler's daughter or as direct as marrying into the dictator's family (Haddad 2011).

Despite these gradations, it is possible to look at politically connected firms as representing their own class versus businesses without political connections. The distribution of political connections tends to be strongly skewed (Rijkers, Freund, and Nucifora 2014; Diwan and Haidar 2020). Even if some oligarchs protest at their relative outsider status, when their shipments of goods are stopped in customs, they know who to call to make sure that the pallet is delivered. Given how crucial these political connections are to firm revenue, profit and survival, it is no wonder that firms will spend considerable time, resources, and effort to maintain them.

The result of these processes is that firms in developing countries operate under different constraints than those in developed countries with relatively strong institutions and well-respected property rights. As institutions become more personal and less rule-bound, the personal relationships of firm owners can become more crucial to the firm's performance than conventional criteria like productivity, value added, and product differentiation (North, Wallis, and Weingast 2009). The reason that theories about firms and politics cannot be imported directly to contexts without strong state institutions is that firms themselves undertake a different set of roles and obligations when a relatively neutral "free" market does not exist. Entrepreneurs in developing countries are often as reliant on their ability to make phone calls to powerful bureaucrats to gain access to required licenses or permits, obtain tax relief, or a state-sponsored loan as they are at developing new ideas for business ventures (Autio and Fu 2015; Amorós et al. 2019; Urbano, Aparicio, and Audretsch 2019).

My theory starts with this context in which companies require at least some acquiescence from government bureaucrats to operate. The theory explains the situation in which these defined hierarchical relationships are upset by a political event unforeseen by either business, bureaucrats, or top political leaders: regime change.

1.2 THE OUTCOME: BUSINESS POLITICAL ENGAGEMENT FOLLOWING TRANSITIONS

To begin my analysis of the causal graph, I first define the outcome that I want to explain: business political engagement, especially in countries where corporate political activity is lightly regulated if at all. As I mentioned in Section 1.1, I intend to explain the difference between two types of political engagement, what I call *broad* rent-seeking and *narrow* rent-seeking. However, these are concepts, not activities in a strict sense. Rent-seeking only implies that companies engage in some kinds of activities to gain rent, not that these activities are necessarily political. As such, in order to make the concepts concrete in political terms, I focus on four main activities that companies may use to try to influence politics and by doing so obtain rents:

1. Instructing their employees to vote for a specific set of politicians
2. Hosting campaign rallies or other events in favor of politicians
3. Providing donations to political campaigns
4. Distributing literature to employees about political campaigns or candidates.

What may be immediately apparent from this list is that certain types of common political activities by companies are missing. In particular, I do not include lobbying or participation in business trade groups as possible strategies (Blau, Brough, and Thomas 2013; Kim and Kunisky 2017). The reason for this omission is due to the domain within which I am examining business political activity: specifically, states with weak institutions, significant problems with corruption and rules biased in favor of those with political connections. In these types of states, lobbying is unlikely to be a particularly important activity as it requires a state that can enforce lobbying rules, that is, such as the registration of representatives of the firm and a record of their activities. In the absence of these rules, it is difficult to describe the informal negotiations that occur as lobbying in the same sense as companies in the United Kingdom or the United States.

Similarly, I do not focus on business political engagement in terms of involvement in business associations because associations tend to represent types of companies and sectors to the government. As a result, they may not help intercede for the particular permits, licenses and protection through the bureaucracy that a given individual firm might need. Business associations are quite relevant for explaining macro policy change, such as the success or failure of trade liberalization and tax reform (Cammett 2007; Fairfield 2015). Much of the work in this area compares business associations in terms of their breadth, commitment and ability to obtain policy concessions (Schneider 2004). Individual business interests are usually not the main focus, but rather the aggregation of interests and their representation through formal institutions. Yet in this book, I am

1.2 *Business Political Engagement Following Transitions*

focusing on informal relationships that businesses lose, which in turn can cause them to become victims of relatively unconstrained bureaucrats.

The lack of attention to business associations is not to say these associations do not exist or are not important in developing countries. However, as previous research has demonstrated, securing a firm's property rights (protection from expropriation by the state) and access to markets (state-sanctioned oligopolies) are highly firm-specific activities, often relating to an individual company's political connections. As such, this conceptualization of business political engagement is relevant to the burgeoning literature on political connections of companies. These types of business political engagement enable businesses to obtain personal relationship with parties and their candidates, permitting exclusive influence which the business can wield to obtain both perks and protection from state-sanctioned expropriation. In addition, businesspeople can have both membership in associations and informal political connections as these two modes of relating to the state have distinct aims (Haggard, Maxfield, and Schneider 1997).

To be more precise about what I mean by political connection, I define these connections as a form of relationship between the firm and the state that involves personal exchange (Haber, Razo, and Maurer 2003; North, Wallis, and Weingast 2009; Frye 2017). Political connections can involve a concrete relationship, such as a former government official or MP who sits on a company's board and assists that company in obtaining rents (Fisman 2001; Faccio 2006). In advanced industrial democracies, firms may employ professional lobbyists to maintain connections with government officials on their behalf (Kim and Kunisky 2017). The cultivation of political connections involves the company's leaders working primarily on their own initiative to offer some kind of perks to power holders. Political connections of companies have become a very large research agenda as it would seem that individualized relationships are very important to crony capitalism.

Rent-seeking usually culminates in political connections because connections are an excellent way to ensure a steady stream of rents. Exactly how firm owners become politically connected is an area that has relatively little research, although a groundbreaking study by Markus and Charnysh (2017) tracking Ukrainian oligarchs over their careers showed that maintaining independent bases of power, such as owning media companies, proved more effective at securing political connections over the long run than simply holding political office. Firm political connections may also have a basis outside of the state in terms of what the firm owners can do for the state. For example, firms with a lower level of political connections may have inroads into the office of the local municipal government due to their influence in that area, but remain helpless when negotiating with the national customs authority.

It is important next to separate out the different political activities listed above in terms of how they relate to *narrow* rent-seeking and *broad* rent-seeking. While rents exist in all political systems, this book is relevant to countries where rents seem to matter more to companies than criteria many would consider core business precepts like productivity, sales, and innovation. By obtaining exclusive access to state-sanctioned privileges, companies can cordon off segments of the market for themselves, raise profits and reduce the need to worry about competitors.

The existence of rents is closely tied to corruption as companies have an incentive to circumvent regulations by obtaining the consent of those who have the authority to provide these rents. Nominally, these people are bureaucrats, but often the true principals with control over this distribution are important politicians, and in authoritarian systems, the dictator and his or her inner circle (Magaloni 2006; Egorov and Sonin 2011). For this reason, companies can use these political activities to cultivate relationships with the bosses of bureaucrats and ensure that permits, licenses, and even judicial decisions break their way (Claessens, Feijen, and Laeven 2008; Li et al. 2008; Malesky and Taussig 2009; Sukhtankar 2012).

It should be noted here that I am also excluding direct bribery of bureaucrats as a type of political activity. Again, my focus is building on existing research showing that in states with extensive issues with corruption, companies do not need to rely on bribes to ensure access to state favors. Rather, companies work hard to obtain political connections by adding politicians to their board or providing other favors to political elites (Faccio 2006). These kinds of relationships reduce the burden of bribery by subtly merging the interest of the politician with that of the company, and ultimately result in a more stable policy regime, though not necessarily one that is more open or fair to outsiders (Haber, Razo, and Maurer 2003). In other words, politics is a way for companies to avoid having to pay very high amounts of bribes and being subject to the arbitrary whims of individual bureaucrats (Olson 1993). Nature, and business, abhors a vacuum.

Given this brief discussion of the concept of rent-seeking, *narrow* rent-seeking can be more clearly defined as political activities that are partisan in nature, such as instructing employees to vote for a particular candidate or holding rallies on behalf of parties, while *broad* rent-seeking represents political activities that do not commit a business to a particular side. These activities are more likely to involve providing funds to candidates as businesses are able to distribute funds across the political spectrum. Political parties may even be unaware that businesses are funding all sides as this type of activity is usually hidden. Other activities which can be more ambiguous, such as distributing literature, although in general it would seem that a company distributing partisan leaflets is pressuring employees to support that political side.

This definition or view of rent-seeking does depart somewhat from its use in existing research. I am essentially putting more substance into the term by detailing how exactly businesses will try to obtain rents given institutional conditions. As Moore (2009, 83) wrote in his study of state–business relations in Jordan and Kuwait, "[r]ent-seeking can display different features, and can

1.2 Business Political Engagement Following Transitions

yield different outcomes depending on political conditions." It is one thing to say that in a corrupt society, businesses will have to find ways of securing their livelihood, and quite another to say how that process will happen given the political conditions within which they operate.

In general then, we can expect narrow rent-seeking to manifest itself in a greater prevalence of the most explicitly partisan activities, of which the most significant in the list above is employee vote coercion. We would expect funding parties to be less emphasized, at least when comparing it to a country where broad rent-seeking is more in play. Distributing literature is usually a more partisan activity, unless the company distributes literature from multiple parties. Holding rallies likewise has a partisan connotation unless a party took the rare step of holding rallies for candidates across the political spectrum.

Partisanship is an important consideration in classifying these activities because business generally prefer *back-room* to *front-room* deals when it comes to securing rents. As mentioned previously, relationships with politicians are valuable because they can secure for a given company access to state privileges and perks. For this reason, it rarely makes sense for business to commit to any one politician in a state where this type of access is crucial for their survival because siding with one politician necessarily entails alienating others (Fisman 2001; Earle and Gehlbach 2015). By contrast, remaining somewhat in the shadows yet building rapport and influence with all is the much more efficient strategy to maximizing return on investment and ensuring they have multiple avenues to influence the political system.

Back-room political activities tend to be more closely tied to *broad* rent-seeking because these activities imply that relative secrecy allow businesses to avoid making clear which sides it is backing. As a result, businesses are likely to consider being an ally of ostensible political enemies if this is the optimal strategy to maintain political connections and rents. However, while this type of politicking will tend toward cross-partisan alliances, these activities will necessarily diffuse business' so-called structural power and instead lead to the proliferation of individual corrupt relationships between businesses and political elites, at least in states where these types of political activities are unlikely to be controlled or regulated. In general, without knowing anything else about the political system, I expect that businesses would prefer to engage in back-room deals over front-room deals.

Narrow rent-seeking, which is often constituted by *front-room* deals like ordering employees to vote for a specific candidate or taking public actions like holding political rallies, entails a costly commitment to a certain political side. What is important is that a business' political activity could be observed by others, leading to inferences that the business is backing a political side, potentially making it an enemy to that side's opponents. It is not generally a preferred position for a business operating under the assumption that businesses are mainly interested in obtaining favors from the bureaucracy and judiciary rather than supporting an ideological project. A priori, without knowing anything else about a political system, we should expect this type of business political engagement to be rarer than the relatively less costly actions of providing a one-off campaign donation or distributing literature.

A further observable attribute of narrow and broad rent-seeking is evident in the dispersion of the targets of political activity. We should expect that in periods when narrow rent-seeking is more common that the political activity will be targeted at or in support of the gatekeeper, while in broad rent-seeking, the targets of the political activity will be more diverse. With broad rent-seeking, companies will target the lowest possible broker available to minimize costs associated with winning their support. As such, when examining a cross-section of companies, we should expect that business political engagement – regardless of the type – will be much more diverse across political institutions and actors if broad rent-seeking is the norm.

There is already some initial evidence that the structure of rent-seeking networks may have profound influence on politically connected firms. In a new volume on politically connected firms in the Middle East and North Africa, Malik, Atiyas, and Diwan (2020) noticed that there were peculiar intra-regional contrasts in how politically connected firms were organized. In particular, they pointed out that Lebanon, a quasi-democracy with a weak and fragmented state, had a more "decentralized" rent distribution network than did Morocco, dominated by companies affiliated with the royal family, and pre-Arab Spring Tunisia, where the president's family dominated several sectors through personal ties (Malik, Atiyas and Diwan 2020, 8–9). These differences appear to explain why job creation in Lebanon among crony firms was significantly higher than job growth among crony firms in Egypt. In this book, I will help explain these patterns by specifying how broad and narrow rent-seeking can come into and out of existence due to changes in the distribution of political power.

1.3 THE CAUSES OF BUSINESS POLITICAL ENGAGEMENT

Given this definition of the outcome that I want to explain, I next turn to consider those factors which are most important for explaining how and why businesses react to profound changes in the political system. I divide these factors into those that are more proximate and those that are more distant in the causal framework as seen in Figures 1.1 and 1.2. I first describe the distant causal factors (i.e., those at the beginning of the causal narrative) and move toward the outcome.

Before beginning, however, I must defend to some extent variables which are knowingly left out of the causal graph. One important exception is that I ignore idiosyncratic reasons behind why a businessperson may have a greater taste or preference for politics than other businesspeople. For my purposes, I acknowledge that some company owners seem to have more of a taste for politics (Fox and Lawless 2005), but I will not focus on it as it is a primary

1.3 The Causes of Business Political Engagement

explanatory because these idiosyncrasies are not closely connected to the larger picture of crony capitalism. Some people may have a personality more or less amenable to politics, but the sources of these personalities (as opposed to apolitical personalities) are not the main focus of this work. I acknowledge that some company owners seem to relish more political involvement than others whether in corrupt or transparent systems, but it is unlikely that such personalities alone can explain change in business political engagement over time as I do in this book.

1.3.1 Regime Change and Powerful Competitors

To begin, the initial node in in both the narrow rent-seeking graph in Figure 1.1 and the broad rent-seeking graph in Figure 1.2 is that of a regime change. This event, which is not considered to be caused by anything else in the graph, sets off the chain reaction which ultimately culminates in business political engagement. This is important to note as it is not the aim of this book to explain why regime changes occur, but only to establish that such changes are not necessarily related or caused by other variables such as business political activity and changes in rent prices. The reason for this definition of regime change is because businesspeople are rarely the group that is running the show, despite what some Marxists once claimed. Businesspeople can have considerable influence with a dictator, and that influence can manifest itself as corruption which prompts popular unrest. However, because dictators aim primarily to lengthen their tenure, they proactively take steps to mitigate any threats to their regime, distributing carrots, punishing opponents, and marginalizing un-biased sources of information (Gandhi and Lust-Okar 2009; Pepinsky 2009; Magaloni and Kricheli 2010; Egorov and Sonin 2011).

As a result, it is difficult if not impossible to know exactly when a regime will collapse. Some regimes survive despite both internal and external pressures, such as Jordan's long-lived Hashemite monarchy, installed by a colonial power and often at odds with its neighbors (Herb 1999). At the same time, seemingly powerful regimes can suddenly collapse, such as the bewildering rapidity with which the former USSR unraveled. Rulers have a strong reason to prevent the release of information about their weaknesses, making it harder for people inside and outside their country to judge the true probability of a regime collapse (Kuran 1991; Gehlbach and Keefer 2011).

All this is not to say that businesspeople may not participate in the fall of a regime. The assumption only requires that businesspeople do not have access to the knowledge that only the dictator and his or her inner circle might about the true state of the regime. As such, when not just a leader but an entire regime collapses, businesspeople are caught unawares along with much of the rest of the population. While people always suspect that political change could occur, it is much harder to predict when it will happen in regimes with weak media environments and state institutions.

There is another origin node in the causal graph in Figure 1.1 which is important to describe as well: the existence of a "Powerful Competitor" to the dictator. It is crucial that this powerful competitor – which must be an institutional actor with considerable resources, not just an individual – survive the regime change relatively unscathed (there is no arrow between regime change and powerful competitor in the graph). Of course there are always competitors to dictators and rivals who would supplant him or her. What is meant here, though, is not just influence or credibility, but actual power, or control over state institutions with considerable autonomy from the rest of the government. Perhaps one reason why these types of actors are unlikely to emerge, generally speaking, is that dictators prefer to concentrate power in themselves or their inner circle to avoid creating rival institutions (Marinov and Goemans 2014; Svolik 2015).

However, if such an institution exists such that it has both enough power to influence other state institutions and enough autonomy that it can survive the downfall of the dictator, we can add this variable to the causal graph. What exactly this institution is could vary from country to country as in theory any state ministry or bureaucracy could meet this definition. While I return to this question in the conclusion in this book, emphasis is put on the military as a primary actor in controlling access to rents. The role of the military can be thought of as a sufficient but not necessary criterion for businesses to pool resources into a coalition.

Military influence is not necessary for this to occur because a similar institution or political actor could also centralize rents, such as how rent influence networks changed considerably in East Africa following reforms that changed the distribution of credit by state-owned banks (Arriola 2012). However, the military as an institution has some resources that are peculiarly important in states that are riddled with principal–agent problems described below. As an institution with a near-monopoly on force, the military can act outside of state institutions while still maintaining its own coherence, permitting it to dominate other state bureaucracies. Crucially, for it to play the role in the argument as the powerful competitor, the military must be relatively autonomous from the dictator and his or her inner circle to survive the regime transition. In addition, it should have some kind of economic involvement to permit it to have an influence on business.

In developed countries, military involvement in economic activity is restricted to projects that involve supplying the military with equipment, or what is known as the military–industrial complex (Alptekin and Levine 2012; Dunne and Tian 2013). However, in developing countries, the military may take advantage of its control over coercion to run its own network of firms with relatively little connection to the military's imperative to defend the territory – although these justifications are still given for the military's economic privileges (Izadi 2022).

In countries where enforcement of property rights is uneven, the military retains a natural advantage if it enters economic activity. It is difficult for

1.3 The Causes of Business Political Engagement

competitors to employ the same forms of bureaucratic intervention to hinder military-affiliated companies. In addition, the military's special status may exempt firms it controls from taxes and regulatory inspections. While the military is unlikely to run enterprises that compete against the frontier in economic efficiency, it will excel in obtaining the same kinds of perks and advantages that politically connected firms obtain. As I have already established, access to this kind of political capital vis-a-vis regulators and other influential officials is of greater importance for running a successful business than maximizing economic efficiency.

Despite the clear incentives that militaries have in many developing countries to develop parastatal economic enterprises, research into this phenomenon is relatively sparse. I can confirm that in Latin America, Africa, south and southeast Asia these forms of military economic activity do exist (Mani 2011; Golkar 2012; Myoe 2014; Moyo 2016; Chambers and Waitoolkiat 2017; Staniland, Naseemullah, and Butt 2020). Some of these economic activities seem to follow a coup-proofing logic where military generals are given lucrative opportunities in military-affiliated companies as a way to keep the peace among the officer corps (Marshall and Stacher 2012; Abul-Magd 2017; Sayigh 2019; Staniland, Naseemullah, and Butt 2020; Izadi 2022). However, we lack comparative data to be able to say which militaries have obtained the greatest presence in civilian economic activity. The best existing work shows which countries in the world have a military economic presence, but not the relative size or type of these institutional links (Izadi 2022). In the following empirical chapters, I show that the Tunisian and Egyptian militaries diverged at an early period following independence in their ability to launch successful commercial projects.

Because this type of military economic activity differs from that which we would expect from purely defense-oriented expenditures, I apply a new term to these military-affiliated companies: *the military-clientelist complex*. I employ this label to contrast these types of economic activities from the more commonly known military industrial complex in which companies exist to serve the military's needs for equipment and supplies. The military-clientelist complex, by contrast, has relatively little to do with the military's combat needs and much more to do with spreading wealth around. The fact that military-affiliated companies are under state control is what creates the clientelist tinge. The military is able to determine who its suppliers and consumers are, and its capture of monopoly profits provide it with a potent weapon over economic elites. Operating within restricted domestic sectors with ease, the military-clientelist complex represents a tangible reality that businesspeople must come to terms with.

The reason that I emphasize the military-clientelist complex in this study is because this institution is able to survive a regime transition. Newly elected parties in a transitional democracy will struggle to impose control on a powerful coercive institution, especially given the military's ability to claim special status as a defender of the country's sovereignty (Magnusson 2001; Brownlee 2002; Kim 2021). In addition, democrats must fear the military's willingness to stage a coup, a threat that is backed by the military's direct control over coercion. For all these reasons, it is very unlikely that in a democratic transition in a country with weak state institutions will we observe a rapid loss of economic privileges for the military so long as the military retained some autonomy from the prior dictator. Of course, if the military did not have extensive linkages to the business community, its relevance to business politics would be tangential. The deeper those links, the more that the military's political actions will spill out into the wider business community.

As a consequence, when a military-clientelist complex exists, there is a possibility that pro-authoritarian movements will have an array of tools they can use to coerce business support for their movement. Of course, it is unlikely that the military-clientelist complex, even when it is quite large, will be able to impose threats on all firms in the country. Nonetheless, there will be a sizable number of firms who rely on military-affiliated companies as either suppliers or consumers, and for these firms, it will be individually rational to support the military's side. Although militaries can in theory be in favor of democratization, the military often is a naturally conservative institution (Huntington 1957; Geddes 1999), and in the context of regime transitions implies a bias in favor of authoritarianism.

In sum, for both outcomes of broad and narrow rent-seeking, the causal graph begins with a massive disruption of state institutions through a regime change. This kind of political event is relatively rare and for that reason very hard to predict, so I treat it as an exogenous shock in the causal chain. What separates the two causal chains at this early stage is whether or not a powerful competitor to the dictator exists who also survives the downfall of the regime. In this work, this institution is the Egyptian military-clientelist complex, but it is entirely possible to have other institutional actors such as a powerful new political party who could likewise exert pressure on businesses via control of state institutions.

1.3.2 Loss of Principal

I move next to the second node in the graph, which is labeled "Loss of Principal." At this early stage, the causal process is the same for both the narrow and broad-rent seeking pathways. By principal, I mean the person or institution whom people in the government feel responsible or accountable to. Of course, lower-level bureaucrats are directly accountable to their superiors, and so on, but there is still a sense in which the dictator and the dictator's inner circle are those to whom bureaucrats are ultimately accountable. This concept is also known as the residual claimant in economic theory. As such, after regime change occurs, there is a sense in which state institutions are decapitated, that is, the head or responsible organ is suddenly removed. As a result, bureaucrats

1.3 The Causes of Business Political Engagement

and those who rely on them enter into a period of profound uncertainty until new rules can be written that decide who gets what and when.

This is a similar trend to research based on post-Communist states in which the loss of the single party led to unconstrained bureaucrats holding up businesspeople for more bribes (Shleifer and Vishny 1993). As the number of bureaucrats who can ask for bribes increases, the total amount of bribes will necessarily increase because the pie of available bribes is not fixed. With no one to punish upstart bureaucrats, each will aim for as great a share of bribes as possible (Shleifer and Vishny 1993).

Mechanism M_1 is based on the contention of Dahl (1971) that these transitions will occur when the costs of tolerating the previous dictator are greater than the costs of repression, or of removing whatever political problems caused the regime transition to occur. The principal, or dictator, can only be removed when it is in the interest of those in power – or at least, those who remain in power following the dictator's fall. However, once this decision point is reached, the real distribution of authority in the state will necessarily change as well.

The reason that I discuss the removal of the dictator as the removal of the *principal* is because principal–agent issues are the dominant mechanism used to explain the constraints on bureaucrats in performing their duties. The principal–agent framework has long been used to understand the discretion that bureaucrats, or the agents, have in their jobs (McCubbins, Noll, and Weingast 1987; Dixit 2002; Gailmard and Patty 2007), and it is also a core idea behind how political scientists explain differences in state capacity (Evans and Rauch 1999; Dal Bó, Dal Bó, and Di Tella 2006; Besley and Persson 2009; Ma and Rubin 2018). States with fewer principal–agent problems, or more control over bureaucrats, have higher capacity as they can enforce laws more strictly and collect taxes more comprehensively (Pepinsky, Pierskalla, and Sacks 2017). Crony capitalist states, almost by definition, have lower state capacity in part due to close relationships between businesspeople and bureaucrats that often involve off-the-books transfers (Svensson 2005).

The principal–agent relationship that matters here is between the bureaucrat and political leaders, even if the relationships are not entirely formal. Due to the fact that rules and policies may not be strictly followed in states with weak institutions, the informal nature of how power is distributed is a more significant determinant of how the government allocates rents. Political connections are a way that firms can protect and stabilize their interactions with bureaucrats who may not be otherwise constrained by policy rules (Haber, Razo, and Maurer 2003; Marcus and Davis 2014). When bureaucrats threaten firms, they are often abusing state institutions to their own advantage, perverting rules about taxes or business licenses to unfairly punish companies. Conversely, when bureaucrats reward companies with contracts or special licenses, they often circumvent rules designed to secure the best value for the state by awarding contracts to the highest or most competitive bidder.

24   *1 How Firms Respond to Regime Change*

When bureaucrats do the bidding of ruling politicians in these states, they often do so outside of the legal and regulatory framework of the state (Gingerich 2013; Gehlbach and Simpser 2014). The interests of the common welfare are then short-changed in favor of the political patron and his or her cronies, which often includes businesses. The bureaucrat usually receives a cut of the profits, though they may also take action simply to avoid the politician's wrath. In either case, the bureaucrat is no longer faithfully implementing the state's rules and regulations, but rather is acting either for their own interests or for an actor who, while they may themselves be a part of the state, are acting quite outside their official capacity.

The reasons why principal–agent problems in bureaucracies are high, and state capacity is low, is somewhat beyond the scope of this book, but are certainly rooted in long-term political-economic trajectories of countries (Tilly 1992; Evans 1995; Waldner 1999; Kohli 2004; North, Wallis, and Weingast 2009). It would seem that only seismic shifts in how political elites relate to each other can push states to become more organized and coherent. Much research has been devoted to this particular question, but answers about when and why states develop more capacity elude general theories so far. While this book operates a much lower level, it may shed some light on the mechanisms that help sustain low-capacity states.

The importance of principal–agent issues will be seen in the next section because of its relation to determining the price of state privileges for businesspeople.

1.3.3 Increase in Rent Prices

While the loss of a principal in any government will result in profound consequences for how governments function, for the purposes of this book the important consequence is the effect on business access to crucial government rents. To understand the reason why this occurs, I use a second network in Figure 1.3 that might be thought of as a model-within-a-model that captures the mechanism M_2: following a loss of principal, bureaucrats are no longer accountable as they once were. Though not strictly a causal graph, it encapsulates how relationships between businesspeople, bureaucrats and dictators are likely to occur in practice. This model could also represent the mechanisms connecting loss of principal with the increase in rent prices.

To explain this mini-model, it is important first to understand why businesses require rents from bureaucrats, and what they require them for. As previously mentioned, in countries with significant issues with corruption, it is often a necessity for companies to obtain rents, or unearned privileges, from the state (Li, Meng, and Zhang 2007; Gehlbach, Sonin, and Zhuravskaya 2010; Szakonyi 2018). These kinds of perks and benefits are quite diverse, from winning supply contracts, securing access to protected markets to obtaining direct government subsidies through low-interest loans and export promotion

1.3 The Causes of Business Political Engagement

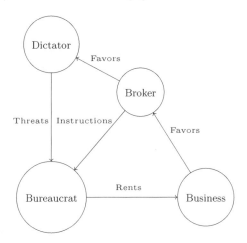

FIGURE 1.3 Causal diagram for rents, firms, and brokers

(Diwan, Keefer, and Schiffbauer 2015). These kinds of goodies are distributed through personal relationships in crony capitalist states in which the metric is the political influence of the business leader rather than the company's performance or importance to economic development goals (Bellin 2002; Haber, Razo, and Maurer 2003; Heydemann 2007; Frye 2017). This type of individualized distribution of perks and privileges to individual companies is often seen as the hallmark of crony capitalism.

The model in Figure 1.3 describes the relationships that govern how a given business – denoted by the node on the right-hand side – is able to obtain favors and perks from bureaucrats without requiring direct interactions such as bribes. The business wants some kind of rent – loosely defined, as it could be a form of property right protection – but they do not go to the bureaucrat. Instead, they develop a political connection with a broker by providing favors, such as election financing (Stokes 2011; Aspinall 2014; Larreguy, Marshall, and Querubin, 2016). The broker passes on some of these favors to the dictator while keeping some of them for him or herself. The broker then passes instructions to the relevant bureaucrats to provide rents to the business. If the bureaucrat disagrees or tries to obstruct, the broker can use his or her influence with the dictator (or the dictator's inner circle) to force the bureaucrat to act. While simple, this diagram captures how these relationships are likely to happen in practice.

While the plot shows businesses trying to obtain rents, there is another reason why companies might seek individualized relationships with state bureaucrats and politicians, and that is to protect the firm from harm inflicted by the state (Olson 1993; Acemoglu, Johnson, and Robinson 2004). The line between benefit and harm can blur, but it remains an important conceptual distinction as it reflects different frameworks for why firms engage in politics. Again, there are a variety of reasons that firms might seek protection from the state. It could be due to the need to obtain permissions to operate or register a business, or to secure permission to import and export goods. The company may need to defend itself from expropriation, whether this be expropriation of income via excessive/unregulated taxation/fees, or through direct expropriation, such as state bureaucrats (acting independently or as agents of powerful politicians) using quasi-legal means to obtain ownership over the firm (Haber, Razo, and Maurer 2003; Markus 2015; Frye 2017).

Generally speaking, prior research on politically connected firms and crony capitalism has not differentiated clearly between threats and benefits or carrots and sticks with companies and political behavior. The observed behavior is likely to be similar as in both cases businesses need to influence the behavior of bureaucrats. However, the underlying utility calculus is likely to vary. Political engagement to avoid threats is relatively straightforward: The company will expend resources to political activity up to the amount of harm it believes may befall it in the future. However, incentives to obtain goodies from the state involves additional costs beyond those of the bribes, funds, or board seats that a company may need to give to play the game. Earning perks from the state may earn it the enmity of others, such as companies associated with rival politicians.

In this book, I incorporate both reasons that might drive political engagement in crony capitalist systems. The primary variables that affect political engagement will also affect firms regardless of whether their engagement is based more on sticks or carrots. While an interesting empirical question in its own right, it is not necessary to separate these two incentives for the argument to explain the outcome.

In order to obtain these relationships, businesspeople can negotiate directly with businesspeople by paying bribes on a per transaction basis, by co-opting bureaucrats in a phenomenon known as state capture (Szakonyi 2018; Canen and Wantchekon 2022), or by using some kind of political broker who can arrange for the necessary transfers. The emphasis in this book is on the third kind of exchange as it is very much the heart of crony capitalism: informal relationships used by companies to capture perks and goodies from the state. As has been discussed previously, obtaining some kind of relationship as opposed to a series of one-shot bribes promises to restrain predatory behavior by bureaucrats and ensure continued access from companies to government resources (Haber, Razo, and Maurer 2003).

State capture, on the other hand, can certainly occur, though it can be somewhat difficult to separate this empirically from the model shown in Figure 1.3. Capture requires replacing the dictator as principal in the top node with the firm itself, or perhaps replacing the broker with the firm. The problem is that it can be difficult to know whether a broker is in fact a broker or a member of the firm; in these relationships, the separation between official and unofficial duties is difficult to characterize. In any case, the model in Figure 1.3 can be thought of as a generalization of the process; a company may succeed in moving up the

1.3 The Causes of Business Political Engagement 27

value chain and replacing brokers, but every company in theory can participate in this process without needing to do so.

The inclusion of brokers is important as it is not the case that dictators have either the time or the resources to individually dole out rents to companies. As Markus (2015) showed, expropriation and other issues can be motivated by bureaucrats outside of the direct purview of the sovereign or ruler of a country. While some companies with the highest level of political connections may be able to intercede with the dictator personally, most others will likely need to use some kind of proxy for the dictator's influence.

While a broker could be anyone with influence, it is especially helpful to think of them as part of the dictator's party. Parties have been shown to be crucial in authoritarian stability by permitting the resolution of conflicts (Brownlee 2007; Gandhi and Lust-Okar 2009; Meng 2020) and providing rules for how rents are distributed (Reuter and Gandhi 2010; Blaydes 2011). It is important to note that through the broker, the business can essentially make use of the dictator's threats or ability to punish shirking in bureaucrats to ensure they obtain the necessary permits, favors, and privileges. Crucially, it is not necessary for the business to have direct relationships with bureaucrats for the model to work. In addition, through connections businesses can obtain support in working with bureaucrats from across the state.

The change in the cost of bribes, so to speak, can be thought of as a form of transaction costs for rent seeking. Corruption is, after all, a way of avoiding state regulations, and obtaining favorable policy decisions is a transaction between a company and the state (Husted 1994). When businesses have to pay more bribes to obtain the same level of state favors, it represents an increase in the "cost of doing business" that they will have to absorb or pay on to consumers. In all cases, rising transaction costs reduces the expected payoff of the rent to the company (Méon and Sekkat 2005).

This explanation of the mini-model is necessary to show why the price of rent will increase following the collapse of the dictator's regime and party. Stripped of these relationships which previously smoothed business-government interactions, businesspeople are left to deal directly with bureaucrats who suddenly do not have to fear any principal (or at least are much less constrained than they were before). As a result, if businesses are to obtain the same privileges and benefits, they face a hold-up problem where they can no longer make use of brokers and other proxies to obtain what they require. In addition, the dependence of the business on the rent through the institutionalization of the broker–business relationship means that businesses can be particularly vulnerable to hold-up problems following a regime collapse. The very benefits described by Haber, Razo, and Maurer (2003) can come back as vulnerabilities.

This increase in bribes, though, will be a temporary phenomenon. As business adjusts to the new situation, they will build personal political connections that allow them to identify lower-cost methods of obtaining their necessary

28   *1 How Firms Respond to Regime Change*

rents. As Kang (2002) showed, business can benefit from a democratic transition as politicians need funds from businesspeople to run campaigns. Over time, new principal–agent relationships come to replace the old, and if the number of political actors increases as happens in democratic transitions, business may well end up better off than it was before in terms of state access.

1.3.4   New Gatekeeper Emerges

This node only appears on the graph in Figure 1.1 that explains when narrow rent-seeking is the dominant mode of business political engagement. Again, this process happens independently of what was described in the previous section; businesses are likely to experience an increase in rent prices regardless of whether a new gatekeeper emerges. Gatekeeping later determines how businesspeople react politically to the new situation and attempt to remedy their problem.

As mentioned previously, the institutional actor capable of taking over the state in this book is the military-clientelist complex. This actor must have significant autonomy from the dictator to permit it to subsume the roles of the dictator and any brokers in Figure 1.3 as per mechanism M_4. If the gatekeeper has the requisite autonomy and level of resources, the gatekeeper can seize the opportunity to reconfigure the relationships between businesses and rents by controlling brokers and consequent access to privileges and benefits provided by bureaucrats to companies. Of course, this lucrative type of control is likely to engender significant competition among other remnants of the ancien regime, not to mention incoming democratic reformers, and for that reason for a new gatekeeper to emerge, it must be a powerful institutional actor with the resources to push aside other claimants to the throne.

For this reason, it is important to note the arrow between the loss of a principal and the new gatekeeper nodes. The loss of principal creates the opportunity for a new gatekeeper to emerge, but does not require it. Instead, a network may evolve without such hierarchical relationships and permitting businesspeople to work with brokers who do not necessarily have as direct access to a dictator or other person with extensive power over the bureaucracy. The resulting network is likely to be fragmented and chaotic to businesspeople, and in this situation, it may be more appealing for businesspeople to attempt state capture, though as I will show, that is not necessary for businesses to respond to this chaos.

1.4   COMBINED CAUSAL PROCESS

The outcome that this theory is aimed at explaining is the type of business political engagement following a regime transition. As mentioned before, in both broad rent-seeking and narrow rent-seeking, business political engagement will

1.4 Combined Causal Process

occur post-transition because rent prices increase. The cost of doing business, not in terms of supplies and wages but in terms of government favors and protection of property, necessarily increases in tandem. Unless businesses want to be at the mercy of newly unconstrained bureaucrats, they will seek to recruit new brokers to help them manage the chaos. The difference between the two pathways is that in a broad rent-seeking system, companies only experience the stress of disrupted relationships with brokers. In the narrow rent-seeking system, businesses now face an actor who can centralize control over bureaucrats and the political system, which necessarily limits business' options.

According to mechanism M_5, once a gatekeeper is able to centralize the distribution of rent, it is also able to command a much greater allegiance from crony capitalists and even more ordinary companies who still rely on government permissions to operate. It is not necessary for all businesses to have a direct connection to some military official for this incentive to exist; all that has to be true is that the threat of the gatekeeper's actions could interfere with business operations. As a result, business political activity will revolve around the gatekeeper's central role because the gatekeeper can condition access to the state's resources on businesses supporting the gatekeeper's political goals. Thus, the gatekeeper is able to bring about narrow, or more partisan, rent-seeking as the norm among businesspeople.

As mentioned in the previous node, all businesspeople need to survive a transition is access to brokers who can manipulate the levers of government. As mechanism M_3 describes, businesspeople need new relationships to replace old ones. Absent a new gatekeeper emerging, businesspeople have much more freedom and flexibility to choose the particular broker best suited to their needs, whether that be an elected politician or a power behind the throne. The quotidian interactions described previously in this chapter, such as giving funds to parties to ingratiate themselves, can help reestablish relationships between businesspeople and the new power holders. By so doing, broad rent-seeking becomes the norm among businesspeople: become a neutral party toward most or all political sides, and target those brokers for influence who are best able to deliver.

That is not to say that in the case of broad rent-seeking all is well for businesspeople following a political transition. There are still substantial threats that come about to businesses by virtue of unconstrained bureaucrats, or even worse, government agencies that are forced to divulge corrupt dealings of the past. In the first case, bribery payments and other costs of doing business are likely to increase, in the latter, the business could face the threat of expropriation or even imprisonment. As such, while the type of business political activity will differ as a result of the gatekeeper's influence, the same may not hold true for the level of business political activity. Following transitions, uncertainty requires business political engagement of one sort or another when valuable rents are to be won or lost.

1.5 OBSERVABLE IMPLICATIONS OF THE THEORY

The full causal process shows how I expect all of the variables to produce business political engagement. However, it is unlikely that I could gain information about all of them. For example, it is difficult to know for sure which bureaucrats are under someone's political influence and to what extent they might charge a business for bribes. For this reason, I discuss in this section what I could expect to observe if the causal process is correct. By doing so, I can focus on those observations which could help me know whether the argument is justified or not.

First, I consider what this theory implies for how business reacts to a political transition, especially one toward a more open and accountable system of government such as democracy. In the case of a crony capitalist regime that collapses, businesses are unlikely to be big fans of democratic reformers, though that is not because they have ideological beliefs that democracy is a bad system of government. The businesses that exist in a given country are those that successfully navigated its economic and political institutions, and as such will tend to have a status quo bias. Especially in states with issues with corruption and crony capitalism, the businesses that survived and thrived are likely those with some positive relationship with the state.

Political connections, though, are only valuable with a particular regime or set of officials. Once regimes shift, new political leaders may ignore these connections or even actively discriminate against those who formerly were in favor (Albertus and Menaldo 2014; Earle and Gehlbach 2015). A shift in regime type is an even more frightening prospect for politically connected firms as democracy will likely bring with it demands for redistribution by changing the effective tax rate (Boix 2003; Acemoglu and Robinson 2006). Meeting these demands would require whole-sale institutional change of the sort that would increase state capacity to regulate markets and deter corrupt practices. This kind of true reform would be the death knell for the entire political-economic system. In other words, a transition to democracy entails for politically connected firms not only a loss of connections to one particular ruler, but a threat to the system of connections itself.

It is of course possible that business becomes a force for democratization, as some theory in political science has long proposed (Moore 1966). Research by Mazaheri and Monroe (2018) shows that, on average, small business owners in the Middle East are more in favor of democratization than the average citizen. However, their study also shows that business owners in countries that saw instability after the Arab Spring have less interest in further democratization, and the authors' qualitative research in Jordan showed businesspeople feared the political chaos that regime change could bring.

Costly commitment to regime change is unlikely for companies in the region because, I have previously described, strong selection pressures ensure that the companies that exist have some kind of accommodation with the state. This

1.5 Observable Implications of the Theory

may involve direct partnership with the ruler's family, but even minor business-people require assistance from local magistrates and bureaucrats who control access to necessary permits to operate their business, own land and access bank accounts (Djankov et al. 2002). As Greenwood (2008) writes in his study of business in Jordan and Morocco,

> Entrepreneurs interviewed in both Morocco and Jordan described corrupt links between prominent business families and the palace as a formidable obstacle to democratization. These families strongly oppose democratization because they fear that greater levels of political transparency and accountability will mean an end to the privileged ties to the center of power they have historically enjoyed. (848)

When those relationships are disrupted, such as through incisive and effective economic reforms that make the provision of permits a function of need rather than personal connections, it is plausible that businesses would become more sincere partners in the democratization effort (Bellin 2002; Arriola 2013). For example, Islamist business industrialists in Turkey, which arguably has the most powerful state and successful liberalization efforts of any country in the region, supported democratization with the rise of the Ak Parti in the 2000s due in part to these business' success in export markets rather than domestic protected sectors (Başkan 2010). However, given that economic reforms are difficult in states with weak institutions and powerful political patrons, we cannot necessarily expect this to occur quite often in the countries that the theory would apply to.

Based on this description of firms in authoritarian developing countries, we might expect two results from regime transitions when large numbers of crony capitalists exist: (1) wide-spread redistribution against politically-connected firms and (2) strong pushback from businesses in response. Existing research has shown that the first outcome does not necessarily occur post-transition: Income and wealth inequality does not necessarily decrease following transitions to democracy, and is even less likely when transitioning from one authoritarian regime to another (Ansell and Samuels 2014; Scheve and Stasavage 2017; Albertus and Menaldo 2018). Unfortunately, at present, we lack available comparative data to estimate at what likelihood the second factor, fierce business activism opposing regime change, occurs across countries. But it is apparent that if wholesale redistribution never occurs, then it is unlikely that business collective action in favor of regime change would be frequently observed.

This lack of redistribution post-transition is a puzzling result of research into regime change, especially when new leaders publicly campaign for an end to crony deals. As I show later in this book, it is easy to document the economic distortions created by crony capitalism. These networks of firms and regime officials ought to be straightforward targets for reformers. In some cases, such redistribution does occur, as the case of Trabelsi in Tunisia demonstrated. However, such reformist actions are unlikely to happen extensively. It could be, on the one hand, that people do not actually want redistribution following regime change, as is suggested by Ansell and Samuels (2014). I take the other position, which is that redistribution is not observed because state institutions are not capable of implementing redistribution. Post transition, elites are able to corrupt institutions from within and secure the same kinds of rents that they obtained previously, as suggested by Acemoglu and Robinson (2008) and Albertus and Menaldo (2018). What I offer in this framework is a mechanism for explaining how and why institutions tend to be corrupted, which I argue is often aggressively pursued by politically connected firms.

The primary reason, I argue, that we do not observe greater levels of partisan activity among businesspeople post-transition is that business contain inherent advantages in political competition within emerging regimes. Democratic reformers seeking to consolidate a new regime have a multidimensional problem: they must compete for votes while also constructing the system by which representation occurs. As a result, parties and party systems tend to be inchoate following transitions from dictatorship to democracy, and it may be a significant time before parties are able to form backward linkages (Hagopian 2007). Furthermore, these democratic regimes have to borrow the same state institutions that existed under dictatorship (Levitsky and Way 2010) and which prominent businesspeople already know how to penetrate and manage to their advantage. In a transition from authoritarian rule to a different set of authoritarian leaders, the same challenges are likely to apply to those trying to consolidate their rule even if elections are less important.

As a result, businesspeople can become kingmakers when it comes to electoral competition in new democracies. Parties with weak linkages also lack the ability to raise funds through appeals to a wide social base (Biezen and Kopecký 2001). Prominent businesses, on the other hand, are happy to help with election funding – it merely replaces the cost of doing business with the prior dictator – in exchange for protection of their political-economic privileges. Because these firms already have strong connections to bureaucrats and considerable financial resources due to monopoly profits, they do not need policy changes but rather only a perpetuation of the status quo. For parties trying to seek office without requisite organizational know-how, this bargain may seem like manna from heaven. Unfortunately, as with the biblical manna, too much of this good can create long-term bads.

My contention, as I expressed earlier, is that these kind of deals between businesses and politicians is the most likely outcome for firms following a democratic transition. As companies build new political relationships, their crony privileges are kept sacrosanct. All other things equal, the temptation to corrupt democracy from within is stronger than investing in costly collective action to overthrow democracy. That is not to say that businesses are necessarily in favor of change: there is still plenty to fear from a new regime over the long term. In the short term, businesses may still be targeted for expropriation on a case-by-case basis. However, so long as widespread expropriation does

1.5 *Observable Implications of the Theory* 33

not occur – which is unlikely precisely because of the lack of strong state institutions – businesses are more likely to choose to take the immediate perks of partnering with democratic reformers than the long, hard, and uncertain road of fighting back against the new regime.

The mechanism that underlies business' failure to resist democracy can be understood via the prisoner's dilemma and the role of coordination games. In this case, cooperation around a common political goal would require business pooling resources around an anti-regime change movement, that is, a coalition, either by advocating for a military coup or planning an incumbent takeover where a strong executive overrides checks and balances. As I show later in this book, businesses have substantial and growing economic power in a liberalizing age in which state-owned enterprises have been sold off in favor of so-called private enterprise. If business really did unite around a common cause, their funds, organizational resources, and captive voter base – employees – can prove a lethal weapon against transitional regimes. However, this sort of overt politicking involves many risky front-door deals of the type often avoided by businesses.

There are observable implications that follow from broad business political engagement. First, we should observe delayed or obstructed economic reform efforts, particularly with regard to opening investment and trade regimes and implementing anti-corruption initiatives. These policy changes would undercut the value of firms' political connections, many of whom are heavily involved in party finance or even running for office, and consequently it can be difficult for transitional legislatures to pass these laws even if there is widespread popular demand for these changes. The inchoate party system makes it harder for voters to assign blame for the lack of progress on this front, lowering the cost to political parties of agreeing to table these reform efforts (Cheeseman 2010).

Second, we should observe businesspeople who are politically engaged but also politically neutral (Kim and Kunisky 2017). The political neutrality of business can come as a surprise and may be mistaken for political moderation of business elites. As I argue, business' native preferences in crony capitalist system are usually in favor of the status quo. Neutrality comes rather from individual firms seeking to protect their own privileges regardless of who they must fund to do so. To paraphrase Winston Churchill, firms will give a dollar to the devil if the devil helps them obtain a coveted government contract. Weak state institutions help firms spread their donations around the political spectrum because parties either evade what political financial regulations exist or sit on the information if the regulations do not exist (Hummel, Gerring, and Burt 2021). Parties may believe that they can accept these funds because the means justifies the ends, but firms' willingness to engage with *all* sides can make corporate interests untouchable for legislators in parliament. This type of behavior naturally follows from the demands of broad rent-seeking. To secure rents with a dispersed rent network and principal–agent relations, it becomes important to engage with all stakeholders, so to speak.

Political neutrality also implies that businesspeople will avoid engaging with one particular political party. Partisanship could undermine their ability to work all sides of the table. As a consequence, the most likely form of political activity we should observe from businesspeople is party finance. We should expect to observe other kinds of political activity relatively infrequently, such as businesspeople directing their employees to vote for a particular party or hosting rallies for political parties. As businesspeople become more interested in protecting their interests within the existing party system, they counterintuitively become less interested in advocating for any one political party.

Third, we should either not observe any elite-directed movements against democratization, or if they do occur, we should expect that these movements will collapse due to in-fighting and the very real cost of partisan activity for businesspeople. The logic of this argument is not deterministic – some firm owners, especially very large conglomerates with substantial resources to put to their own ends, may choose still to build a coalition for regime change (or at the very least, move toward an illiberal democracy). However, the success of these movements is undercut by cooperation issues like the prisoner's dilemma and too many focal points. Firms have multiple options to protect their interests in the policy space, and they need not restrict themselves to an anti-regime party even if one exists. At the same time, a narrow focus in political activity may incur substantial costs to the business by displaying partisan affiliation and necessarily alienating part of the political spectrum. Defection away from the anti-regime movement could mean actively supporting a pro-regime party, but it may just imply a firm staying neutral toward the anti-regime faction. If movements against the new regime cannot reach a stage of sustained collective action, they will find it difficult to undermine new state institutions including elections (Brownlee 2007).

As I mentioned, the outcome of individualized firm political engagement (i.e., broad rent-seeking) is most likely to occur following regime transitions with weak state institutions and significant numbers of politically connected firms. In a transition to democracy, such as those studied in this book, democratic competition without regulations on party finance can result in a new dense web of personal relationships between firms and ostensibly reform-minded democrats. Some companies may even be able to expand as those firms that suffer expropriation or lose influence open new opportunities for survivors. However, as I specified earlier, this result is likely to occur *if all else is held equal*. Aspiring pro-authoritarian movements may have some tools at their disposal to sequester business support for their movement.

1.6 THE MODEL IN A NUTSHELL

Given these variables, we can now discuss how they collectively determine the outcomes of narrow and broad rent-seeking. As mentioned previously, these are types of business political engagement, not necessarily levels of engagement. It

1.6 *The Model in a Nutshell* 35

may be that a gatekeeper with control over rents may be able to secure a higher level of engagement from firms in addition to their undivided loyalty, but it is still the case that following regime collapse, many companies that previously depended on mediated access to state institutions will require some kind of political activity to protect their interests. In essence, they need to replace old forms of political connection with new forms of connections lest they continue to face the mercurial nature of unconstrained bureaucrats.

However, I do not think that these kinds of individualized connections are the only way that companies can respond to these challenges, although I do think they are the dominant way. An alternative is for companies to become a part of a political coalition in which their political allegiance grants them special favors or protects them from the ire of unrestrained bureaucrats. This distinction has not been made previously in research on crony capitalism, but is a crucial distinction for this book.

In general, businesses prefer back-room deals to front-room deals – that is, individualized political connections are more prevalent than joining political coalitions. If the aim of the company is to minimize costs, then it should only want to obtain a relationship with the person with influence over the specific area they care about – that is, the relevant broker in Figure 1.3. For example, if a company is in a rural area, and fears visits by the local tax collector, it may only need to curry favor with the town mayor to prevent such visits from occurring. If a company wants to obtain contracts from the Ministry of Industry in order to supply a state-owned company, it may only need influence with the bureaucratic decision-makers who allocate contracts (or with those who have influence over the decision-makers). For these reasons, joining a larger political coalition is unnecessary and may incur substantial costs beyond what purchasing this influence requires.

Furthermore, individualized relationships have an additional benefit for companies: they prevent the firm from taking partisan sides. Political activity, after all, can have a down side, as it inevitably associates the company with the fortunes of a political patron (Albertus and Menaldo 2014). Political activity that is more hidden (in the back room) can hopefully isolate the company from any downfall due to a transition in power (Earle and Gehlbach 2015). Work on lobbying in the United States, for example, reveals that this type of political activity is primarily aimed at those committees with control over relevant regulatory processes and not in terms of partisan divides (Kim and Kunisky 2017).

As mentioned earlier, these different kinds of engagement arise from different kinds of control over rents. For back room, individualized political connections to work, principal–agent relations in the bureaucracy must assume a certain shape. In particular, the bureaucrats' accountability will depend on which broker they are involved with, which can vary significantly across ministries and geographical areas. We could phrase this in social network theory terms as a network with relatively low centrality, that is, many hub and wheel constellations within the network. The more hub-and-wheel constellations, the less hierarchical the network and the less that companies have to worry about politicians up the food chain, so to speak. These hub-and-wheel constellations could arise due to the bureaucrat's own initiative or to involvement with a broker like a politician, leader within the ministry, or member of organized crime.

When a bureaucrat takes their own initiative versus the interests of some other principal, we often identify the result as petty corruption. This label implies that the fee or bribe requested by the bureaucrat is fairly small, and for a business, possibly trivial (or even efficiency enhancing). However, bureaucrats with control over very valuable resources are likely not going to remain accountable to themselves even if the state fails in its oversight role. Rather, the bureaucrats will be co-opted by a power holder, either via greater perks than the bureaucrat could obtain or from threats to the bureaucrat's job or personal well-being (Gehlbach and Simpser 2014).

If a new gatekeeper does not emerge, we can expect that the network with control over rents will become more dispersed. New politicians and political parties entering the system are almost certainly going to attempt to control access to these lucrative rents in order to cultivate support from prominent businesspeople. However, lacking the ability to exclude rivals, different components of the state are likely to be captured by different factions, permitting businesses to potentially play sides off against each other in negotiating for more rents for less cost.

Conversely, if the network grows more centralized with a new gatekeeper, businesspeople may see the need to join the gatekeeper's political coalition with serious ramifications for the political system. Coalition is a diverse term that refers to a general group of people with the same political aim. In the context of crony capitalism and weak state institutions, the aim is often to support a particular leader or elite network rather than to achieve an ideological goal. I use coalitions instead of parties because in countries with weak state institutions, networks of political control may not be defined by formal institutions (Slater 2012). For a business to support a coalition, it will have to engage in some kind of more public display of political support, such as participating in party rallies or ordering their employees to vote for a certain candidate. This kind of more visible politicking may be quite costly to the business as it could alienate both customers and even its own employees over these public stances.

The person who benefits the most from these types of coalitions are the gatekeepers who stand to gain from the increase in political support provided by businesses. The control over rents can then be thought of as a form of a bargaining game (Levi 1989): As the political elites centralize control over rents, they can subsequently ask for more direct political loyalty to themselves. Conversely, as the power of political elites over office holders declines, as is often the case in the context of weak state institutions, loyalty to these national-level leaders declines and the option of joining coalitions seems unnecessary to most businesspeople.

1.6 *The Model in a Nutshell* 37

As mentioned previously, participation in coalitions is not a dominant strategy for companies, whether in terms of this theory or in terms of empirical research to date. Again, companies prefer back-room deals and broad rent-seeking to front-room deals and narrow rent-seeking. Absent intervention, they are unlikely to accept the high cost of more public political participation. There are certainly businesspeople who become political of their own accord, but again, these idiosyncratic individuals, who often comprise a very small sliver of the business world, are rarely representative of companies. Many more businesses will only get engaged in overt politicking if they have no alternative, and in a crony capitalist system, such a world can only emerge when networks of influence are relatively centralized. There has to be a reason for cronies to leave the shadows and reveal themselves to public scrutiny.

All of this discussion is to make the point that business political engagement, even in crony capitalist systems, is a variable. It might seem that all companies in a corrupt, nontransparent market would engage in politics either to win benefits or disrupt threats. However, this may not occur, either because the firm does not believe the perks are worth the expenditure, or because the costs required to enter politics are too high, such as ceding partial control of the company to connected elites who want to extract revenue from the company. Furthermore, there is always the risk of blowback, of a cultivated political relationship suddenly becoming a liability due to the changing winds of regime fortunes.

When a firm does decide to engage in politics, in can largely do so with either a front-door (political coalition) or back-door (political connection) strategy. The reasons that companies adopt either strategy are closely tied to the rents or protections they seek from the state. As control over rents increases, powerful political patrons may be able to coerce clients into a more coherent political coalition. Without such control, businesspeople can focus solely on lower-level decision-makers and power-brokers while eschewing front-door political commitments.

The outcome that has the most danger for nascent institutions is if a powerful actor like the military is able to further consolidate control over rent-seeking networks, becoming an effective gatekeeper even if they are not nominally in control of the state. If that occurs, support for the gatekeeper's coalition becomes a necessary price for businesses to pay. Suddenly, the game changes and instead of the cost of collective action dampening business support, businesspeople become more concerned about being left out than on being the suckers who stayed loyal to the movement. As I demonstrate in this book, businesspeople have multiple levers they can use to influence the political system. In regimes in which employees have few legal recourse, employer attempts to influence their employees' vote choices are a particularly acute problem. Although the ballot may be free, the social environment surrounding voting may not be.

38   *1 How Firms Respond to Regime Change*

If business happens to mobilize against a nascent democracy, pro-authoritarian movements will receive a large boost and a reversion to autocracy becomes more likely. The aim of this book is not to estimate the probability that such collective action decreases the tenure of democracy as that probability depends on other factors, such as the likelihood that the military stages a coup, which are beyond the scope of this book. Businesspeople generally act with other partners in politics who assume a more public and visible role. Nonetheless, it is important to stress that a united business class is a serious problem for the health and longevity of an emerging democracy, a subject to which I return in the conclusion.

1.7   ALTERNATIVE EXPLANATIONS

In this section, I note two competing explanations that could also explain business behavior in these situations. I briefly critique them, and I will present evidence that I believe is inconsistent with both within this book.

The first is that of ideology motivating business interests post-regime change. This formulation can take many versions, but essentially it arrives at businesses having stable preferences in common which they then impose on to a regime. This perspective tends to think of businesses as having a very large amount of *structural* power, which they can employ to barter with politicians to obtain their outcomes (Lindblom 1977; Marsh, Akram, and Birkett 2015). Often businesses are seen as handmaidens to the neoliberal ideology associated with the World Bank and the International Monetary Fund. When analysts discuss corporate leaders desiring a "pro-business" regime, they are implicitly referring to this tradition of analysis. Businesses are fundamentally alike and favor some kind of system that privileges business against other societal interests like workers or consumers.

I do not think such ideologies, though they may be common among businesspeople, are very likely to be a motivating factor when political connections are very important to business survival. Business in these countries does not involve extracting value from labor so much as it depends on state-sanctioned rules to keep out competitors. Liberalizing policies may be seen as profound threats to the system because they allow new entrants, but evidence has shown that businesspeople are able to use political connections to subvert such policies (Sfakianakis 2004).

I am not suggesting that in developing countries there is no such thing as the structural power of business. Rather, I argue that precisely because this power is structural, it is likely to manifest itself in structures of government. It makes sense to talk of this structural power in the context of tax (Fairfield 2015) or monetary (Pond and Zafeiridou 2020) policy, but not necessarily deal-making between individual politicians and companies. As such, I do not take a perspective that assumes that businesses have certain interests in common, or

1.8 How to Test the Theory

that politicians necessarily are aware (even subconsciously) of what these interests are. This book is more about how individual companies may seek influence with politicians. While the aggregation of political influence can have subsequent effects on the government, this happens via active business participation in politics rather than passive threats against policymakers.

The second competing explanation is that what explains business political participation are interests that have little to do with their bottom line. The defining cleavage in the post-Arab Spring political environment is between secularists and Islamists (Stepan 2012; McCarthy 2016), and it is probably true that at least some business political action is motivated by sectarian concerns. Indeed, one of the most prominent Egyptian businesspeople, Naguib Sawiris, is a Christian and was targeted by Muslim Brotherhood officials for tax evasion. He subsequently became one of the prominent leaders of the anti-Muslim Brotherhood movement.

While I acknowledge that sectarianism played a role in increasing polarization and subsequent political involvement, I do not believe that these kinds of issues can explain the action of the majority of companies. Businesses showed a willingness to be involved with both Islamist and secularist politicians following the democratic transition in both countries (Adly 2017), as I would expect given the theory presented in this chapter. Sectarianism can certainly explain some political action, but it cannot explain all of it, especially with respect to business leaders. Electing a secularist may bring government policies closer to the business manager's ideal point *if that manager is a secularist*, but it will not solve the problem of maintaining access to important privileges post-transition. As such, while sectarian polarization certainly matters on the margin of political action, sectarian affiliation on its own does not solve the problems businesses face following a democratic transition.

1.8 HOW TO TEST THE THEORY

Through the course of this book, it is my intention to learn, to the best of my ability, whether this theory can best explain business political behavior in Egypt and Tunisia. It is not enough to simply put forward a compelling story that accords with what we might expect businesses to do; to the extent possible I want to obtain evidence that this causal story is a solid basis on which to understand how businesses in the region think about regime change. Doing so, of course, is no easy task.

In general, I need evidence of how businesspeople in these countries interacted with the state in order to obtain rents, which would allow me to measure the outcome of business political engagement. I also need measures of the major independent variables, especially the nature and long-term trends of rent distribution networks and political institutions. Second, I need variation in the values of the variables to know whether political outcomes change in response. To give just one example, I need to examine situations where rent distribution networks change, as the theory does not predict changes in business political engagement without prior changes in rent distribution.

To accomplish this goal, the book's focus will be on the experience of two countries, Egypt and Tunisia, during the tumultuous period of the post-Arab Spring years. Both countries experienced thrilling regime transitions in early 2011 after mass protests forced out long-standing dictators, Zine Abidine Ben Ali in Tunisia and Hosni Mubarak in Egypt. Both countries also followed a similar trajectory as free and fair elections ushered in new parliaments and presidents in 2012.

As is now widely known, only Tunisian democracy survived past year two with Egypt succumbing to a military coup in the summer of 2013. As of the writing of this book, Tunisia's hold on democracy remains tentative, although Egypt is very much an authoritarian regime. This divergence between the two countries has prompted a host of discussion about why Tunisia remains a democracy while Egypt reverted to authoritarianism. It is not the intention of this book to provide an authoritative account of why Tunisia remained a democracy, although much of the research presented is relevant to this question. By focusing on a neglected actor in these transitions – businesspeople – I help illuminate the inner workings of elite politics in these states and uncover the dynamics behind the rise of a powerful pro-authoritarian coalition in Egypt.

These two countries are a fertile area to test the theory presented in this chapter because they have significant numbers of crony capitalists and the networks of rent-seeking influence have changed dramatically. Furthermore, political changes revealed crony activities in the prior regime as previously taboo subjects like corruption of top-level party officials became an acceptable subject of research. We now know that businesspeople with family ties to Tunisia's prior dictator benefited handsomely from a business empire they built through their influence over state bureaucrats and business rivals (Rijkers, Freund, and Nucifora 2014). The large number of participants in these rent distribution networks strongly implies that broad rent-seeking was the norm for the country prior to the dictator's fall. The Tunisian bureaucracy became riddled with principal–agent problems over decades of mismanagement and later liberalization, producing widely heterogeneous rent-seeking arrangements benefiting influential elites (Hammami 2020).

In essence, based on my theory, I will examine businesspeople choosing between individualized business political engagement versus coalitional engagement in post-transition Egypt and Tunisia. These two types of business political engagement reflect different *changes* to underlying rent distribution networks in both countries. I will show that businesses in Egypt ultimately became absorbed in a coalition that successfully brought down democracy, while businesspeople in Tunisia fractured due to their higher tendency toward striking individual deals with politicians. As a consequence, businesspeople were of little help to the nascent pro-authoritarian movement in Tunisia, while they were a central pillar of the Egyptian military's coalition to undermine democracy.

1.8 How to Test the Theory

Given my causal graph, there are three possible ways to explore whether the empirical evidence aligns with the theory. First, in Chapters 3 and 4, I undertake a qualitative process-tracing exercise that details the nature of political-economic systems in Egypt and Tunisia. I trace out the rise of authoritarian coalitions in both countries and show how businesspeople reacted to these coalitions. My emphasis in these chapters is showing the intermediate steps that explain the ultimate outcome of the failure of authoritarian politics in Tunisia and their success in Egypt, which I believe is at least partly a result of stronger business engagement in Egypt versus Tunisia. By showing evidence of how each variable influenced the next, and as many of the intermediate steps and mechanisms in between, I aim for a kind of causal inference by showing that the causal story happened in the right order and through the right channels as I theorized (Waldner 2015).

Second, I will consider observational evidence analyzing different types and rates of political activity of businesses across the two countries. This kind of inference involves making the assumption that the causal graph is correct, and then examining whether distributions of political activities among businesspeople match up with those predicted by the theory. Crucially for this type of inference to be true, the data must be generated by the causal process I previously described.

As a result, I also look at experimental data. Using an experiment involves directly assigning a value to one of the variables in my theory, or what is known as *do*-calculus (Pearl 2000). This type of inference is very powerful because I can make statements about the values of the variables in my theory change *without needing to worry about whether I have correctly mapped all other variables.* Even if there are omitted factors, directly intervening in businesses' calculations will allow me to isolate the influence of a particular variable. On the other hand, this type of inference is limited by the fact that I cannot change certain variables. For example, I cannot create or remove gatekeepers from countries as that would require unheard-of levels of control over a country's political institutions. Instead, I focus on manipulating variables much closer to the outcome of business political engagement, such as by seeing whether businesspeople are more politically engaged when they have an opportunity to gain support from the military.

To implement these strategies, I must collect data, and I briefly discuss the type of data I collect.

1.8.1 Qualitative Data

Qualitative information about the actions and opinions of businesspeople in Egypt and Tunisia is a valuable resource for knowing whether their experiences line up with the causal model. In addition, because businesspeople are only one part of the broader political spectrum in these countries, I look at other factors that affect both regime change and the rise of crony capitalism. It is important to examine the context of how policies and leaders change because businesspeople in both countries do not exist in a vacuum. To understand why a businessperson in Egypt or Tunisia is likely to have dramatically varying opinions on democracy and government than a similar businessperson in the United States or Europe, we need to comprehend the very different traits that a businessperson must have to be successful. Direct interviews with businesspeople can help undercover the complex relationships undergirding business' political decisions, and in this book I will present the results of dozen of field interviews with Tunisian and Egyptian businesses, political leaders, NGO activists and journalists.

In addition to interviews, collecting historical information about these countries can help substantiate the long-term trends that are associated with crony capitalism. Businesspeople in Egypt and Tunisia have been close allies of the state since their countries' independence, and these dense business-state networks are the foundation for crony capitalism. How these networks arose, and what has sustained them since the Arab Spring, requires a historical examination of the mechanisms through which businesses obtain capital, invest, and compete for market share. While these actions in a developed economy might primarily involve managerial decisions about price competitiveness and product innovation, in the Middle East obtaining political support of one form or another is likely as or more important than the company's own capabilities.

Isolating the role of businesspeople within the myriad actions and consequences of different political actors in both countries is a challenging task. To structure the case studies and ensure that I address all relevant factors, I implement a process-tracing exercise that is aimed at making credible causal inferences about what drove business political engagement. Process-tracing involves creating a narrative based on all of the available data so that I can see whether the causal story in my theory corresponds to the actual, empirical story in each country.

Process-tracing is an emerging method in political science that provides an alternative to statistical inference for data that is essentially qualitative in nature (Bennett and Checkel 2014). Instead of feeding data into a model, I look at the details of these two countries to see if the factors that I believe cause business political engagement indeed do so in the correct order. While there is no consensus as of yet concerning how to judge the credibility of process-tracing in terms of causal inference, I adopt in this study the straightforward method of Waldner (2015) that proposes that a process-tracing study is causal when it can produce a causal graph in which each node (i.e., each stage of the process) is both necessary and sufficient for each subsequent node. While this is an abstract definition, in practice it means that I need to be able to identify all the historical steps of business' political engagement. Leaving out a crucial stage would result in a causal graph that is incomplete and as a result potentially unreliable.

This method formalizes the underlying intuition behind performing a case study. With statistical data it is possible to test for relationships between

1.8 How to Test the Theory

variables by examining the conditional distributions of data generated by these variables. However, the aim with process-tracing is to establish relationships between particular variables located in both space and time, which is a distinct and sometimes neglected aspect of causal inference: making inferences about particular cases instead of aggregate relationships (Woodward 2003). That is, instead of asking in these case studies whether businesspeople on average across time and space tend to have an adverse effect on democratization, I will examine whether the Egyptian military-clientelist complex is linked to business political engagement after the Arab Spring, while the lack of structure affected Tunisian business political engagement.

The advantage of structuring a process-tracing exercise around causal graphs (Waldner 2015) is that it helps unify the particularistic nature of single-event causation with the counterfactual theory of inference (Morgan and Winship 2007). I cannot observe, unfortunately, an Egypt without the military-clientelist complex or a Tunisia with one, which would be the best way to know if these institutions were having a causal effect. With process tracing, I will instead base the credibility of causal inference on the validity of the mechanisms and the completeness of the causal graph. For example, I should be able to identify individual businesses that were actually engaged in politics in both countries rather than just provide generalizations that I believe are accurate. To the greatest extent possible, I want to trace out every link in the causal chain to be sure it is there.

Finding these low-level connections between variables is important because it helps determine if a confounding variable exists that determines both the independent variable (military-clientelist complex) and the dependent variable (business political engagement). If such an alternate explanation for the facts of the case exists, then the causal graph is by definition incomplete (a variable is missing from the graph) and the proposed mechanisms are not actually at work. The presence of mechanisms is a crucial criterion for ensuring that the causal graph is valid by collecting direct evidence that the variables interacting with each other. Some competing explanations can be eliminated through Mill's Method of Difference if these factors are the same in both Egypt and Tunisia, but any time-varying confounding variables – that is, any variables which may have a varying effect on business political engagement – cannot be addressed in this manner. For this reason, the mechanisms should be such low-level human processes – preferably at the psychological level – that they can be described as "invariant causal principles" (Waldner 2015). The mechanisms I have proposed aim to come as close to this criterion as possible by focusing on the specific decision points where politicians and business leaders changed their minds.

What I specifically intend to look for in the cases is evidence of (1) the effect of the transition on businesses in both Egypt and Tunisia, (2) the nature of the political system post-transition, and (3) the eventual political response of businesses to their political environment. Finding evidence of the first factor is important for learning whether businesspeople report the types of disruptions which should motivate them to engage in politics, such as increases in bribe costs and predatory bureaucrats. The second area involves learning about the nature of political institutions post-transition and whether these would tend toward more centralization or decentralization as new political leaders and parties enter the system. In particular, I need evidence that a gatekeeper either did or did not emerge in each country.

Finally, the third area centers on the actions that businesses did or did not take in response their dilemmas. While I cannot gather data on all businesses, I can also learn more about the motivations behind their political engagement as well as details about how this engagement took place. Learning whether the causal process worked for companies that are central to this study – in other words, crony capitalists – is an important test of the theory. I need to have evidence that crony capitalists did try to reach out to political actors, and that their aspirations were determined by the institutional system. In case of rent centralization, they would need to work with the gatekeeper, while if not, they should maintain relationships with any party that might aid their cause.

1.8.2 Quantitative Data

Quantitative research can help test the theory by enabling to collect data on a much broader swath of the business community in these countries. At the same time, quantitative data necessarily lacks context that is helpful in knowing whether or not the data are relevant to the research question. For this reason, I do not rely on quantitative data alone, as I described in the previous section. However, this type of data is still crucial in establishing the argument by providing a much broader application of the argument than I could possibly hope to achieve via field research.

Most of the quantitative data that I will present later in this book is collected directly from businesspeople using online surveys. To recruit businesspeople, which is a difficult task in survey research, especially in authoritarian countries, I employed Facebook ad targeting. By using Facebook's proprietary user information, I was able to target ads at business managers, enabling me to collect data securely and anonymously on sensitive topics.

This relatively new form of data collection has numerous advantages in this context because I can implement the same surveys in both authoritarian (Egypt) and democratic (Tunisia) countries, and I have significant control over what kind of data I choose to collect on companies. For example, I can get much more precise, company-level data about the type of political activities they have engaged in during the five years following regime transitions.

Another crucial advantage of this type of quantitative data collection is that I can employ randomization to directly test certain parts of my theory. I use survey experiments in which I randomly present hypothetical scenarios respondents, and then see if they respond to these prompts in the way my theory predicts. While limited in that I cannot test my theory with actual institutional

1.8 How to Test the Theory

changes, it is still an important component as it provides a controlled setting within which I can see how businesspeople react to different political opportunities.

For this reason, I also put forward experimental data in the last two chapters in this book. The experiment I employ loses realism – external validity – but allows me to control some of the factors that lead to business political engagement, even hypothetically. The trade-off enables me to be less concerned about selection bias as I can equalize the political opportunities that are given to companies, but at the same time, I potentially lose relevance to the particular political problems that companies face. In order to manipulate, I have to abstract away from the background conditions from which political activities arise.

In summary, both qualitative and quantitative data provide overlapping and complementary ways of understanding and evaluating the argument at the core of the book. While I do not expect the argument to explain all outcomes perfectly – there are inevitably factors that are ignored and outcomes that cannot be fully explained – it will have observable implications in all of these domains. By using all of the evidence available, I aim to show how the theory can help explain a relatively difficult subject, that of business strategy in response to political transitions, and the subsequent effects of these strategies on transitions. It is up to the reader, ultimately, to decide whether the evidence presented enables me to claim that the variables in the theory are in fact causally related, as that is certainly the aim of this book.

2

Case Study

The Egyptian Military as the Gatekeeper

Having set out the theory and provided some context for the study of political connections, I now turn to the more detailed analysis of Egypt and Tunisia. This section of the book, comprising this chapter and the following one, offer qualitative evidence that substantiate the model of business political engagement presented in Chapter 2. The emphasis will be on showing how businesses in these two countries became involved with crony capitalism, and how they subsequently reacted when the institutional arrangement suddenly changed.

In this chapter, I describe how the theory can explain the decisions of businesspeople in Egypt during the turbulent post-Arab Spring period. As mentioned in Chapter 1, I organize the case studies by tracing out the factors that produced the outcome of business political engagement. To do so, I construct a narrative of what happened in Egypt by process-tracing each step of the causal graphs shown in Chapter 2. To do so, I must construct an event map that marries each causal factor to an actual historical event in Egypt. To make credible causal inferences, I need to have a valid argument and show how each component of the argument maps on to a specific event in Egypt's recent history.

The event map for Egypt is shown in Figure 2.1, which follows from the causal diagram in Figure 1.1 in the previous chapter that explains when narrow-rent seeking will emerge. I employ this causal graph because Egypt represents the case where businesspeople largely engaged in narrow rent-seeking centered around the gatekeeper, the military-clientelist complex. This narrow-rent seeking directly led to a more cohesive business coalition which was better able to achieve its goals. I also reproduce the mechanisms from Table 1.1 in Table 2.1 as a reference for the reader. The intention of the case study is to provide empirical justification for the theory laid out in the diagram. Of course, there are other influences on business behavior that are not captured completely in the theory, and as such I do not expect businesspeople to mechanically respond to the changes in political institutions. Rather, I expect to see trends and patterns that show influences on business behavior in the aggregate and especially among powerful business actors.

46

2 Case Study: The Egyptian Military as the Gatekeeper

TABLE 2.1 *Mechanisms for narrow rent-seeking causal graph*

Mechanism	Definition
M_1	Costs of repression exceed the costs of tolerance.
M_2	Bureaucrats no longer accountable to former dictator's and his/her party.
M_3	To offset higher bribe costs, firms invest in political relationships.
M_4	Greater institutional resources allows actor to compel support and give orders.
M_5	Gatekeeper provides rents only to those who support its political movement.
M_6	Loss of ruler as principal creates opportunity for others to seize control.

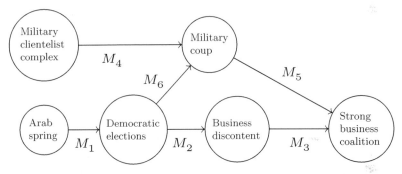

FIGURE 2.1 Event map for Egypt case study

The strength of the case study approach is that I am able to examine particular businesspeople, politicians and political parties in considerable detail as well as to focus on the difficult-to-quantify mechanisms undergirding decision-making. The main limitation is that I cannot possibly cover all companies nor all politicians within the country. As such, my focus in this chapter is on powerful and influential actors, while in the final two chapters I cast a much wider net by using survey data to recruit a diverse set of businesspeople from both large and small firms. However, it is difficult to substantiate all the parts of the causal story with quantitative evidence, and as such the case study is presented as a way of observing all of the causal variables in operation with attention to the mechanisms that show influence from one variable to another.

As shown in Figure 2.1, I identify a critical institution – the military-clientelist complex – as an important factor which emerged historically in Egypt but not in Tunisia. By the time the Arab Uprisings succeeded in overturning dictatorships in 2011, these differences in political-economic institutions would have important consequences for how businesses engaged with politics in these two countries. The success of pro-authoritarian coalitions opposing democracy differed due to varying levels of engagement by businesspeople. The causal process unique to Egypt, which is in the top part of Figure 2.1, shows how the military emerged from outside the crony capitalist system, permitting it to influence businesspeople post-transition as it claimed ever-increasing power over the state.

Businesspeople in Egypt also suffered from the same loss of privileges and need for political action as their counterparts in Tunisia, but the institutional context differed. This led companies to focus their political engagement around the military's plans for the country, becoming an inadvertent prop to a pro-authoritarian coalition. Business in Egypt had suspicions about democracy, but was willing to reach a compromise with democratic reformers. On their own, they would not have coalesced into a powerful political movement without the incentives provided by the military-clientelist complex.

2.1 EVIDENTIARY BASIS

The case studies are based on a variety of both secondary and primary sources. Primary data collection occurred during 2016 when I spent eight months in Tunisia, followed by a shorter trip to Egypt in September 2016 and a return trip to Tunisia in the summer of 2019. In total, I completed thirty-four interviews with managers of Egyptian and Tunisian companies, in addition to dozens of interviews with policy makers, activists, legislators, scholars, and business associations. I also collected microeconomic data on conglomerates and a complete rollcall vote dataset of Tunisia's first and second parliaments. I also draw on online surveys I implemented in Egypt and Tunisia over the past several years that targeted business employees in both countries.

These primary sources are complemented with a diverse array of secondary sources, including French and Arabic language news sources and scholarship from French and Arab political economists. In general, I rely more on the secondary literature in Egypt because the research environment there has been severely restricted after the rise of military dictatorship and because Egypt has a much more established tradition of political-economic research on which to draw. By comparison, in Tunisia I rely much more on my own interview-based research to understand linkages between firms and parties.

Due to anonymity offered to interviewees, and the sensitive nature of some discussions I had with businesspeople, I only provide dates for interviews and do not refer to their companies by name. While this does inhibit the narrative to an extent, anonymity was important for respondents to provide detailed information without fear of repercussions. In addition, anonymity allows me to focus on the outcome I am trying to explain, which is general patterns in business political engagement, rather than the involvement of any one company or conglomerate.

2.2 HISTORICAL POLITICAL ECONOMY IN EGYPT

I begin my discussion of Egypt with a general overview of the distinct nature of the country's political economy. This section explains how crony capitalism arose in the country. As will be seen in Chapter 3, the political-economic foundations of the state are broadly similar in nature to Tunisia's, permitting valid comparisons to be drawn. The nature of state–business relations in Egypt today can be traced to wrenching changes in political economy following Egypt's independence the 1950s as the region's colonizers, notably Britain and France, turned over sovereignty to indigenous political movements.

Egypt's brief experiment with democracy ended with the rise of a military-led regime under the aegis of Gamal Abd El Nasser, who launched into state-led industrial development to correct the perceived imbalances of the colonial economy in which the colonizing country was given distinct economic privileges (Waterbury 1983; Barnett 1992). While the aim of state-led development was to create an environment in which indigenous business became competitive on international markets, in practice this outcome did not occur. Instead, state-led development resulted in a sticky web of relationships between firms and states that obstructed economic growth and innovation. The political-economic system that arose out of the postcolonial period has been described as precocious Keynesianism (Waldner 1999; Henry and Springborg 2010; Diwan, Keefer, and Schiffbauer 2015; Hertog 2016), meaning that political leaders wanted to implement aggressive Keynesian policies to stimulate private sector investment with government-led initiatives, but lacked the political capital to do so. Instead, relatively weak modernizing rulers had to make concessions to rural producers and urban consumers in order to maintain their regimes. While politically effective, these bargains had the unfortunate side-effect of undercutting state capacity and making it impossible for postcolonial states to realize their developmental goals.

It was in the transition from an agrarian colonial economy to an industrialized postcolonial economy that many of the long-standing patterns of political-economic relations formed. Industrialization had begun under the pre war colonial era, but it primarily consisted in downstream processing of cotton for textiles and other applications rather than wholesale industrialization across sectors (Waterbury 1983, 58–60). Nasser's military regime, of course, preferred to have industrialization in sectors that conferred greater state (and military) power, such as automobiles, airplanes, and chemicals (Barnett 1992, 81–93). As a result, the state intervened through the variety of policy options common to import substitution industrialization (ISI), restricting foreign exchange in protected industries while simultaneously launching state-backed and state-owned companies to produce for the domestic market (Waterbury 1983, 63–65). Nasser's regime did not take on a particularly ideological hue when it came to economic policy-making, but was rather driven by the exigencies of fighting foreign threats (Israel) and excluding rivals, such as landowning elites allied with the overthrown monarch and the Egyptian Muslim Brotherhood (Waterbury 1983, 52–53, 63; Barnett 1992, 97; Eibl 2020, 68–71). Consequently, these policies often amounted to granting economic fiefdoms to regime allies rather than causing truly disruptive economic change.

Ultimately, the industrializing and land production policies of the Nasser regime led to a policy mix common in the Middle East and Africa of ISI married with the inclusion of agriculture (Bates 1981; Waldner 1999; Waldner, Peterson, and Shoup 2017), in which urban businesses, rural framers and urban consumers were all appeased. Unfortunately, political-economic policies that aim at large-scale transformation are unlikely to work if everyone is better-off (Gerschenkron 1962).

Eventually, Nasser nationalized major industries after his initial attempts at industrialization proved largely unsuccessful (Waterbury 1983, 68–69; Barnett 1992, 95), a solution to such obstacles in the short term but a signal of weak state power and a lack of the "embedded autonomy" necessary for sustained development (Evans 1995; Adly 2020). While manufacturing as a percentage of GDP increased in the 1960s, by the end of the decade the state suffered from a serious balance of payments crisis as projected national savings failed to keep up with currency restrictions (ISI assumed that national saving could be stimulated through currency restrictions aimed at lowering consumption of foreign goods) (Waterbury 1983, 92). The dismal performance of the ISI regime can be attributed to the same factors that made it politically appealing: The Nasser regime was unwilling to discipline the state-directed companies it helped create, instead using them as a source of revenue and a safety valve for employment for the masses (Waterbury 1983, 108–9; Adly 2020, 86–97).

However, despite the economic inefficiencies and the risks to state finance, this system proved to be difficult to unwind because of its political importance. In the five decades from the end of Nasser's tenure until the Arab Uprisings, Egyptian policymakers made important modifications that attempted to save the system without fundamentally altering it, a risky proposition that proved disastrous (Adly 2013). However, it did provide regime stability for five decades, which is an accomplishment not to be diminished. The trade-off was that the Egyptian state never established strong measures of control over bureaucrats or powerful elite actors who remained able to take advantage of institutions and policies.

Egypt experienced economic crisis at around the same time as Tunisia in the late 1970s and 1980s. Given the political foundations of ISI, it is in hindsight unsurprising that the well-intentioned development policies failed to achieve their goals. The aims of the ISI program – to replace foreign capital in manufacturing with domestic Egyptian companies – never lived up to its promise, resulting in high levels of indebtedness and mediocre rates of industrialization (Bechri and Naccache 2006). Similar to Tunisia, Egypt experienced a debt

2.2 *Historical Political Economy in Egypt*

crisis in the 1980s in large part driven by domestic policies that made the country vulnerable to dramatic changes in currency rates and capital flight. As Waterbury (1999) argued,

[S]tagnant economic growth and rising interest rates in the industrial core countries in the early 1980s made it impossible, even for the export pioneers, to export their way out of debt or into growth. The 1980s (really beginning with Turkey and South Korea in 1979) witnessed a string of debt crises and partial defaults. Almost nowhere did ISI survive intact. (335)

In Egypt, it was Sadat who was the first to tinker with the trappings of an ISI regime that was clearly failing to meet its production goals. He attempted to move Egypt away from a state-driven economy by enabling private enterprise and reducing the size of the welfare state, a policy known as Infitah, or opening (Adly 2020, 98–100). However, Sadat kept many of the import controls and other restrictions on foreign exchange, which enabled Egyptian state-owned enterprises (SOEs) to continue to provide necessary employment while a new entrepreneurial class flourished with their new role as brokers and contractors of the political economy regime (Soliman 2011, 38–39). As a result, although consumption increased, state finances lagged, which prepared the way for a major fiscal crisis in the 1980s (Soliman 2011, 44–45).

Despite economic reform (of a sort) and fiscal pressures, Sadat's actions did not fully disestablish Nasser's policies. His decision to rescind the public subsidy of basic foodstuffs led to the infamous Bread Riots in 1977, and these subsidies have been a third rail of Egyptian politics ever since (Stacher 2012, 68–69). What Sadat managed to do was to empower some of the business owners and former landowners who had suffered under the nationalization under Nasser, but most of the ensuing foreign and domestic investment went into service sectors, rather than manufacturing, as he had hoped (Waterbury 1983, 145). A select few Egyptians became wealthy through joint ventures with foreign companies that were granted monopoly concessions, such as Michelin and Goodyear's monopoly on certain kinds of tires for the automobile market (Waterbury 1983, 151; Sfakianakis 2004). Rather than ushering in a liberal capitalist utopia, Sadat layered institutions on top of the existing ISI infrastructure that enabled rapid wealth creation for existing elites via a new license raj on investment (Adly 2020, 210–11).

The outcome of economic reform in Egypt also entailed the empowerment of crony capitalists (Cammett et al. 2015, 282–286; Diwan, Keefer, and Schiffbauer 2015; Malik, Atiyas, and Diwan 2020; Rijkers, Freund, and Nucifora 2014). Sadat's policy of liberalization was later completed by his successor, Mubarak (Stacher 2012, 70), especially after a debt deal reached with the United States as a result of supporting Operation Desert Storm. These policies initiated wide-scale privatization of SOEs dating back to Nasser's era, some of which ended up in the hands of wealthy elites (Clement Moore Henry and Springborg 2010, 169–70; Adly 2020, 105). Furthermore,

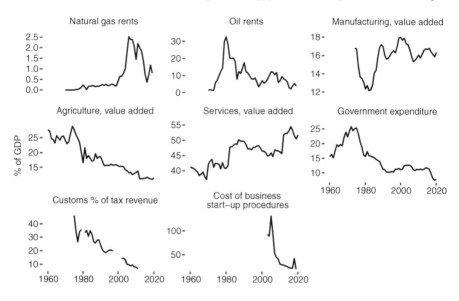

FIGURE 2.2 Egypt development statistics

the IMF reforms led to Egypt's adoption of a flat tax, reducing the state's revenue base (Farah 2013, 61–62).

The nature of the IMF program followed the Washington consensus orthodoxy in forcing the government to reduce expenditures while opening up trade and investment ("Egypt – Human Development Report 1995" 1995; Cammett et al. 2015, 275–81). By so doing, IMF conditionality successfully dismantled the remaining bulk of the import substitution regime begun under Nasser's tenure, although it left in place some important pockets of import protection that catered to politically connected businesses (Adly 2013, 70–115). As mentioned earlier, this conditionality program was implemented not only because of high Egyptian indebtedness, but also because it represented an opportunity to incorporate newly minted capitalists through managed elections (Blaydes 2011). While remaining in many ways a military regime, the tactics of controlled liberalization enabled Egypt to pivot under Mubarak from a state-controlled economy to one with economic freedom and enforcement of property rights for a set of business elites (Brownlee 2007).

Liberalization did result in some changes, as is shown in Figure 2.2. The government received far less of its revenue from custom duties as trade policies opened, and total government expenditure also fell. Meanwhile, the cost of business creation decreased as the state adopted pro-market policies advocated by the IMF. However, while the value added of agriculture fell over this time period, services came to dominate a larger share of the economy rather than

2.2 *Historical Political Economy in Egypt* 53

manufacturing. Given that Egypt's service sector is relatively low value as an emerging market, the plot reveals that the country's liberalization shrunk the government sector without stimulating the kind of growth which could result in high-paying jobs and competitive products. As a result, Egypt's conversion an open market economy did not result in much export growth, despite some natural gas rents as can be seen in the figure. Rather, economic production has shifted to activities catering to a still closed domestic economy.

Despite this relatively dismal economic performance, it is clear that Sadat's initiation of the Infitah liberalization in the 1970s led to the rise of a business-oriented class that was previously less influential under Nasser's statist regime. As Blaydes (2011, 36) describes, Sadat's domestic policy calculation was to move away from some of the pillars of support for Nasser's regime who promoted socialism in favor of "the Egyptian business community." Consequently, he was able to incorporate a rising capitalist class into nascent liberalization of the political sphere, a policy continued and deepened by his successor, Hosni Mubarak (Tarouty 2015, 85–112).

The way in which Sadat and Mubarak pivoted after the debt crisis set in motion selection processes that were biased in favor of businesspeople with the ability to obtain favors from the regime. Waterbury (1983) first identified the infitahiyeen, or the beneficiaries of Infitah, as a set of merchants who successfully exploited Egypt's highly skewed import regime. While there are rags-to-riches stories in these countries, generally speaking the business elite made their fortunes during ISI, and there is a high level of stability (and low level of firm turnover) among big business. In order to grow a firm to an acceptable size, internal connections with bureaucrats and dictators were necessary to navigate the web of rules and regulations governing ISI, with the end result that those who were most adept at the process were most likely to succeed (Adly 2020, 76–79).

Although it is not easy to directly tie the rise of crony capitalism to rare events such as the outbreak of mass protest movements, secondary sources argue that Egypt was experiencing a form of rising inequality during the lead up to the Arab uprisings in 2011. This sentiment did not track with macroeconomic indicators of increased income inequality, but rather perceptions of reduced opportunities for non-elites. Cammett and Diwan (2013) describe how the process of privatization in the Arab world in the 1990s led to the capture of SOEs by private elites, an assertion echoed by a wide array of sources from both before and after the Arab Spring (Lesch 2012; Stacher 2012; Farah 2013; Noueihed and Warren 2013). In particular, Prime Minister Ahmed Nazif, a close associate of Mubarak's son Gamal, is blamed for promoting wide-scale privatization and ensuring that Gamal's business associates were in line to receive lucrative deals on Egyptian SOEs (Tarouty 2015, 55–83). However, these well-known accusations of corruption were apparently not enough to influence structural indicators of income inequality within the country, although survey evidence revealed that perceptions of inequality were increasing during the 2000s (Cammett and Diwan 2013, 407–12).

The loss of rural and urban incorporation came with benefits for Mubarak. He allied himself with a new wave of businesspeople who joined the National Democratic Party (NDP) and made the party an electoral and patronage juggernaut. Expanding the elite coterie to include rising capitalists helped Mubarak build his own base of support, and this group also stood by the planned succession of his son Gamal, which the military vehemently opposed (Tarouty 2015). Due to this enlargement of the ruling coalition, Egypt appeared stable to most observers, having survived several attempts by professionals to foment mass movements for regime change in the 2000s. Yet it was ultimately the political-economic foundations that crumbled, leading workers and farmers to join forces in a colossal overthrow of the Mubarak regime.

It is worth noting as well here why I specify that the military's influence over the economy is separate from the causes of the Arab Spring in Egypt as shown in Figure 2.1. While we do not have precise data on the growth of the Egyptian military's economic enterprises, we do know that they extended back at least as far as Nasser's regime, who relied on officers to run many of the big SOEs in his industrialization efforts (Waterbury 1983, 63–65). Of course, when Sadat liberalized the economy, many of these officers-turned-bureaucrats moved into manager roles in the growing private sector due to their superior ability to obtain licenses and financing (Sfakianakis 2004, 19; Sayigh 2019; Abul-Magd 2017).

While these types of relationships were more informal in that individual generals pursued wealth and prestige, more formal involvement by the military seemed to take off in the 1970s as well, initially in manufacturing (Marshall and Stacher 2012, pp. 19–20; Marshall 2015; Sayigh 2019). The military also diversified its commercial interests as the economy liberalized, though these were threatened by Mubarak's drive for privatization and foreign investment (Marshall 2015, 5, 20–21; Sayigh 2019). In other words, Mubarak's economic diversification combined with his push to create a new pro-business elite seemed to be an effort to marginalize the military. However, the military's power was never seriously threatened (Cook 2007), and the military also proved adept at changing its own investment strategies, pursuing joint ventures with foreign partners to upgrade and compete with the new crony capitalists (Marshall and Stacher 2012). While we do not know for certain the extent of the military's commercial holdings on the eve of the Arab Spring, existing accounts argue that they were vast and went far beyond defense manufacturing to managing crucial infrastructure and ports (Marshall and Stacher 2012; Abul-Magd 2017; Sayigh 2019), though Sayigh (2019) thorough study suggested that the military's prominence came from its ability to occupy crucial sectors rather than dominating the Egyptian economy in a macroeconomic sense.

The reason why the military invested so heavily in commercial activity is likely due to the need for coup-proofing (Izadi 2022). While Nasser, Mubarak and Sadat all arose to power through the military, they had to worry about others taking the same path and supplanting them (Sayigh 2019, 19). Allowing

2.3 *The Arab Spring* 55

military officers to run public–private enterprises as private fiefdoms permitted them substantial autonomy and riches in exchange for acquiescence to the dictator's plans (Sayigh 2019, 22). While Mubarak may have had designs on reducing the military's influence, he was never rash enough to cut off the military's core interests or its lucrative economic base. As a result, the military's economic and political power remained crucially separate from Mubarak's, permitting the former to escape the fate of the latter.

As I discuss in Chapter 3, this distinction in terms of military economic involvement is one of the profound differences between Egypt and Tunisia. While it is not my aim to explain why the military become more involved in the economy (Izadi 2022), it is still important to this study that these crucial differences appeared long before the Arab Spring came to be. By the time that the authoritarian regimes in both countries collapsed, the bases of political and economic power differed between the two countries. At the time that the Arab Spring occurred, few would have thought that these historical trajectories would matter so much for the health and survival of democracy in the two countries.

2.3 THE ARAB SPRING

Having established why Egypt is a country that suffers from long-standing issues of crony capitalism and rent-seeking, I now turn to the momentous political events which define this case study. Regime transition is the first causal factor in the causal diagram, and as such represents the beginning of the setbacks that businesspeople experienced. Despite big business' political connections, companies were quickly rendered vulnerable to the rapid shift in control of the state.

The Arab Spring did not in fact begin in Egypt. The rapid mobilization of the Tunisian country-side in late 2010 quickly translated into popular protest in Egypt (Weyland 2012). The sudden demise of the Egyptian regime in early 2011 likewise came as a shock, not because everyone assumed that the state would always endure, but rather because the coup de grace came from a massive and nearly spontaneous social movement. Egyptian politics had exhibited contestation and unrest for some time, but it should be noted that the most visible signs of social movement formation in Egypt in the 2000s were elite-directed. Sources examining Egyptian politics written after the Arab Spring note the rise of the Kefaya movement, Egypt's first protest movement with an emphasis on regime liberalization, if not full regime change, as a potential predecessor of the Arab Spring (Dunne and Hamzawy 2008; al-Sayyid 2013). This movement was composed, however, of wealthier members of Egyptian society, even though it was led by "veteran left-wing activists" (Tadros 2014, 10–15). Kefaya primarily drew support from Egypt's new middle class, not from impoverished residents of Cairo, as might be supposed (Tadros 2014, 10–15). Analysts say that this movement drew its inspiration from protests in 2000 in league with the Palestinian intifada and the 2003 protests against the war in Iraq (Tadros 2014; Mossallam 2013), but it is important to note that Kefaya had a domestic focus and for that reason is a fully distinct movement.

The second major political movement of the mid-2000s came via the protest of Egyptian judges against government interference in the judiciary (Gohar 2008, 177–78), which would also reflect political discontent among elites, not the poor. These movements were partially successful at forcing the regime to permit more open elections in 2005, but the success of the Muslim Brotherhood prompted the regime to clamp down on any further liberalization (Dunne and Hamzawy 2008, 21–22). Ayman Nour, who ran in the 2005 presidential elections and received an unprecedented 8 percent of the vote against Mubarak, was summarily sentenced to five years in prison (Dunne and Hamzawy 2008, 23). Mubarak's National Democratic Party made some concessions to the judges' movement by permitting judges to oversee elections (Dunne and Hamzawy 2008, 25), but this limited liberal measure was followed by a higher level of electoral fraud in the 2010 parliamentary elections than had been seen previously in Egypt (Stacher 2012, 7).

The Kefaya movement and the judges' movement were eventually quashed or dissolved, although some of activists did re-emerge during the Arab Spring. The one truly worrying sign of what was to come, which is only very clear in hindsight, had to do with the rising level of labor unrest. In the few years preceding 2011, strikes by "illegal" labor unions grew in number, although at the time few thought that a revolution was in the making. Labor union fervor has a history tracing back to Nasser's Egypt (Vatikiotis 1961), although this particular wave of activism was noted for its persistence and ferocity. Labor activism restarted despite the fact that Mubarak had prevented any independent unions from forming during his rule; the only official union was the Egyptian Trade Union Federation, which was notable mostly for its whole-hearted support of government policies (Gohar 2008, 183–84). Labor acceptance of the status quo began to change by 2008 with the Malhalla worker's demonstration. Organized by a young Egyptian woman who wanted to support striking textile workers, a Facebook page she created led to 70,000 members and 30,000 turning out in demonstrations, dwarfing the earlier Kefaya movement (Rashidi 2013, 59–60). The protest was held on April 6, which coincided with the anniversary of Gandhi's famous march to the sea in colonial India on April 6, 1930 (Rashidi 2013, 59). The April 6th Movement, which would rise to prominence during the Arab Spring protests of 2011, was born during this episode of labor unrest.

The Malhalla demonstration was followed by a series of labor strikes erupting around the country at regular intervals. By 2010, there were approximately thirty-two worker protests per month in Egypt, according to newspaper reporting (al-Sayyid 2013, 24), and prior to 2010, there were "more than 1,900 strikes" incorporating "more than 1.7 million workers" (Farah 2013, 56). While the April 6 Movement was ostensibly led by young activists from an educated background (Tadros 2014), the strength of the movement was found in

2.3 The Arab Spring

the intensity of worker mobilization outside of official channels. Indeed, early accounts of the Arab Spring tended to overlook the fact that the protest movement spread quickly from Tahrir Square to other cities around Egypt because of the willingness of workers to mobilize (Faiola 2011).

As would be expected given the crumbling nature of Egypt's long-standing political bargains with workers, a substantial share of these worker strikes were in SOEs which could be targeted for further privatization (Farah 2013, 56). The regime had crossed a red line in its dismantlement of employment guarantees through state institutions; as a result, a groundswell of discontent emerged that the April 6 Movement was ready to tap in to. The fact that both labor and rural farmers had an axe to grind against the regime is what put Egypt's elites in such a tough spot: there was no ability to divide and conquer or pin social groups against each other given shared feelings of economic grievance based on decades of crony capitalism. As such, the costs of repression rose higher than the costs of changing long-standing political institutions (Dahl 1971; Acemoglu and Robinson 2006; Boix and Stokes 2003), per mechanism M_1.

However, the actual spark that led to the downfall of Mubarak's regime was as unforeseen as Bouazizi's immolation had been in Tunisia. As I have demonstrated in this analysis, it does not appear that Mubarak's end was directly related to a short-term cause. Egypt had been suffering after the Great Recession, but wide-spread protests did not occur until 2011, by which time Egypt had begun to recover from the recession. Some analysts have speculated about a fluctuation in food prices prior to the outbreak (Johnstone and Mazo 2011; Ansani and Daniele 2012), but while that may have been a contributing factor, it was the slow erosion in both rural and urban bargains that undermined the Mubarak regime's ability to enforce compliance. The exact trigger of the uprising in Egypt – a protest movement in a different North African country – could not have been foreseen by the regime's strategists, intelligence officers or corrupt businesspeople, leaving all of them equally vulnerable to its scale and ferocity. As a result, I know that the subsequent changes in the political activities of businesspeople were a direct result of the transition as opposed to preexisting political strategies, which were rendered irrelevant by the sudden loss of political patrons.

In a story that has now become legend, Egyptian activists accidentally launched the revolution when they scheduled a "Day of Rage" on a national holiday celebrating the police. However, instead of the expected turnout of a few hundred, several thousand appeared ("Timeline: Egypt's Revolution" 2011). Protests kept growing larger and larger until they were able to occupy all of Cairo's Tahrir Square, cutting off access to major bridges and effectively crippling the city. Pitched battles with plain clothes security officers followed, but people refused to leave until on February 11, Hosni Mubarak resigned as president. Unlike Tunisia, however, where power transitioned to a prime minister with a care taker cabinet, in Egypt the Supreme Council of the Armed Forces (SCAF) took over, and as was later evident, stage-managed Mubarak's

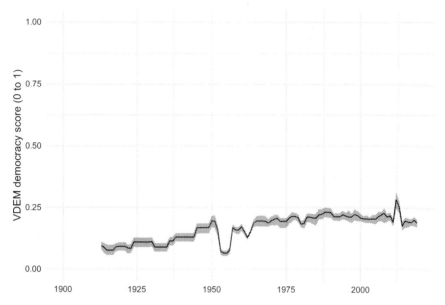

FIGURE 2.3 Varieties of democracy values for Egypt

resignation. While at the time few international observers paid much attention to that detail, it was a worrying sign of what was to come.

The important point to make in this section is that while there were some precursors to the Arab Spring and that protester grievances were related to crony capitalism, crony capitalists and other regime elites did not have a hand in the creation or even control of the movement in its early stages. While prior political movements were successfully contained through divide-and-conquer tactics, no one in the regime anticipated the broad popular movement. As such, the Arab Spring represents a true shock to the system that resulted in real if temporary political change as Figure 2.3 shows occurred during 2011–2013.

2.4 DEMOCRATIC ELECTIONS

The fall of Mubarak proved sufficient to open up the political system, ultimately leading to free and fair elections, which is the next step in the causal process. By the fall of 2011, Egypt held its first truly open elections since Nasser's coup in 1952. These initial steps toward democratization revealed that Egypt's elites, at least for the time being, had succumbed to "people power" (Lynch 2013; Pearlman 2013). The mechanism, M_1, describes the well-known tolerance-repression trade-off. The high level of political mobilization made it too costly for elites to continue repression and democracy became the only viable outcome (Dahl 1971).

2.4 Democratic Elections

Yet later analysis revealed that not all power holders were affected in the same way. In particular, it was the military acting through its governing body, the SCAF that made the decision to depose Mubarak on February 10 (Albrecht and Bishara 2011, 16). Furthermore, the SCAF took control over legislative authority before the elections took place, issuing laws and even a constitutional declaration in March 2011 (Sallam 2014, 40).

Given that the nascent democratic regime lasted for only two years (see Figure 2.3), it can be difficult to classify the interregnum as a period of democracy. Nonetheless, prominent indices of regime change do code single-election cases as democratic based on qualitative evidence of unrestricted political competition (Boix, Miller, and Rosato 2013; Geddes, Wright, and Frantz 2014). The proof in the pudding for Egypt's transition came when Mubarak's former nemesis, the Muslim Brotherhood, won a commanding majority coalition in the bicameral legislature in 2011 with the Salafist party al-Nour as a coalition partner, permitting the Islamist organization to also control the staffing of the committee set up to draft Egypt's new constitution (Sallam 2014, 41–42). Given that the Brotherhood had been a long-standing opponent of the regime, their assumption of power represented a clean break from Mubarak's dictatorship and a sign that the elections were conducted equitably. In addition, Morsi was able to fire Egypt's highest-ranking military officer during his tenure, along with other high-ranking figures of the ancien regime ("Crowds in Cairo Praise Morsi's Army Overhaul" 2012). Thus, it does appear that the military was willing to concede to losing a share of its authority, and there is evidence that the military negotiated this transfer of power with the Muslim Brotherhood prior to the 2011 elections (Tadros 2014, 65–66). The military's calculation, which ultimately proved quite accurate, centered on the favorable treatment they could receive in this new regime once Mubarak's elite allies had been removed from the system (Sayigh 2019, 3–4).

In a very similar story to Tunisia, only the Muslim Brotherhood was fully organized and prepared for the elections that occurred only a few months after Mubarak's downfall. The April 6 Movement that had successfully orchestrated the protests split when the group's prominent leader tried to structure the amorphous coalition into a political party (Elshami 2011). The NDP, as mentioned previously, had suffered grievously from the ire of both the protesters and the empowered military, and was officially banned. Thus, elite politics were very fractionalized and disorganized as in Tunisia, permitting a quick and easy victory for the Muslim Brotherhood (MB) in the legislative elections in 2011.

The MB benefited in particular from two advantages which had little to do with the organization itself. First, none of the legal opposition parties could compete with the MB because the Egyptian regime had long fostered a policy of preventing opposition parties from building mass followings, especially among leftists (Lust-Okar 2005; Lust and Waldner 2017). As a result, the MB had a critical informational advantage, which meant that many voters in the initial elections assumed that the MB was farther to the left than it in fact was

(Masoud 2014). Combining both of these favorable elements with the MB's well-known social and medical institutions (Brooke 2017) meant that it won a commanding majority in the legislative assembly that had the responsibility for writing a new constitution for the country in 2011.

These prevailing winds did not propel the MB to similar success in the later presidential election, although again the field was divided among too many candidates, including Amr Moussa, a long-time Egyptian diplomat and representative of Egyptian secular liberalism. Despite obtaining only a quarter of the vote each, only Mohammed Morsi, the MB's candidate, and Ahmed Shafik, a former air force general with support from old regime elites, survived to the runoff election in which Morsi narrowly won by 51 percent of the vote (Kirkpatrick 2012b). With Amr Moussa's defeat, Egypt's secularists and liberals were forced to choose between two unpalatable options, with the result that the election came down to the MB's resurgent base and the old NDP's decaying networks. The victory of Morsi over the remains of the NDP dealt a critical blow to the old authoritarian party and signaled that democracy had come to Egypt – at least for the time being.

To summarize, the explosive nature of the protests, which were themselves a product of decades of decaying institutions, overwhelmed Egyptian security forces and led to Mubarak's ouster. The brute force of mass protests is the mechanism, M_1, that led to Egypt's free and fair parliamentary elections by changing the cost of tolerance for elites. However, as is so often the case, elections do not a democracy make, and the polarizing contests and dismal performance of the Egyptian left and center, along with military interference, were worrying signs for the nascent democracy. While the dictator and the dictator's party's control evaporated, other elites remained able and willing to compete for power.

2.5 BUSINESS DISCONTENT

The sudden loss of Mubarak and his party, the NDP, resulted in a rapid change in the behavior of both politicians and government officials. This next variable in the causal graph is crucial because it is the ultimate source of business' negative reaction to the democratic transition. The principal with ostensible control over Egypt's sprawling bureaucracy had disappeared (mechanism M_2), setting off a chain reaction as previously well-established relationships between brokers, companies and politicians ruptured. The loss of political backers meant that the expropriation of influential businesspeople closely connected to the old regime proceeded in fashion similar to that of Tunisia after the uprisings. However, unlike Tunisia, it was the military that prevented any close examination of its economic assets by imposing anti-privatization measures, arguably because privatization threatened SOEs run by military elites (Marshall and Stacher 2012). By doing so, the military preserved its economic prerogatives even as Mubarak's son Gamal and his business allies fled the country or ended up in jail (Sayigh 2019, 22).

2.5 Business Discontent

These rapid moves against business, even if it was centered on close allies of the former dictator, spooked business elites. The Egyptian Central Bank imposed limits on capital flight soon after Mubarak's downfall. Capital flight continued despite these limited controls, however. In September 2011, the Bank for International Settlements reported Egyptians had transferred nearly $7 billion worth of domestic assets to foreign banks, likely a sign of "elevated levels of political and economic uncertainty" (Cohen 2011). In the beginning of 2013, the company with the largest capitalization on the Egyptian stock market, Orascom Construction Industries, abruptly transferred its shares to the New York Stock Exchange out of concern for "paralyzed economic policy-shaping" (Halime 2013). Those who had the most to fear were businessmen like Ahmed Ezz, an Egyptian steel magnate who held leadership positions in the NDP and was very close to Gamal Mubarak. While his businesses were never seized outright, he was prosecuted for corruption and jailed (Adly 2017).

In addition to high-level expropriation and corruption initiatives, businesspeople in Egypt also had to grapple with rising levels of petty corruption and labor unrest. The loss of the dictator and the ruling party as a principal to bureaucrats and other state agencies meant that competition over power and influence spread into previously tame sectors. For example, labor repression had been common in Egypt prior the Arab Spring, so the sudden onset of new political freedoms brought with it a massive surge in strikes in both public and private sectors ("2012 Worker's Protests in Egypt" 2013; Benoit-Lavelle 2016). Businesses which could have previously relied on connections to regime officials to quell or target labor dissidents instead had to negotiate or risk real loss to their business, although these negotiations were a most dire threat to firms in export sectors with lower margins.

In addition to contestation from previously marginalized actors, businesspeople had to contend with newly empowered bureaucrats, no longer as fearful as they once were of businesses' political connections. For this reason, petty corruption has become more of a thorn in the side of business in both countries since the Arab Spring. An online survey of businesspeople I conducted in 2017, analyzed more in depth in Chapter 5, provides concrete evidence of this phenomenon. Sixty-six percent of Egyptian respondents said that it was much more likely or more likely that bureaucrats asked for "informal payments" since the outbreak of the Arab Spring. In addition, only 13 percent of Egyptian respondents said that these informal payments had become less likely or much less likely since the Arab Spring.

It is not surprising, then, that businesspeople had ambiguous opinions of the process of democratization. Figure 2.4 shows data from a survey of Egyptian businesspeople implemented in 2018 in which respondents were asked about their CEO's level of support for democracy. The plot shows very mixed feelings toward democracy, with respondents rating their CEO's support for democracy at roughly 5 to 6 on a scale of 1 to 10. While this plot only shows preferences, not actions, it does indicate that business did not find democratization to be an enjoyable experience. These grievances, though, were not enough to spur

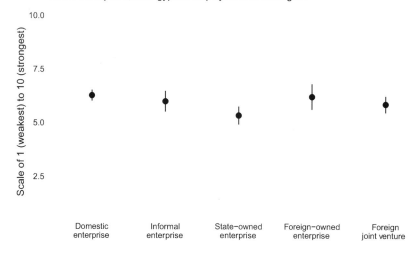

FIGURE 2.4 Average affect toward democracy among business employees and managers in Egypt, online survey in Summer 2018

rapid or systemic mobilization against democracy. Broad rent-seeking could have become the norm for Egyptian business just as it did for Tunisian business.

2.6 MILITARY COUP

I now turn to the rise of a new gatekeeper, shown in the upper part of the causal diagram in Figure 1.1. It is the presence of a powerful gatekeeper that forces a shift in the way that businesspeople engage in politics. However, it took time for these changes to manifest themselves. Early in the transition process, business elites in both Egypt and Tunisia reacted negatively to democratization and offered at least tepid support of parties opposing further democratization. The Egyptian authoritarian coalition's longevity and near monopoly on support among business elites is what separates it from its Tunisian counterpart. Over time, Egyptian businesspeople became more and more likely to engage in narrow rent-seeking in support of the pro-authoritarian coalition as the list of potential political patrons narrowed.

The Egyptian business community's initial reaction to the Arab Spring came in the form of a marriage of some powerful businesspeople with elites tied to the old regime. Despite the failure of the NDP in Egypt's first round of elections, there was evidence that elites had begun to coalesce again into a nascent coalition through their support of the presidential candidate Shafik. A fascinating piece of evidence was a meeting that Ahmed Shafik held at the American

2.6 Military Coup

Chamber of Commerce in Cairo in 2012. Incorporating many wealthy elites, he received a standing ovation when he extolled Mubarak's virtues and pledged to "use executions and brutal force to restore order within a month" (Kirkpatrick 2012a). However, with the military willing to let the NDP take the blame for Mubarak's dictatorship, the movement was not able to generate enough support even with the MB's considerable handicap as a polarizing force in Egyptian society.

In the aftermath of Shafik's defeat and the military's acceptance of Mohammed Morsi as the new Egyptian president, Egyptian businesses had to respond to this shift in power. As mentioned earlier, some prominent businesspeople were directly targeted in corruption scandals and suffered fines and in rare cases asset seizure. In general, however, the Muslim Brotherhood did not launch a campaign to root out corruption (as they saw it) or to otherwise antagonize the Egyptian business community. In fact, the Brotherhood launched its own "public–private partnership" organization, the Egyptian Business Development Association (EBDA), to reach out to business leaders and build support for needed reforms to secure IMF loans (Adly 2017). Adly argues that EBDA reflected an "ecumenical mindset" by incorporating business leaders who had had ties to the Mubarak regime, such as Safwan Thabet, who had been a member of the NDP. Other business elites forced their way into this group to protect their own interests, such as Mohamed Abul-Enein, who despite being criticized by Mohammed Morsi used his media outlets to congratulate Morsi on his presidency. Abul-Enein was rewarded with a trip to China as part of an Egyptian state delegation (Tarouty 2015, 79–80).

This evidence, while anecdotal in nature, does show that businesspeople had an opportunity for broad rent-seeking, that is, to work with whomever would offer them the best deal in obtaining valuable rents. The ideological nature of the MB did not preclude them from working with secular Egyptians who thought little of their Islamicizing project. Lacking a solid grip on governing institutions, the MB came into office with an attitude of rapprochement toward existing elites, creating opportunities that businesspeople could exploit as they worked to reestablish their rent-seeking networks.

For example, while Morsi had fired the ranking leader of the Egyptian Armed Forces, he appointed another leader from within the institution and did not try to challenge the armed forces' prerogatives, which were themselves written into Egypt's new constitution, including the military's right to try civilians in military courts ("Egypt: New Constitution Mixed on Support of Rights" 2012). The Muslim Brotherhood appeared to be adopting a strategy of reform and wait: If they could deliver economic revitalization to the Egyptian economy, then they could change their image as a fundamentalist Islamic group and earn a much wider base of support. The strategy also appeared similar to the AKP model from Turkey, which also successfully implemented pro-EU reforms that led to considerable export-led growth in the 2000s.

However, as has been covered so far in this chapter, Egypt's political economy rested on coalitions that had been forged by Nasser decades earlier and variously modified by his successors. What the MB needed was elite allies to create its own coalition and take control of the state. Instead, the group appeared to be too weak either to compel elites to support it or to punish those who criticized it. The most well-known story of MB's difficulties concerns Naguib Sawiris, a charismatic leader of Egypt's largest firm, Orascom, which was also one of the country's few international companies with operations across the Arab world and beyond. In the chaotic media environment of post-revolutionary Egypt, Sawiris was able to set up his own television station, ON-TV, which he used to great effect against the Muslim Brotherhood (Tarouty 2015, 148). In response, the regime launched a "tax evasion" case against his company, which was ultimately only resolved when Sawiris agreed to sell ON-TV (Adly 2017). Despite this momentary victory, it apparently did not intimidate Sawiris, who continued his resistance to the Muslim Brotherhood through the growth of the Tamarod, or rebellion, movement for early presidential elections. Sawiris is the counterpart to Tunisia's Fawzi Elloumi described in Chapter 3: A powerful businessman with such an outsize role in the economy that he could take on the patronage of a political movement without expecting immediate returns. Other businesses did not have as much liberty to consider voicing their opinions about the Muslim Brotherhood while it held power.

As such, Sawiris' actions cannot be directly explained by the theory I proposed. Sawiris' business empire was so massive, with investments in dozens of countries, that he could plausibly undertake the sponsorship of a political movement without regard for the potential cost to his company in either money spent or lost opportunities for rents. However, despite his wealth, on his own Sawiris would have been unable to upend democracy. It was military involvement that proved crucial to the authoritarian movement's success.

During the second year of Mohammed Morsi's brief term, an apparently spontaneous movement, which bore the name Tamarod (rebellion), attracted people to protest the MB's rule. Tamarod is a peculiar movement because it is not entirely clear how much of it was actually due to popular unrest with Morsi's regime and how much was due to elite backers from business (namely, Sawiris) and the military with support from the intelligence apparatus (Khalaf 2013). The campaign began initially as an online petition to hold early presidential elections; the petition reportedly obtained over twenty million signatures (Hussein 2015). The leaders of the movement were all activists whose secular inclinations led them to oppose the Muslim Brotherhood, some of whom had been involved in the much earlier Kefaya movement (Meky 2015).

However, what is clear is that Sawiris used his media outlets to greatly amplify the movement's message (Tarouty 2015, 148–49). In addition, further research has uncovered close links between Tamarod and Egyptian intelligence services, including accusations of funds being transferred and intelligence officers working in the movement. Members of the military and the Ministry of Interior were quick to trumpet and inflate the movement's supporters, at one

2.6 Military Coup

point claiming that nearly a third of Egypt's population had turned out to protest (Ketchley 2017). Given this mixed genesis, it is perhaps not surprising that the movement split after the military coup in 2013 when some of the members, including the founder, endorsed the military general Abdel Fattah Al-Sisi for president (Hussein 2015). Some of the movement's members saw it as a legitimate effort to reform Egypt's nascent democratic institutions, but its successful co-optation meant that it instead became a prop for a coup.

As a popular movement, Tamarod's complaints against the Morsi regime centered on the failing economy and Morsi's heavy-handed institutional reforms. Despite two years of negotiations, by the summer of 2013 the MB had yet to sign an agreement with the IMF, apparently because the IMF was not satisfied with the pace of economic reforms (Khalaf 2013). As a consequence, Egyptian debt continued to rise and unemployment and growth both remained at dismal levels (Khalaf 2013). Second, as Morsi continued to find resistance to policy reforms, he pushed through a new constitution via referendum that gave the presidency veto power over legislation and the ability to appoint heads of most agencies, a move that added fuel to Tamarod's fire (Sein 2015, 191–93). Perhaps even worse, the MB took on labor unions that disliked the MB's neoliberal agenda, using state-owned media outlets to argue that strikes were un-Islamic (Sein 2015, 193). As mentioned previously, labor unrest was one of the groundswells of the original uprisings, and without a new political economy with which to form a new coalition, Morsi's attempted power grab via institutional changes amounted to nothing more than throwing around empty pieces of paper.

Tamarod represents the authoritarian reactionary counterpart to Tunisia's Nidaa Tounes described in Chapter 3. Old regime elites and powerful businesses came together to support a new movement that aimed to use democratic processes to subvert democracy from within. Ancien regime elites had suffered grievously in the initial round of elections and had had to accommodate themselves to the new regime, which they did even as they looked for alternative avenues for political action. Neither Tamarod nor Nidaa Tounes initially called for the overthrow of democratic institutions or an end to civil liberties, instead they exploited the open media environment to fashion a new message that would appeal to citizens tired of revolutionary chaos. Thus, the mechanism which connected elections with the growth of these movements was the threat created by the downfall of the prior regimes and their party institutions. As is so often the case, ancien elites were able to regroup and refashion their coalition for democratic competition (Loxton 2015; Grzymala-Busse 2019), and the manner in which this occurred in Egypt and Tunisia is remarkably similar through mechanism M_3 as prominent businesspeople like Sawiris and Elloumi were willing, at least initially, to fund the start-up costs for the movement to avoid potentially catastrophic losses from a newly hostile political environment.

Without any expansions in its Islamist base, the Morsi regime was vulnerable to challengers, and the military was more than ready to seize the opportunity when Tamarod made its initial debut. Whether or not the military was responsible for starting Tamarod, it quickly became a firm supporter of the movement and helped it achieve its goals. One of the big advantages of the military, relative to the MB, is that it had a natural constituency of firms it could compel to join or at least avoid opposing the movement. The military's ability to control valuable rents in the chaotic state bureaucracy and its uncontested primacy in the security arena meant that businesspeople had to consider whether sitting out would bring costs to their company. Over time, narrow rent-seeking in support of the military's agenda became a necessity if businesspeople were going to obtain the rents they depended on.

While Tunisia's pro-authoritarian coalition reached its apogee after only a few years, Egypt's coalition grew from a conspiracy to a powerful force that remains dominant in the country. On July 3, 2013, after Tamarod street protests had roiled Cairo, General Al-Sisi announced that Adly Mansour, a justice, would replace Mohammed Morsi, effectively ending the MB's tenure as head of state (Kirkpatrick 2013). The regime that Morsi had never fully controlled quickly let go of him: apparently even members of the elite presidential guard waved flags in celebration from the presidential palace after his removal (Kirkpatrick 2013). As has been well established in political science, institutions without credible threats are rarely enforced (Shepsle 2008; Levitsky and Murillo 2009; T. Pepinsky 2014), and in this case Morsi's aggressive posturing only made it easier for his enemies to stir up enough public unrest to grant the coup legitimacy.

2.7 STRONG BUSINESS COALITION

The final part of this case study explains why the combination of the military coup and existing business discontent combined to push businesspeople toward narrow rent-seeking. Narrow rent-seeking, targeted at the military and its bureaucratic allies, had its visible effect through lock-step business support for the military's political prerogatives. There was little room for businesspeople to avoid a relationship with the military, even if it was only aimed at preventing military companies from pushing businesses out of their existing markets. As it increased its control over the state and all channels to obtain perks and favors, the military helped build a durable elite coalition.

It is not the object of this case study to establish why the military wanted to switch from ruling to governing (Grewal 2016). Rather, I focus on the built-in advantage that the military had as a coalition leader in encouraging a critical number of firms to not only consent but also directly participate in its coalition. The military's ability to exclude rivals by using economic assets to encourage consent represents the third-party enforcer (mechanism M_4) that can help a nascent antidemocratic movement reach the point at which it is the only game

2.7 Strong Business Coalition

in town. As a result, the military-led dictatorship has been far more successful than its Tunisian counterpart as it has survived for nearly four years despite a violent insurgency and continued economic decline. The military's ability to compel assent does not mean that it is able to punish all firms in Egypt, but rather that its power is sufficient to enjoin enough firms to participate given the risk that they could become targets. Unlike the Muslim Brotherhood, the Egyptian military has been able to forge a new political economy that produces consent among citizens even though it has had deleterious effects on a wide swath of Egypt's population.

The primary way that the military has gained this level of influence among the business community is by becoming the de facto and de jure gatekeeper for many valuable rents. While the military has had economic influence in Egypt for some time, as documented in Chapter 1, the military's economic enterprises have grown significantly since the Arab Spring. As I describe in this chapter using qualitative evidence and in Chapter 5 with quantitative evidence, the military has expanded across sectors while also taking over many forms of government contracting, restricting previously influential crony capitalists to subcontracting roles. The military's ascendancy over the state is so complete that it has created a perception that all businesspeople should have some kind of relationship with it if they are to be at all successful in the Al-Sisi regime. Unlike in Tunisia where the loss of the dictator led to increased bureaucratic autonomy, in Egypt the military replaced the dictator and other former power holders, concentrating control over rents in its own institution.

This divergence between Egyptian and Tunisian business communities, I argue, occurred about the time that both Tamarod and Nidaa Tounes gained momentum. While Tunisia's authoritarian successor party quickly splintered into competing factions, Tamarod had reached the point at which firms believed that other firms would also participate, creating a self-sustaining movement. This transformation happened as Egypt prepared for a new round of legislative elections in 2015, this time under the watchful eye of the armed forces.

While Tunisia's would-be authoritarians squabbled and undercut each other, Egypt's elites were busily building a new dictatorship to permanently end Egypt's experiment with democracy. General Al-Sisi stepped down as head of the armed forces to run as a candidate in new presidential elections in 2014 in which he won a commanding majority of the vote. However, the military's assumption of power would not be complete until it had a pliant legislature to grant it the ability to control at least two out of the three branches of government. For that reason, the parliamentary elections in 2015 represented the introduction of the new coalition of elites that would help usher in a new regime. This election was the end outcome, from the military's perspective, of the Tamarod movement, and for that reason it is the one on which I focus as a comparison point with Tunisia. It also represented a test of the strength of the coalition underpinning military rule. The military had the independent power base to seize control from Morsi; it did not have the ability to create political parties out of whole cloth and to find suitable candidates. Rather, business elites allied together to forge new political parties and jump-started the military regime by providing funding and candidates for elections. This wide-spread business collective action is strong evidence of mechanism M_5 as businesses began to coordinate around a pro-authoritarian equilibrium in which alternative political options to the military simply did not exist.

My interviews in Cairo, along with secondary source materials and the survey research I present in Chapter 5, all suggest that at some point in the runup to these elections, businesspeople had to adjust their political strategies to account for the new unipolar environment. While Tamarod attracted the support of businesspeople like Sawiris who had a bone to pick with the Morsi administration, it eventually came to dominate the political scene as it closely allied with the military. This shift had a band-wagoning effect on Egyptian firms: as the perception that other firms were supporting the military increased, so did the incentives for all firms to support the military lest they be the only ones to not do so (Lohmann 1994; Kuran and Sunstein 1999; Gehlbach and Keefer 2011). The fewer businesses that did not express explicit support for the military, the easier it became to identify the holdouts. These strategic complementarities helped the military consolidate its new coalition in the run-up to parliamentary elections.

Because there is less information available on the Egyptian parliamentary elections in 2014, I use the survey data I collected to provide a general sense of how businesspeople acted. Figure 2.5 shows that Egyptian companies were far more likely than their Tunisian counterparts to order their employees to vote for a certain candidate. Between 10 and 15 percent of firms did so according to the survey, which represents a substantial level of employer-based vote coercion. Furthermore, due to social desirability bias, this number is very likely a lower bound of the total level of firms that instructed their employees how to vote in the elections. Considering that turnout in the 2015 elections was a meager 26 percent of Egyptians (Fahmy and Noueihed 2015), it is quite likely that employer-based vote persuasion had a large effect on those who did turn out to vote.

The candidates for the 2015 elections included a large number of independents who were not affiliated with any party, which is a strategy that Mubarak had previously used to diversify the parliament instead of having everyone become a member of the NDP. The process of becoming a candidate was described to me as a "pay to play" procedure, and unsurprisingly many businesspeople participated.[1] Several businesspeople were well-known former NDP members, including Nabil Dibis, owner of a private university, and Sahar Talaat Mostafa, the sister of Hisham Talaat Moustafa, who owns a real estate construction conglomerate (Messieh and Mohamed 2015). The final elected

---

[1] Interview 5.

2.7 Strong Business Coalition

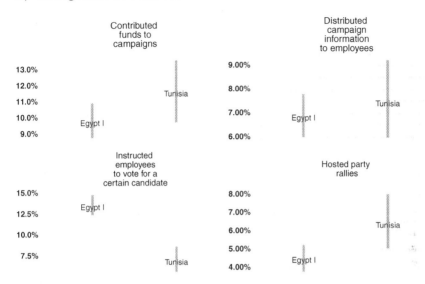

FIGURE 2.5 Political activities of firms as reported by employees

parliament comprised about two-thirds independents and one-third from a handful of parties, only two of which are worth discussing.

The largest party is the Free Egyptians Party, which was set up by Naguib Sawiris after the Arab Spring to put forward a neoliberal agenda for Egypt (Tarouty 2015, 98–99). This party represents the only one that has a policy agenda that can be spoken of, and it is at least nominally independent of the ruling coalition thanks to its sponsor. Yet the party does not seem to have had much of an effect on guiding the new military regime, and instead argues that it needs to support Al-Sisi because he is a bulwark against the Muslim Brotherhood and Morsi.[2] The second-largest party is the Nation's Future Party, a bizarre conglomeration of ex-NDPers and sycophants. Mohamed Badr, the 24-year-old head of the Nation's Future Party and a former Tamarod leader, received significant support from the military for his party even though he lacked prior experience in political organizing (Sirgany 2015). Despite his apparent political ambitions and the outstanding success of his new party in Egypt's elections, Badr is currently in the United States pursuing further education.[3]

Ultimately, the resulting parliament seemed to replicate the dynamics observed by Blaydes (2011) in her discussion of the political economy of the NDP. Powerful businesspeople have claimed a seat at the table through their

---

[2] Interview 5.
[3] Interview 5.

70   2 *Case Study: The Egyptian Military as the Gatekeeper*

apparently willing use of resources to fund campaigns. In addition, vote turnout is managed by having companies order employees to cast ballots for specific candidates, effectively blurring the line between political parties and firms. In a stunning reversal, the military has replaced Hosni Mubarak and his meddling son Gamal at the head of this state-business nexus (Aziz 2017).

By contrast, Egypt's new military-led regime is noteworthy for its ability to punish even elites in its reach for power. While the military's ability to punish firm defection (M_4) can explain the rapid formation of Tamarod, those same factors cannot easily explain the longevity of this coalition when compared to Tunisia's ill-fated Nidaa Tounes. Rather, it is the self-enforcing dynamics created by narrow rent-seeking among elites (M_5) that explains the near-uniform consent by the business community to the new regime, even though it would appear that the policies backed by the military are particularly harmful to business interests.

The military had several primary levers for creating the critical mass of firm support, including monopolizing primary materials manufacturing, withholding contracts for goods and services, exploiting conscript labor and making use of military courts for economic disputes. The growing economic clout of the military makes it very difficult for some businesses to operate without residual uncertainty about what could happen if they oppose the regime. Once businesses began to believe that other businesses supported the military coalition, actionable support for authoritarianism became widespread among the business community because no one wanted to stand out (M_6). Furthermore, once all businesses are cooperating to help build a dictatorship, it became much easier for the military to identify and punish any firms that still resist or simply choose not to participate.

Compared to Tunisia, the stability of the military-led coalition is remarkable. While Tunisia's pro-authoritarian coalition fractured due to infighting and continual party splits, the military regime remained far more in control of potential opposition than the previous dictatorship. While Tunisia's pro-authoritarian coalition's greatest accomplishment is to undermine some civil liberties and prevent further democratic reforms, Egypt's new authoritarians have crushed civil society while pushing through economic reforms and even auctioning off sovereign land to secure Gulf financing.[4] The military government's policies may have been devastating for the country's economic outlook and social cohesion, but its record of sheer accomplishment is astonishing compared to its North African neighbor.

To understand how the military has been able to maintain its coalition requires an examination of the mechanisms through which business has been kept in compliance. Powerful business leaders supported the military coup,

---

[4] See the sale of the Red Sea islands of Tiran and Sanafir to Saudi Arabia in 2017: www.bbc.com/news/world-middle-east-40278568.

2.7 *Strong Business Coalition*

such as Naguib Sawiris, and many others came along for the ride. But the military's disastrous economic policies should have brought about defection of these businesspeople and the formation of opposition groups with elite backing (or at the very least, detente with the Muslim Brotherhood). To understand how firm collective action reached this durable, self-enforcing stage, it is necessary to explore in detail the military's ability to push a critical mass of firms to support dictatorship. The military has two basic methods for encouraging business compliance: sticks such as the threat of expropriation and withholding of supplies, and carrots with the provision of contracts to smaller enterprises.

The military's economic franchise began in the 1980s as a way to reward generals with additional benefits when they were willing to retire from the chain of command, a very useful coup-proofing mechanism.[5] Since then, the number and variety of military-controlled firms has expanded with the military controlling much of the state's transportation infrastructure and also investing heavily in fertilizers, oil and gas, and even computer manufacturing (Marshall and Stacher 2012). These same interests are cited as one of the reasons for the military's deep mistrust of the liberalizers allied with Gamal Mubarak prior the Arab Spring, as well as a justification for the military's rapid halt to the privatization program in its aftermath (Marshall and Stacher 2012). The military has certainly kept its dominance in the post-Arab Spring by keeping formerly influential businessmen, such as Ahmed Ezz, a steel magnate, completely marginal while supporting the rise of new steel entrepreneurs who are less of a political liability.[6]

However, the military's economic interests do not only explain the institution's resistance to privatization and businessmen competitors. In addition, the military has considerable advantages that enable it to pressure rivals, and since its accession to power, to pressure businesses to support its political interests. Firms controlled by military generals, although they are nominally independent, have access to military courts when adjudicating disputes, which ensures that any contractual negotiations will always end in the favor of the military firm.[7] Furthermore, these firms are also exempt from taxation due to their definition as companies in the defense industry.[8] Finally, military-linked firms can rely on conscript labor, which gives them nearly zero labor costs and a considerable advantage over any rivals.[9] As a result, the military can easily threaten firms with either expropriation via contractual dispute or by flooding the market with cheap products.[10] In an interview with an Egyptian factory owner, he described his political frustration with military repression, but he also opined that he was forced to acquiesce to the dictatorship because

---

[5] Interview 4.
[6] Interview 5.
[7] Interview 4.
[8] Interview 4.
[9] Interview 4.
[10] Interview 5.

his firm depended on military businesses to supply critical raw materials.[11] This qualitative information is further validated by the survey I conduct in Chapter 3.

These built-in advantages accruing to the military have been considerably advanced by the military's quick domination of economic policy-making. In fact, the military regime's thirst for economic gains through the whole-hearted exploitation of the country's resources is more akin to what an invading army might do to a new colony rather than its home territory. President Al-Sisi's first major economic plan was to bring in liberal Gulf aid to fund mega-projects, including an expansion of the Suez Canal ("The Mega National Projects ... A Locomotive of Development" 2017), probably because of the military's long-standing ties to Gulf contractors (Marshall and Stacher 2012) and the Saudis' eagerness to support the overthrow of its nemesis, the Muslim Brotherhood (Hearst 2013). However, these mega-projects were largely targeted at the military's own companies, who maintained a favored list of subcontractors but otherwise isolated previously well-connected Egyptian contractors.[12] Only some of Egypt's largest firms, such as Orascom headed by Sawiris, were able to profit from these massive development projects in part because these firms had monopolies on certain construction supplies and the military had to do business with them.[13]

The scale with which military-backed firms have expanded is dizzying. Within the first year, the Defense Ministry was authorized to operate for-profit companies, giving military-linked firms yet more advantages over their rivals. In addition, the military's vast land ownings in Egypt are now approved for economic development, and military courts have been a greater prerogative in trials of civilians (Linn 2016). Attalah and Hamama (2016) chronicle the extent of military contracting, including the military's management of a farm subsidy modernization scheme, road construction, solar energy installation, importation of baby formula, state-run fish farms, restoration of archaeological sites, pharmaceutical production, medical device importation, and perhaps most bizarrely, the operation of an international school and running cafeteria services for Egyptian universities. The colossal scope of these additions to military businesses, in addition to the billions funneled into Sisi's megaprojects, have undoubtedly enriched this generation of the officer corps to previously unimaginable levels.

Thanks to Sayigh (2019) massive study of the Egyptian military's conquest of the Egyptian economy, we know much more how the military was able to expand its influence so dramatically. Following the coup, the Egyptian military ensured that state contracts would go to military-owned enterprises like the Arab Organization for Industrialization and the National Service Projects

---

[11] Interview 6.
[12] Interview 2.
[13] Interview 2.

2.7 Strong Business Coalition

Organization (Sayigh 2019, 56). They did this by creating rules allowing for no-bid contracts (Sayigh 2019, 28–29), and also by staffing many of the cabinet and lower-level agencies with current and retired military officers (Sayigh 2019, 157–59). Military control over lower levels of government has likewise increased as "retired" military generals now account for the majority of provincial governors, and even lower-level staff members may be ex-military (Sayigh 2019, 169–70). These moves helped military-owned enterprises expand considerably in terms of domestic production, particularly in cement and steel production, driving prices lower and making use of their freedom to import raw materials and employ conscript labor to be price competitive (Sayigh 2019, 191).

There are only two ways that Egyptian businesspeople can respond to these changes beyond participating in politics as mentioned previously. The first is a Mubarak-era standard: pay large bribes to attempt to become a military subcontractor (Sayigh 2019, 29). The second is to add a military officer on to the board of the company as a "fixer," a practice which predated the Arab Spring but has become more important since the military's rise (Sayigh 2019, 191–93). Although the military's own generation of economic activity does not yet amount to considerable fraction of GDP, its ability to expand into new sectors and its control over state agencies and available rents have made it an actor who can no longer be ignored by businesspeople. It is worth quoting in full from Sayigh on this point:

> [A] significant shift has been underway since 2013, as the military's considerable economic, bureaucratic, and political autonomy allows it to reshape much of the context within which the private sector operates. Its accelerating expansion in a number of economic sectors that have long been dominated by private sector companies is turning it not only into a direct competitor but also into a disruptive market actor as its behavior is not conditioned by normal calculations of commercial cost-benefit. In parallel, the military has realigned its strategic relationships with big, medium, and small businesses. (200)

As such, Egyptian businesspeople need to be aware of the military's existing economic activities, its possible future economic activities and its increasing control over seemingly mundane levers of government. This process describes in full mechanism M_5 in which bureaucrats become beholden to a single gatekeeper, who subsequently can reward or deny privilege and access to elites. It is not necessary for the military to have de facto control over all economic activity in the country, only to create a credible threat that a business' livelihood is threatened if it takes an action which would put it at odds with the coalition. Unwilling to take this risk, businesses increasingly engage in narrow rent-seeking aimed at building a positive relationship with the military-clientelist complex.

This transformation of Egyptian political economy could be palatable to businesspeople if it came with economic growth or its own patronage benefits. However, as I have already covered, military-linked firms have benefited at the expense of private firms, while even large businesses like Orascom have been hurt because of continuing macroeconomic decline. Somehow, despite tens of billions in Gulf aid, Egypt suffered a currency crisis in 2016 as its fixed exchange rate diverged from the black market rate.[14] The most recent projections are not particularly optimistic: as of 2017, the country's debt to GDP ratio had risen by $19 billion in the previous quarter alone to nearly $80 billion ("32.5% Increase in Egypt's Foreign Debt: CBE" 2017). Based on my observations from my trip to Egypt in the fall of 2016, the economy struggled with the fall of tourism revenues and loss of foreign investment, though government statistics showed only modest unemployment that is slowly falling, which seems implausible ("Egypt Unemployment Rate Eases to 12 Percent in Q1 2017" 2017).

As the Gulf funds were lavishly spent on megaprojects, and Egypt's fixed exchange rate came under assault, the Sisi government turned to its other international ally, the United States, and the International Monetary Fund for a bailout. Again, the strength of the military's coalition proved enduring. Al-Sisi and his government successfully negotiated an agreement within a few months in 2016 that offered the IMF more than it could have dreamed of in recent years, including a very high increase in the VAT and civil service reforms. In addition, licenses to operate and other barriers to entry have been significantly lowered in previously protected domestic industries.[15]

However, the burden of these reforms have largely fallen on the formally established businesses which are the nominal allies of the military-led regime. Military firms will not pay the VAT, nor will the many informal establishments that operate outside of the legal framework.[16] Instead, the revenues obtained from the reforms, which have already helped improve government revenues ("Egypt Sees Value-Added Tax Revenue up by 8 Billion Pounds in 2017–2018" 2017), are likely to make life even more difficult for Egypt's business community that helped create a regime which they are now forced to carry on their backs. In addition, the floating Egyptian pound has made life very difficult for Egypt's importers who could formerly profit from Central Bank controls protecting the value of the pound, which is causing additional distress among Egypt's businesses ("As Austerity Pummels Egypt's Importers, Dollar Resources Grow" 2017; "Egypt Reserves Reach Record High of over $36 Billion" 2017).

For these reasons, the military-led coalition in Egypt appears to be remarkably durable, especially when it is compared to Tunisia's less successful authoritarian coalition in the next section. Businesspeople have been forced to stick with the military despite the higher costs in bribes they needed to pay

---

[14] During my trip to Egypt in September 2016, the black market rate was several times the official rate, and money changers at airports outside Egypt refused to convert pounds to hard currency.

[15] Interview 3.

[16] Interview 4.

2.8 Conclusion

and despite the overall limitation in rents. The military's stranglehold over the state has occurred simultaneously with dismal economic performance, preventing businesspeople from being able to grow by expanding into new sectors and markets. Regardless of businesspeople's own ideology, they have become a pillar of Al-Sisi's coalition and an important way that military control is mediated to society at large.

2.8 CONCLUSION

The final and most difficult test for the transformation of Egypt's political economy rests on Al-Sisi's pledge to reform subsidies. Ever since the Bread Riots in the late 1970s, Egyptian rulers have hesitated to modify subsidies even though the IMF has urged reform, especially to tamp down on subsidies such as fuel that are not means targeted. The deal signed with the IMF requires subsidy cuts, including fuel, but gives a three-year time window for the cuts to be implemented ("Egypt Sets $18 Billion for Subsidies in FY 2017–2018 Budget" 2017). In July 2017, Al-Sisi's government initiated cuts by raising gasoline and electricity prices, especially for firms (El-Tablawy and Wahba 2017). The first cuts aimed at bread subsidies – which amounted to restricting the number of loaves and also digitizing subsidy cards – were met with widespread protests in March 2017 and had to be quickly rescinded (Youssef 2017). Most recently, the government has capped the number of Egyptians who can obtain new food subsidy cards for staples while keeping the current system – amounting to 20 million card holders – in place ("Egypt Tightens Eligibility for Food Subsidy Cards" 2017).

It is too early to tell whether the Al-Sisi government will be able to accomplish a task that has eluded all of his predecessors since Nasser's rise to power. However, the evidence presented in this case study suggests that his elite coalition is remarkably firm, and that should give him the ability to continue push through legislation. The risk, of course, is that he inadvertently triggers mass collective action of the scale that brought down the Mubarak government. The military has successfully repressed the democratic activists who led that movement, and the Muslim Brotherhood is still present but suffering considerably. Thus, it is harder for collective action to start, although it can never be ruled out completely. If Egyptians lose their livelihoods, they may have few options other than protests, and even the Egyptian military cannot control all of Egypt's 90 million people if there is an uprising.

An intriguing episode in the fall of 2019 suggests that even though the military's growing dominance is formidable, it still could fall to popular mobilization. In September 2019, YouTube videos appeared from an Egyptian businessman named Mohammed Ali who in colorful, colloquial language described his work for the Egyptian military, including building a palace for President Al-Sisi. Though it is not clear why Ali posted these videos from his apparent self-exile in Spain, his portrayal of corruption associated led to the largest protests in Egypt since the military takeover in 2013.[17] While these protests did not endure, we also do not know what would have happened in the absence of the COVID-19 pandemic which disrupted political contention. As of the present writing, Al-Sisi's regime remains firmly in control of both the country and the business establishment (or what remains of it).

In conclusion, the strategic complementarities that helped Egypt's authoritarians build a new dictatorship in 2014 and 2015 have further sustained it through a difficult period of policy reform and wrenching economic adjustment. The lack of credible rivals proved both necessary and sufficient through the mechanism of the coordination game to produce an elite coalition that was willing to suffer economic harm rather than oppose the regime's new policies. The military's near total control over the provision of rents gives it enormous influence in the country, far eclipsing that of the former dictator. By comparison, Tunisia's pro-authoritarian coalition has failed to pass core policies to its business constituents, much less pose a credible threat to democracy. As I will show in Chapter 3, while Tunisia's democracy is far from a solid footing, it has survived its own authoritarian movement intact, and parties are currently preparing for the upcoming round of municipal elections in 2018 and legislative elections in 2019. In this case, although Tunisia had plenty of elites who would have preferred a reversion to autocracy, the lack of business unity inhibited the growth of the pro-authoritarian movement and, arguably, increased the likelihood of Tunisia's democracy surviving.

---

[17] See www.bbc.com/news/world-middle-east-49777287?ocid=socialflow_twitter.

3

Case Study

Broad Rent-Seeking and the Collapse of Tunisia's Antidemocratic Coalition

In Chapter 2, I showed how the unique presence of the military-clientelist complex in Egypt precipitated a very distinct form of political engagement – narrow rent-seeking – among businesspeople following the Arab Spring and the military's subsequent rise to power. The military's gatekeeper role pushed for a remarkable level of elite unity, resulting in a powerful coalition backed by widespread business participation – or at least acquiescence. In this chapter, by contrast, I will show that Tunisian businesspeople were freer to choose their own path following the Arab Spring, and that they made full use of these freedoms to advance their own interests, even at the expense of an antidemocratic coalition which ostensibly represented them. As a consequence, businesspeople were able to overcome efforts to dramatically reform corruption within the country without the necessity of committing their resources to one political side.

The difference between these political trajectories in the two countries is a direct result of the incentives for business engagement that existed in Tunisia, but not in Egypt. Much of business activity, of course, is hidden as companies prefer to avoid being recognized for having political influence. Yet through careful introspection of political coalitions and interviews with business leaders, I will show that the results of Tunisia's democratic system do follow a predictable, if fairly depressing, trajectory.

Due to the different contexts in which businesses found themselves in Tunisia, I will also use a different event map that shows the causal factors as they collectively produced the outcome. Figure 3.1 shows how the causal diagram from Chapter 2 for broad rent-seeking maps on to specific events that occurred in Tunisia following the Arab Spring, while Table 3.1 shows the mechanisms that explain how the variables affect each other. Of course, there are similarities between Egypt and Tunisia's trajectories: businesspeople in both communities suffered from disrupted political relationships, rising bribe payments and worry over political instability. As a consequence, Tunisia also witnessed the rise of an antidemocratic coalition under the guise of the Nidaa

77

TABLE 3.1 *Mechanisms for broad rent-seeking causal graph*

Mechanism	Definition
M_1	Costs of repression exceed the costs of tolerance.
M_2	Bureaucrats no longer accountable to former dictator's and his/her party.
M_3	To offset higher bribe costs, firms invest in political relationships.

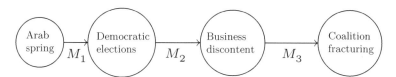

FIGURE 3.1 Event map for Tunisia case study

Tounes party, which successfully manipulated sectarian cleavages to achieve a historic electoral victory, unseating the Islamist Nahda party from its electoral domination of the parliament.

Yet even despite these initial successes, Nidaa Tounes never achieved a monopoly on business support like the military-led coalition in Egypt. The reason for this divergence is due to a missing causal factor in Tunisia. In particular, the causal graph for Tunisia in Figure 3.1 does not contain the influence of a state actor capable of managing the transition process, mounting a coup and using economic levers to influence business. Businesspeople remained free to engage in side deals with Tunisian politicians of their choosing, often preferring to play all sides: back both Islamists and secularists without siding with one against the other. This level of elite disunity augured in the collapse of Nidaa Tounes into underlying factions, and to an extent, helped confound the kind of damage to democratic institutions that the leaders of the coalition clearly intended.

While the antidemocratic coalition in Tunisia never reached the level of mobilization of its Egyptian counterpart, that does not mean that Tunisia's democracy showed robust health. As I describe, business influence tended to reduce policy innovation and entrench corruption, prompting popular disenfranchisement with governing coalitions. As I discuss in the conclusion, these weaknesses ultimately created an opening for the most recent chapter in Tunisia's transition, which may augur a reversion to autocracy. However, even the events of the past year show that Tunisia's path remains starkly different than Egypt's despite nominal similarities in regime type.

3.1 HISTORICAL POLITICAL ECONOMY IN TUNISIA

Tunisia's political economy evolved in remarkably similar ways to Egypt despite the differences between both countries in terms of colonial origin, initial

3.1 Historical Political Economy in Tunisia 79

economic conditions and regime type. Unlike Egypt, Tunisia's independence from France came through the mobilization of a single party known as the Neo-Doustour and headed by the charismatic Habib Bourguiba. As such, upon its founding Tunisia was often referred to as a single-party state that had an impressive level of penetration across classes and rural-urban divides, leading to a quick rise in development outcomes such as education (Moore 1965). Immediately upon its founding, Bourguiba expropriated assets of French and Tunisian businesspeople closely associated with the colonial regime, creating an opening for wider economic reforms (Hammami 2020, 96).

After Bourguiba managed to expel Ahmed Ben Salah, the early unity of the revolutionary coalition foundered as he centralized power. As a result, Tunisia's peak labor association, the Tunisian General Labor Union (UGTT), lost its ability to influence policy because its leftist economic ideology went much farther than Bourguiba, a product of Tunisia's commerce-oriented coastal areas, would tolerate (Ashford 1965; Eibl 2020, 92–95). After a purge of Ben Salah, Bourguiba switched directions and pursued a path that would try to integrate Tunisia with world markets, albeit with significant help from the state.

As a consequence, Tunisia became one of the first Arab states to switch from a socialist emphasis on state-driven development to a somewhat more open state-directed capitalism (Bellin 2002, 19–21). This period witnessed all of the hallmarks of ISI, including the growth of public-sector monopolies in important markets and the protection of indigenous industries through the use of import and export controls (Bellin 2002, 21). While Bourguiba liberalized import and export controls to an extent, the state remained highly involved in economic decisions, especially through powerful state-owned enterprises like the state-owned phosphate and chemical production company Groupe Chimique Tunisien and the insurance company STAR, in addition to maintaining control of domestic credit markets via banks (Henry 1996). The Bourguiban approach amounted to an open invitation to foreign investors to set up shop in Tunisia in clearly defined roles, such as garment production, which were subsequently walled off from the international economy through strict regulation (Bellin 2002, 26–40). The modern class of businesspeople largely dates from this time period, and is closely affiliated with state largesse as Bourguiba sought to grow domestic industrial production through various kinds of subsidies and privileges granted to domestic producers (Bellin 2002, 25–26).

As a result, the business class that developed in Tunisia remained in the coastal areas which had long dominated commerce in the country. The repudiation of Ben Salah and his radical areas, especially for the creation of agricultural cooperatives in rural areas (King 2003, 47), continued a long policy of ignoring the rural tribal hinterland in favor of Tunisia's three main cities: Tunis, Sousse, and Sfax. Despite the Neo-Doustor's revolutionary inclinations, the elites who made up the party were tightly interconnected. For example, many leaders of the party attended a single high school in Tunis known as the Sadiki school, which offered French-style education to members of elite Tunisian families

(Hammami 2020, 92–93). These educational divides persisted in the post-colonial period despite Neo-Doustour's efforts to expand education due to the existence of private and elite high schools in the coast (Blackman 2020).

As a result, the type of private industry that developed under Bourguiba remained closely linked to the state despite its nominal independence. For example, the development of private banks in the 1970s reflected the exploitation of the new regulations by politically connected insiders. One of Tunisia's largest banks, the Banque Internationale Arabe de Tunisie, was founded by one of Bourguiba's ministers who helped oversee the liberalization program (Hammami 2020, 103). As a result, by the 1990s, Tunisia had both a seemingly diverse number of private banks and a strong sense of oligopoly in a sector in which markets were highly segmented and financial growth was limited (Henry 1996). This stratified social hierarchy meant that loans from private and especially public banks were usually only available to those with either political or social connections. As a result, Tunisia's public banks were often widely under-capitalized due to their willingness to make loans without exercising due diligence, requiring periodic interventions by both the state and international financial actors to resolve nonperforming loans (Hibou 2011).

Habib Bourguiba's reign lasted until 1987, when his Prime Minister Zine Abidine Ben Ali staged a coup by having Bourguiba declared medically unable to perform the duties of his office (Grewal 2020). At first, Ben Ali promised dramatic democratic reforms, and he permitted more open political competition for a few years before repressing the same activists he had embraced (Murphy 1999, 200–10). In terms of political liberalization, he is credited with launching Tunisia into an experiment with pro-market liberalism that emphasized export-led growth and successfully privatized numerous state companies, though the state retained at least some influence over their operations (Cassarino 2004). As a consequence, Ben Ali is identified with the growth of crony capitalism as he permitted interlocking relationships between companies, bureaucrats and members of his own family to flourish. It is estimated that companies with a familial link to Ben Ali in the 2000s "appropriated 21% of all net private sector profits and accounted for approximately 3% of private sector output" (Rijkers, Freund, and Nucifora 2014, 3).

The trend of market liberalism combined with cronyism is also evident through research on Tunisia's export upgrading program in the mid-2000s, Mise à Nouveau, which received extensive funding from international development institutions in an attempt to mitigate the harm of freer trade on Tunisian companies. Mise à Nouveau was Ben Ali's signature effort to increase Tunisan firms' ability to export successfully to European markets. Taking place in the context of global trade liberalization which threatened Tunisia's garment and textile manufactures (Cammett 2007), Mise à Nouveau attracted funds from European donors to provide technological and managerial upgrades to Tunisian firms (Murphy 2006, 526). The policy aimed to push Tunisian firms into higher-quality exports so that they could compete with lower-cost

3.1 *Historical Political Economy in Tunisia*

producers in Asia (Murphy 2006, 525). However, while the program did affect a significant number of firms, the total benefits were significantly undermined by the fact that businesspeople in politically important areas, notably coastal provinces, along with firms in the offshore export sectors, benefited dispro-portionately from the program, while firms that had greater need of technical assistance but were less politically connected were generally excluded (Murphy 2006, 532–34). Although the program did increase exports for those firms that were involved (Murphy 2006, 531), the program's macroeconomic impact was limited as unemployment remained in the 10–15 percent range through the 2000s.

If access to business assistance is only available to companies with elite con-nections, then inevitably businesses with those connections will last longer and grow bigger over time. These selection dynamics for firms are important to emphasize to understand businesses in the region. A comprehensive report by the World Bank in 2015 documented the difficulties of job creation in the Mid-dle East, which the Bank argued was a result of companies in the region that lacked dynamism and relied on political connections instead of innovation for success:

The report shows that policies which lower competition in MENA also constrain pri-vate sector development and job creation. These policies take different forms across countries and sectors, but share several common features: they limit free-entry in the domestic market, effectively exclude certain firms from government programs, increase the regulatory burden and uncertainty on nonprivileged firms, insulate certain firms and sectors from foreign competition, and create incentives that discourage domestic firms from competing in international markets. Such policies are often captured by a few privileged firms with deep political connections and persist despite their apparent cost to society. (1)

The political role of Tunisians businesses rests on these trends. Those compa-nies that exist in the country are, generally speaking, those that successfully took advantage of government programs and regulations structuring who can invest in which industry. There are relatively few, if any, businesspeople in the country who resemble the cutthroat capitalists of Silicon Valley, capturing mar-ket share and driving out rivals. By contrast, Tunisian capitalism is much more an arrangement of mutual benefit and limited competition, in which the coun-try's small markets are carved into fiefdoms controlled by powerful business families. While the arrangement is remarkably stable for these families, it also limits growth and innovation, especially for the younger generation.

From an international perspective, the structural adjustment program was a success as Tunisian economic growth and exports increased through the 1990s and early 2000s (Murphy 2006, 531; Cammett et al. 2015, 299–302). Yet none of this liberalization threatened the political underpinnings of the regime because the relationships between firms and the state remained unchanged (Hibou 2011, 41–44; Cammett et al. 2015, 282–86). In addition, rural areas continued to fall behind the coastal regions that received most of the new private investment in manufacturing. Increases in agricultural productivity came at the expense of increasing land concentration among wealthy elites, undermining traditional Tunisian farmers. In addition, the state decreased price support for crucial crops, especially olive oil, the price of which fell by 40 percent in 1993 (King 2003, 117). The loss of these state protections meant that large landowners, who had the capital and wherewithal to shift to new farming methods, were able to gain compared to smallholders who were less able to adapt to the changing policy environment (King 2003, 118).

In sum, by the outbreak of the Arab Spring in 2011, Tunisia's economy remained dominated by a set of elites whose origins dated back to precolonial times in many cases. A set of superelites who were closely affiliated with Ben Ali and his family managed a growing business empire, while the less-connected captured the lion's share of the remaining benefits of liberalization in wealthy coastal areas. The legacy of state linkages to both state-owned enterprises and ostensibly private firms through the provision of credit meant that the state indirectly and directly sustained a large number of businesspeople and entrepreneurs whose livelihood depended on their ability to maintain important political and social connections (Hibou 2011). This high level of social stratification, even in the context of an improving macroeconomic picture, led to bitter grievances that later suddenly erupted, as will be covered in the next section.

Given the discussion in Chapter 2, it should be obvious at this point that Egypt and Tunisia share a lot of similarities in terms of the institutional foundation of their economies. However, it is important to note at the same time crucial differences in the historical origins of Tunisian institutions are compared to Egypt. Tunisia's independence advocates made the crucial decision to negotiate an end to colonialism rather than engage in armed conflict, as their neighbors in Algeria did. This turn toward peaceful relations with their former colonizer permitted them to separate without needing to engage in military mobilization. As a result, the military remained so diminutive that the country was virtually unprotected from foreign invasion until Libya's incursions into the country in the 1970s (Ware 1986, 52–53). For this reason, the military never achieved political prominence in the country (Grewal 2016), and it never had the wherewithal to develop commercial enterprises of the scale of the Egyptian military.

That is not to say that the incentives did not exist for them to try: one of the earliest Tunisian companies, the Banque de Tunis, counted a Tunisian military general as one of its board members at incorporation in the late nineteenth century (Hammami 2020, 81). Intriguingly, Ben Ali's coup against Bourguiba in 1987 preempted another coup plot attempt that involved members of the military (Grewal 2020, 3). If Ben Ali had not been successful and continued Bourguiba's policy of marginalizing the military as a political actor, Tunisia might have taken a trajectory more similar to Egypt's. Instead, the differences

3.2 Regime Transition: The Arab Spring

in how the Tunisian and Egyptian regimes formed – one reliant on a powerful single party and the second on the military – led to differences as well in how political-economic privileges were distributed. By the time that the Arab Spring arrived in 2011, the two countries shared a history of corruption and cronyism at the highest levels, but differed in the prominence and power they gave to military leaders.

3.2 REGIME TRANSITION: THE ARAB SPRING

So far I have described the background conditions that led to the unique mix of capitalism and cronyism in Tunisia's long-lasting dictatorships. The causal process that led to business political engagement begins with the political upheaval of the Arab Spring, which originated in the Tunisian countryside. The Arab Spring is the first stage of the causal process shown in Figure 3.1. This event upended decades of political coalitions, spurring radical change and instability. While there were political-economic issues prior to the uprisings, it is impossible to find any one factor that predicted the protests of late 2011. Rather, it would seem the Arab Spring grew out of long-standing perceptions of corruption and incompetence in governing institutions. Tunisian elites, though they certainly knew of the unpopularity of corruption, were stunned by the rapid spread of the protest movement and were unable to defend their regime. For that reason, the causal story begins with this break with the normal way of doing business.

At the same time, it is important to connect the Arab Spring to the structural factors that preceded it. The unraveling of the ISI bargain dating back to independence, and in particular the loss of privileges for rural producers, set the stage for the sudden wave of protests that broke out in Tunisia's interior regions. While much of the media coverage of the Arab Spring focused on massive protests in urban areas, the origins of the movement are strongly rural. Mohammed Bouazizi, a street vendor in the interior region of Sidi Bouzid, lit himself on fire after police confiscated his street cart. Protests broke out in rural areas (Chomiak 2014, 40–45), and only later spread to Tunis and from Tunis to other countries. While it is true that without urban support, the revolution could not have succeeded so quickly, it is also true that the rural strength of the movement left the regime particularly vulnerable because it did not have the capacity to pacify the entire country at once. This hidden weakness in Ben Ali's regime was foreseen by King (2003):

> The regime's ability to consolidate the emerging authoritarian system described in the last chapter may well depend on the state party's ability to maintain authoritarian controls in the countryside (42).

The sheer size of protests, combined with their geographical spread, brought down the regime by making repression a practical impossibility. Faced with massive popular mobilization, elites in Tunisia democratized per mechanism

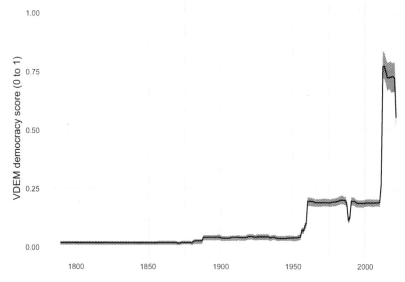

FIGURE 3.2 Varieties of Democracy values for Tunisia

M_1 because of the threat that this mobilization posed to their property and even their own lives (Dahl 1971). The principle that democracy is often demanded by the poor instead of granted as a gift from the rich has a strong foundation in both empirics (Przeworski 2009a) and theory (Acemoglu and Robinson 2006). It is important to note that this begins the causal process outlined in Figure 3.1. The Arab Spring caused an exogenous change in elite relations which came from outside of the system of crony capitalism and preferential access I described in the previous section. As can be seen in Figure 3.2, Tunisia experienced a sustained increase in its Varieties of Democracy electoral democracy score following 2011, evidence of a broad improvement in civil liberties and electoral competition.

As a result, the importance of the Arab Spring revolution to this study is the fact that the element of surprise caught political elites off guard, which consequently allows me to study the reactions of businesspeople during a rare moment in which their political strategies must adapt. In ordinary periods of regime politics, business strategies are determined by a number of factors that are difficult to observe, such as their assessment of the probability of obtaining connections or the likelihood of expropriation by bureaucrats. After an exogenous event like a sudden revolution, however, all businesses had to reset their political strategies, creating an excellent area in which to see whether political trajectories followed those predicted by the model presented in Chapter 2. Because businesses could not have anticipated the massive changes due to the Arab Spring, I can better identify the variables that affect their engagement, that is, principal–agent relationships between bureaucrats, businesspeople, and politicians and both the supply and demand for economic rents.

3.3 Democratic Elections

While there were some signs of popular discontent in Egypt prior to the downfall of Mubarak, it is difficult to point to similar signs of unrest in Tunisia. The Ben Ali's regime tight grip on political participation in the country, which involved restrictive regulation of what little civil society existed and banning of most public displays of political opinion, even opinions that were not threatening to the regime, served to artificially lower the public display of grievances (Chomiak 2011, 70–75). That is not to say, as argued in the previous chapter, that grievances in the country did not exist (Chomiak 2011, 71). Perversely, the regime's repression of most forms of political expression meant that any kind of collective action opposing the regime was likely to be rapid and unpredictable because of the high costs associated with revealing one's true preferences (Kuran 1995).

The one factor that seemed to immediately precede the Arab Spring was the release of a trove of alleged US State Department cables describing corruption within Ben Ali's immediate family (El-Khawas 2012, 8). However, this information primarily served to confirm people's prior suspicions rather than generate novel information. The actual spark came from the self-immolation of Mohammed Bouazizi, a street vendor persecuted by the police in a rural Tunisian town, but the reason why his story mobilized people while Ben Ali's many other acts of repression did not is difficult to assign any causal reason to. For this reason, it is a useful starting place to examine how business strategies adjusted to an unanticipated shock to the political system.

3.3 DEMOCRATIC ELECTIONS

Once Ben Ali had been forced to leave the country in February 2011, Tunisia began a rapid transition to democracy with a quick election in 2011 to form a constituent assembly that would help draft a new constitution. This next stage in the event map in Figure 3.1 was the logical consequence of a successful democratic revolution. However, democracy entails responsiveness to public opinion, and in Tunisia's case, the empowerment of long-marginalized rural voices. The results of the first elections in 2011 were a resounding disappointment for the former "legal" opposition under Ben Ali and for secular reformers who had hoped for a move toward European-style social democracy. The elections to the National Constituent Assembly, a unicameral legislature dating back to Tunisia's independence, resulted in a highly fragmented parliament with only one party, the Islamist Nahda, receiving more than forty percent of the popular vote (Allani 2013, 3) after its return from repression and exile under Ben Ali.

Secular and leftist opposition parties dating back to the old regime lost considerable support, none more so than the Parti Démocrate Progressiste, which came in a dismal fifth and blamed its loss on unnamed electoral consultants who advised the party to invest heavily in TV advertising (Stepan 2012, 91). In reality, these parties were simply unprepared for open democratic competition despite having adequate electoral funds due to the elitist nature of these parties under the Ben Ali regime.[1] This unpreparedness is not accidental, nor was it merely a result of poor leadership. Rather, party fragmentation post-Arab Spring has been shown to be a direct result of policies under the previous dictatorships that divided opposition groups through selective legalization (Lust-Okar 2005; Lust and Waldner 2017). Because the Nahda party was entirely banned under Ben Ali, it also retained a level of organizational autonomy, and it quickly reactivated its networks of Islamic activists after the downfall of the regime (Nugent 2020). The second-highest share of seats went to the Congrès Pour la République, which combined an Islamist orientation with a discourse of human rights (Storm 2014, 85–118). Thus every other party, whether remnants of the former regime's party or secular liberals, were relegated to a voiceless minority in the first parliament.

These lop-sided electoral results led to a growing polarization of political discourse and a forced reevaluation on the behalf of the many failed political parties of their political strategies. Per mechanism M_2, the change in political institutions ended previous one-party control over state institutions and inaugurated a new set of rules and relationships governing power. While elections did not immediately change the full set of bureaucrats who made up the state, the new constitution and the free and fair elections meant that the previously all-powerful influence of Ben Ali over the state suddenly disappeared. Of course, individual bureaucrats retained considerable influence within their ministries, but there was no longer any conductor or residual claimant who could bully and command underlings to follow his bidding. From the perspective of connected businesspeople, chaos ensued.

3.4 BUSINESS DISCONTENT

As I argued in Chapter 2, many businesspeople in states with weak institutions depend on cronyist relationships with bureaucrats to secure access to important types of rents. As such, the disruption of these relations consequently led to a loss of rents for businesses, especially for crony capitalists who were closely allied to the dictator. Thus, it is not surprising that following parliamentary elections, businesspeople came under unheard of scrutiny for crony deals made under the previous regimes. In addition, business could no long rely on long-established relationships to ensure that they could navigate the state bureaucracy to their advantage.

While Nahda had its difficulties in governing, which I will describe later, in the aftermath of the revolution both secular liberals and Islamists were eager to prosecute what they saw as the primary actors responsible for corruption under the Ben Ali regime. Given the dramatic losses in elections, politically connected businesspeople had relatively few allies in the parliament to turn

---

[1] Interview, January 18, 2011.

3.4 Business Discontent

to in order to delay or tamp down on anti-corruption and economic reform drives. The most immediate and dramatic acts of expropriation centered on the former dictator Ben Ali and his relatives, who through his wife Leila controlled a sprawling business empire that focused on imports and services in domestic retail markets. These assets were evaluated at USD $13 billion and involved over hundred people, so this targeted confiscation was a bit more than a family affair (Rijkers, Freund, and Nucifora 2014, 114). In addition, members of this influential network were imprisoned or had arrest warrants issued against them, most notably Imad Trabelsi, Leila's brother (Dejoui 2017).

Expropriation of corrupt businesspeople, however, did not extend as far as some democratic reformers wanted. In addition to the list of Ben Ali affiliates who were targeted for expropriation, a much wider list of businesspeople was put together by the same committee that seized Ben Ali's family's assets.[2] This list was never released to the public nor referred to the prosecutor's office, and I have never been able to obtain a copy of it. The untimely end of this second list was very likely due to intense lobbying by politically connected businesspeople who saw their own assets on the list.[3] While cronyist influence was able to avoid this threat to the broader business community, business elites learned a powerful lesson about the threat that democratic accountability posed to the way things normally had been done.

As a result, many established companies in Tunisia reacted nervously to these attempts at expropriation. Even more ominous to businesses was the creation of a transitional justice committee, written into Tunisia's new constitution, that was given a mandate to investigate "all of [the State's] domains" and for which no statute of limitation applied ("Constitution of the Tunisian Republic" 2014, Article 148). Furthermore, the authorizing legislation in 2014 for this commission included within its mandate "economic crimes," and the commission invited any accusations of such crimes from all Tunisian citizens for the entire period of Tunisia's dictatorship (Malki 2017). Given this broad mandate, the aura of expropriation survived the initial spate of confiscations focused on Ben Ali's inner circle and the demise of the infamous second list.

A second source of concern for businesspeople was the increasing difficulty in managing a bureaucracy which their hard-earned connections had made navigable. An excerpt from a translated interview I had with a hotel manager in August 2016, as shown in Table 3.2, was particularly revealing in this regard.

In other words, bureaucrats reacted to the demise of the Democratic Constitutional Rally (RCD) by holding up businesspeople for additional rents and competing with each other for a greater share of the bribery pie. Lacking powerful political figures who could enforce access for businesspeople, especially as these types of accesses were based on informal relationships, meant

---

[2] Interview with Journalist, February 2, 2016.
[3] Interview with Journalist, February 2, 2016.

TABLE 3.2 *Interview transcription, 2016*

INTERVIEWER	Yeah. Has the, I mean, have people in the customs tried to collect bribes and stuff from you? We've had a lot of people complain about that.
INTERVIEWEE	Yes.
INTERVIEWER	But it doesn't seem like it really matters. It's slow, it's slow, it's slow.
INTERVIEWEE	(In English) Because before the revolution, it was simple. You had to pay one person and you'll have exactly what was the amount.
INTERVIEWER	And now it's ...
INTERVIEWEE	Now, it's a lot of people! And you never know the amount, and in this company, we do not choose this process, but I know that other companies don't have another choice. Now the problem is, you pay someone, and when you go to pick the parcel, you find someone else and you have to pay them, too.

that business were left with little recourse as they would be unlikely to find sympathetic ears in the midst of a democratic revolution.

These mixed feelings toward democratic reform manifested themselves in a yearly annual survey of business executives by the consulting firm Ernst & Young. While their survey did not touch on sensitive topics like cronyist relations and largely maintained the fiction of the separation of big business and the state in Tunisia, it nonetheless represents a compelling picture of how business leaders reacted to the changes especially as their survey included many of the largest companies. In 2012, an overwhelming majority of respondents (76 percent) selected "political and security instability" as their biggest worry in the run-up to parliamentary elections, and 84 percent described the political climate as "bad" or "very bad" (Hajji and Zaoui 2012, 13). Interestingly, twice as many CEOs selected political instability compared to problems with economic conditions as their main concern in the country (13). Furthermore, a plurality (46%) believed that the political situation would only get worse (13). Oddly, CEOs were also concerned about a decline in Tunisia's image in the world (70%), a revealing sentiment as widespread media coverage at the time tended to paint Tunisia as embarking on a bold democratic experiment.

These dismal views of Tunisia's nascent regime, however, did not prevent business managers from opining that the disruptions would not last beyond the medium term. A strong majority (65%) of respondents predicted that they would see a "return to normal" within two to five years (14). It is somewhat puzzling why business executives were so convinced that they could weather the new political changes even as they cited them as a formidable obstacle to their business. Unfortunately, the Ernst & Young survey did not ask about any political activities of businesspeople, abiding by the self-serving myth of

3.4 *Business Discontent* 89

business as a separate realm, leaving us to infer that the CEOs had plans for reestablishing their relationships with government officials which they believed would ultimately prove successful.

I am able to replicate these CEOs perceptions through an online survey of Tunisian businesspeople I completed in the summer of 2017 and that is described more in Chapter 5. For respondents at large firms in the survey, 63 percent of Tunisian respondents reported that informal payments had become more common since the Arab Spring. This high percentage is a good indicator of the phenomenon of "agent predation" (Markus 2015) in which bureaucrats become more unconstrained in their positions and feel more comfortable holding up firms for additional revenues. The networks of cronyist relations had become unbalanced following the swift exit of the dictator and ruling parties, permitting an increase in bureaucrat autonomy vis-a-vis business.

Given high-level expropriation, labor unrest and growing corruption, the democratic transition brought little of good to the established business communities in Tunisia. Of course, the change in rules could have created new openings for entrepreneurship and competition in the country, and during my field research, I met several innovative Tunisians trying to do exactly that. However, entrepreneurs faced not only the normal difficulties of building a business, but also the necessity to obtain the licenses, permits, and banking privileges which established firms had already obtained (Batjargal et al. 2012; Boudreaux, Nikolaev, and Holcombe 2018; Ge, Carney, and Kellermanns 2019).

For these reasons, established companies were predisposed to dislike democracy because they had prospered under dictatorship, and any increase in political competition could usher in more economic competition as well. While a process of managed liberalization could benefit well-connected domestic firms, true economic reform would be harmful because it could attract high-quality entrepreneurship that would compete away the rents that these businesspeople had worked so hard to secure for themselves.

Figure 3.3 reveals the middling support for democracy among employees and managers in another survey of Tunisian companies I conducted in the summer of 2018. The figure shows average responses on a scale of 1 to 10 for a question that asked respondents whether their bosses support democracy. The values for different companies are very similar and display middling support for democratization. It is useful to compare these numbers to the Arab Barometer's regional surveys that show around 90 percent of respondents believe democracy is the best type of government (Jamal and Tessler 2008).

Interestingly, respondents at foreign-owned firms reported more positive views toward democracy among their bosses, suggesting that the outsider business community had a different take on Tunisia's institutional trajectory. The poor views toward democracy among domestic businesspeople in Tunisia are very likely a reflection of the difficulties faced by firms in navigating an uncertain institutional terrain where old certainties and relationships were put under significant strain.

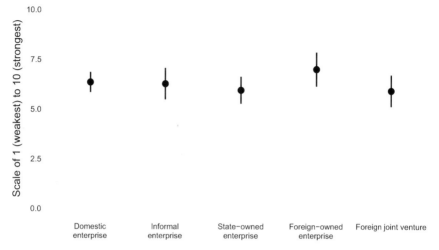

FIGURE 3.3 Average affect toward democracy among business employees and managers in Tunisia, online survey in Summer 2018

As I identified in Chapter 2, there were various incentives which would impel businesses toward political engagement during the post-Arab Spring period, and the sentiment among business owners toward regime change was largely negative. For businesses that depended on access to rents from the state, favor from new political elites was a necessity to survive. For other businesses that feared expropriation from newly empowered reformers, obtaining protection became a significant priority. The need for political engagement also varied with the extent of disruption in terms of the increased autonomy of bureaucrats. While no two companies are of course alike, in the aggregate it is not surprising that both countries witnessed the rise of pro-business and pro-authoritarian politics, which is the next stage in the causal process in Figure 3.1.

3.5 COALITION FRACTURING

Many Tunisian businesses at this point had a clear interest in political action, but the incentives that encouraged them to do so differed from those in Egypt. Tunisian businesses had much more freedom to consider which and how many political sides to support, which involved broad rent-seeking across the political spectrum. The lack of campaign finance regulation meant their donations were hidden from public scrutiny. Ultimately, the role of secrecy helped Tunisian firms protect their business interests, though often at the cost of transparency and political reforms. Although Tunisians' political engagement was

3.5 Coalition Fracturing

not necessarily higher than Egypt's, it did have a different focus thanks to the country's lack of a powerful political patron capable of requiring narrow rent-seeking.

At first, Tunisian businesses seemed to have a similar negative reaction to democracy as their counterparts in Egypt did. Elite turnover in both Tunisia during the 2011 parliamentary elections led to the creation of a reactionary pro-authoritarian coalition. This coalition married former officials from the dictatorship eager to rebrand themselves in the new political system and businesspeople looking to head off the zeal of democratic reformers. However, not all good (or bad) intentions make their mark, and in this case, the intentions of coalition formateurs in Tunisia proved to be much less successful than their counterparts in Egypt. In both countries, prominent businesspeople became the patrons of coalitions and used their considerable resources to jump-start collective action, but only in Egypt did the movement reach a critical size beyond which it could become self-sustaining, which I argue is a result of the military-clientelist complex. Tunisian pro-authoritarian leaders had fewer sticks and carrots to use to grow their coalition and curtail businesspeople from reaching a separate peace with new parties via broad rent-seeking.

Instead, businesspeople were too willing to reach across the aisle for political support, networking with Islamists and reformers with equal relish. The loss of authoritarian controls meant that the remnants of Ben Ali's RCD party had little threats to use to push for elite unity, especially once it became clear that stymieing radical reforms would not be too difficult. The authoritarian reaction in Tunisia became a vehicle for protecting elite interests, but these interests never coalesced to the point that regime change became a possibility, as many of Ben Ali's former cronies devoutly wished. While the RCD successfully employed state resources to maintain business allies and isolate rivals during Ben Ali's tenure, following the RCD's collapse its survivors had little to use to discipline rivals.

3.5.1 Nidaa Tounes' Origins

As previously mentioned, the fragmented party landscape and consequent loss in the 2011 elections by non-Islamists meant that old regime supporters, businesspeople, secular liberals, and leftists all had to reevaluate their political strategies to adjust to the rise of Nahda. The opening for a return of pro-authoritarian actors to politics came about through growing polarization between Islamists and secularists in the country. Inside the parliament, secularists quarreled with Islamists over whether the constitution should state that Tunisia was or was not an Islamist country (McCarthy 2016, 170–71). To make matters worse, discursive polarization gave way to Islamist-inspired terrorism in the summer of 2013 with the assassination of popular leftist MPs Chokri Belaid and Mohamed Brahmi.

Facing protests and falling public support, Nahda chose to transition out of its leadership role by resigning from the cabinet in favor of a transitional government composed of technocrats. This transition was managed by a loose association of Tunisian power brokers, including the peak employer association, the Tunisian Association of Industry, Trade, and Handicrafts (UTICA), and the peak labor union, UGTT. It was this group, the Quartet, that later earned a Nobel Prize for helping avoid sectarian conflict as occurred to a much greater extent in Egypt and Syria. Whether or not this group did in fact avert civil war, it is apparent that Nahda changed its tactics following the spread of extremist ideology through radical groups like the Islamic State. Instead of an explicit Islamicizing project, Nahda came to emphasize its appeal to lower-class interests and its commitment to continue an overhaul of state institutions to remove prior remnants of the regime (McCarthy 2016, 172–74).

Out of this political confusion emerged a nascent alliance between well-connected businesspeople, secular liberals, and former regime elites, while leftists continued to oppose both the Islamists and politicians with ties to Ben Ali. A political consultant described a series of secretive meetings in early 2012 hosted by the prominent businessman Fawzi Elloumi, CEO of the Elloumi group, known for manufacturing and several related businesses across sectors. The meetings included Mohsen Marzouk, an employee of the NGO Freedom House and a well-known liberal intellectual; Taieb Baccouche, an academic and former minister of Education, and Ridha Bel Hadj, a former RCD party apparatchik.[4] This peculiar configuration of politicians would have been implausible apart from Nahda's rise in the polls; however, it was not polarization alone that gave Nidaa Tounes its motive force.

By the time that the party was officially announced in the summer of 2012, it was clear that Fawzi Elloumi's resources and business networks had contributed to the group's coalescing. The Elloumi Groupe is one of the largest in Tunisia, and is by far the most successful private exporter. The Group's reported revenues approach 5 percent of Tunisia's GDP.[5] In addition to Elloumi, other "elite families" who wanted to "preserve [their] wealth" flocked to this party, which quickly became a symbol of political stability in a turbulent time.[6] However, many of the other elite businesspeople kept a lower profile in their support for Nidaa Tounes, as is common with businesses in virtually every democracy. The notable exceptions include Chafik Jarraya, an influential businessman who was very active politically under the Ben Ali regime, and Nabil Karaoui, who as the head of the largest private TV station provided ample cheap advertising for the nascent political movement.

While I was unable to definitely ascertain the level of support for Nidaa Tounes among all of the top conglomerates, most of the thirty-four managers

---

[4] Interview January 18, 2011.
[5] Author's calculations based on data from L'Economist Maghrebien.
[6] Interview January 18, 2011.

3.5 Coalition Fracturing 93

that I spoke to expressed varying levels of support for the party. At the very least, virtually none of these businesses has been an outspoken champion of the socialist trade union party, Front Populaire, or even the ostensibly neoliberal party, Afek Tounes. Afek's message of reform appears not to have resonated among established businesses that would stand to lose from serious efforts to overhaul Tunisia's investment code and trade regime. What is crucial about the top conglomerates in Tunisia is that all of these businesses became successful under the Ben Ali regime, and change is not necessarily a benefit from their perspective. Some of the managers I talked to complained of the avarice of Ben Ali's family, but in general they viewed Ben Ali as an asset because he could ensure that they received favorable treatment from the bureaucracy. This powerful selection effect is the underlying reason for the support of the dictator among big business: it is not that business itself has any direct affinity with dictatorship, but rather that the businesses that thrived under the former system were those that were optimally adapted to those institutional conditions (Acemoglu 1995). Powerful pro-democratic businesspeople, who may readily appear in more liberal economic systems (Arriola 2013), represent the unobservable outcome among Tunisia's business class due to decades of institutional selection.

For this reason, it would be wrong to characterize Nidaa Tounes as a purely secularist party. The presence of businesspeople and former regime elites provides a second context to the party's goals. While both secular liberals and former RCD-ers were concerned about Nahda's rise to power, they viewed the threat from very different lenses. Secular-liberal polarization induced by Nahda did not create the movement, but rather provided an opportunity for this alliance to form, an opportunity that disenfranchised RCDers reached for eagerly and secular liberals acquiesced to with some reluctance. Beji Caid Essebsi, a government official under both the Ben Ali and Bourguiba regimes, became the octogenarian symbol of this movement by launching a presidential candidacy in 2014, and called for a return to "bourguibisme," a term refers to a supposedly idyllic phase of Tunisia's post-independence existence under its first dictator. He argued forcefully against Nahda's Islamist project, implying that the movement would return Tunisia to a medieval era of under-development (McCarthy 2016, 171).

The extent of the presence of the former dictator's party, the RCD, in Nidaa Tounes is difficult to document, but it was frequently alluded to in my interviews in Tunisia. Probably the most telling story came from a political consultant who described a training of Nidaa Tounes vote mobilizers. One of the Nidaa Tounes campaign workers listened attentively to the presentation, and then described how he used different tactics with the same goal of voter mobilization during the Ben Ali period:

One guy came to me after this training, and he was like, "Hey, come here, let's talk. I've been doing [get-out-the-vote efforts] for 25 years." "How have you been doing this for 25 years where there were no elections?" "You know, I was with the old party. We

94   *3 Broad Rent-Seeking and Collapse*

would go to people, and we would say," "I will give you twenty dinar if you vote for us." And if they say no, then I say, "I'll break your jaw."[7]

Between 2012 and 2014, Nidaa Tounes became the most well-financed operation in Tunisian politics. From my interviews, it appears that the party's funds came from three sources: (1) local Tunisian businessmen like Elloumi, (2) European parties (Konrad Adenauer Schiftung) and states (France), (3) the United Arab Emirates, which supported Nidaa Tounes and Beji Caid Essebsi as an alternative to the (allegedly) Qatari-supported Nahda, and (4) border smugglers who wanted extra-legal protection for their lucrative trade with Libya and Algeria.[8] It is impossible to know the exact makeup of the party's funding, but even with foreign assistance, businesspeople like Elloumi had both the interest and means to build Nidaa Tounes into an electoral juggernaut. Elloumi's assistance helped overcome the collective action dilemma at the initial stages because his group's resources dwarfed other firms, and so he could take on the risk of funding a party even if he did not receive a great share of the benefits. If the secular liberals made a deal with the devil to gain electoral ascendancy, it worked. After a bitter, polarizing campaign, Nidaa Tounes took eighty-nine seats in the 2014 elections to Nahda's sixty-nine ("Tunisia: Majlis Nawwab Ash-Sha'ab" 2017).

At this point, it would appear that Nidaa Tounes was poised to push Tunisia away from democracy and toward dictatorship. All the cards had fallen into place: A large party with cross-class support incorporating former figures from the regime along with powerful businesspeople had won in the elections, and the party's figurehead was a nascent strong man who could make use of the presidency to undermine democratic constraints. Dismal economic growth and regional instability thanks to Libya's civil war provided credible contexts for democratic backsliding and even incumbent takeover. Indeed, after Nidaa Tounes' electoral success, protests broke out in rural areas against the return of the RCD, the party that controlled the state under Ben Ali (Lefèvre 2015, 308).

Up to this point in late 2014, it would appear that Tunisia and Egypt were following parallel paths. Both had rising pro-dictatorship coalitions that seemed capable of subverting democratic norms. It is true that the nature of democratic threats differed between Tunisia and Egypt. Tunisia did not undergo a military coup, as Egypt did, which was due to the long-term historical processes producing a military without the clout to stage a coup. In essence, Tunisia's military had been politically marginalized for a long time, and the democratic transition brought a larger budget, so it had little to fear from further democratization, whereas a reversion to dictatorship would deprive the military of these new-found benefits (Grewal 2016). But given that transitional democracies are at risk to incumbent takeovers for much longer periods of

---

[7] Interview January 18, 2016.
[8] January 18, 2011.

3.5 Coalition Fracturing

time (Svolik 2015), we know that the relative probability of Tunisia experiencing a democratic reversion was still substantial due to the threat of incumbent takeover. For these reasons, Tunisia could well have moved toward its own form of dictatorship in 2014 despite the fact that it had survived the apparent (but ultimately unobserved) coup threat. President Kais Saied, as I discuss later in the chapter, finally broke through democratic institutions by staging his own coup in July 2021, though the aftermath of his coup showed how hard it is to build a new dictatorship without a powerful coalition to support it.

The political demobilization of elites brought on by the popular uprising in both countries had clearly ended, and a new wave of authoritarian politics had begun. Aside from the different propensities toward military coups, the key difference between the two countries was the longevity of these movements, which would in turn depend on the underlying incentives of participating and non-participating elites. The military in Egypt took the lead in opposing democracy thanks to its hegemonic institutional position, but the coalition that the military headed was much larger than just military generals. Similarly, in Tunisia, the Nidaa Tounes party stood for a much larger coalition of people sympathetic to the old regime, but compared to Egypt, this coalition proved to have less durability. The breakdown of this coalition, I argue, is related to the types of rent-seeking that business in both countries could pursue. In the Tunisian case, the much wider menu of options for political brokers encouraged business to play all sides of the table.

3.5.2 Broad Rent-Seeking

Explaining the failure of a coalition is no easy in task, in part because political science theories are often set up to explain success. However, broad rent-seeking among Tunisian businesspeople does help explain Nidaa Tounes' surprising lack of resilience, especially when compared to the relatively enduring coalition in Egypt. My field research in 2016 revealed that powerful businesses still maintained political connections, but that they did not see it in their interest to support each other's political efforts. Rather, they would rather follow a dominant strategy of supporting a broad swath of political parties in the hope of obtaining the best outcome for their donations; that is, engaging in broad rent-seeking. This outcome follows from the theory presented in Chapter 2 because business only requires relationships with those bureaucrats or brokers who can provide rents, a goal that unflinching partisanship may impede.

During my research in Tunisia, I met with managers at thirty-four firms from a wide variety of sectors, although all of them were medium to large-sized firms. The majority of Tunisians work for small establishments that may or may not be officially registered, but the politically influential businesses are those with formal recognition that also maintain significant resources in capital and labor. I interviewed companies in diverse sectors from car dealerships to construction to agricultural processing to pharmaceuticals, including five of the twenty largest companies in the country. These firms were located in the three largest coastal cities in Tunisia: Tunis, Sousse, and Sfax. The majority of these firms had several hundred employees, reflecting my sample construction that aimed at larger firms capable of influencing the political system.

Overall, I found that these managers tended to favor Nidaa Tounes. A plurality, 21 percent, said that Nidaa Tounes had the best economic policies of any party in Tunisia. However, in an indication of the coalition's poor performance, by the time of my interviews in the summer of 2016, the number of managers reporting that no party had a sound economic policy (44%) dwarfed those who still supported Nidaa. Similarly, a majority (54%) said that none of the presidential candidates had a good economic policy, a strong rebuke of President Beji Caid Essebsi. Thus, while Nidaa Tounes appeared to have wide support among the business community, by two years into its tenure the party was widely perceived as ineffective even among firm managers who should be natural supporters of the party. Furthermore, Nidaa Tounes' middling support did not appear to be driven by pro-Islamist sympathies among managers in the sample. Nahda fared even worse among firm managers, gathering only 10% of managers' support despite the fact that Nahda had an aggressive economic reform plan during its time leading the parliamentary majority.

Rather, firm managers largely see the current parliament as a failure, at least from a point of view that touches upon their firms' interests. A majority of managers said that the political system in general was worsening (37.5%) or had experienced no improvement (25%) over the past year. When managers were asked why they believed that the political system had failed to improve, several cited "conflictual interests" resulting from "the formation of political coalitions." Furthermore, those who saw improvement in the political system primarily cited general amelioration of civil liberties, such as "liberty of expression" and "more space for debates and discussions" rather than any kind of noticeable policy change.

Despite these pessimistic assessments of Nidaa Tounes' performance, it is clear from these interviews that many firms had the option of participating in the coalition, and some indeed did so. Of the thirty-three firm managers with whom I did structured interviews, sixteen reported that they had some contact with political parties during the elections. This high number is a lower bound given that these managers may not have been aware of all attempts by parties to contact their firm. Furthermore, 39 percent of firm managers reported that their firm supported a party in some way. Of these firms, the most common type of support was financial (45%), followed by distributing party information to employees (32%), hosting party events using firm resources (25%), and instructing employees to vote for the party (20%).[9] Given that these firms

---

[9] Percentages do not sum to 100 because some firms engaged in multiple kinds of activities on behalf of parties.

3.5 *Coalition Fracturing* 97

represent a convenience sample, and that some managers may not have wanted to share all this information given social acceptability bias, these numbers represent only approximate estimates of the true levels of firm political engagement in Tunisia. On the whole, however, these numbers give evidence to the fact that firm political participation is a common phenomenon in the country, and that the failure of Nidaa Tounes to represent the interests of powerful businesspeople does not appear to be because of a lack of interest of firms in political issues. The quantitative data presented in the next chapter drawn from online surveys presents a similar picture of business political activity in Tunisia over the past few years.

The process through which the business community failed Nidaa Tounes was laid bare in an interview with a powerful business owner who had supported the party wholeheartedly.[10] This business owner described his work raising funds for Nidaa Tounes in the lead-up to the 2014 elections, which involved meeting with CEOs from a number of large firms across the country. Surprised at the widespread participation from a number of well-known figures, I asked this owner if all of this mobilization had made Nidaa successful. The owner winked at me, and then proceeded to tell me that while many of these businesses did contribute to Nidaa Tounes, at the same time they were giving similar contributions "under the table" to Nahda. That is, businesspeople saw opportunities to gain particularistic advantages for their firm and little to lose by supporting political rivals. A different business owner emphasized to me his commitment to neoliberal political philosophy, but then told me he had contributed funds to the socialist Front Populaire, a party associated with trade unions, to ensure that his firm's interests would be respected.

As another firm manager described his firm's willingness to engage in politics, "businesspeople have to make strategic coalitions." Without any penalties to supporting multiple parties, a rational firm leader will support rivals in an effort to ingratiate themselves with all sides. While this widespread participation is an effective strategy from the firm's point of view because it will secure the firm's property rights and any monopolistic privileges, this flexibility also made it difficult for Nidaa Tounes to consolidate power. Companies do not need to be on the "right" side, nor do they often prioritize ideology in political action if it would undermine their access to needed rents. Rather, their politics will tend to be very general and open insofar as it allows them to secure necessary relationships with state officials.

This level of business disunity can be seen as a status quo of sorts in democratic systems that lack any institutional actor capable of punishing defection. While many businesspeople in my interviews expressed sympathies for Ben Ali and his regime, when they came to engage in politics, they preferred pragmatic

---

[10] I cannot give more details of this informant for reasons of confidentiality.

strategies benefiting their firm instead of over-arching goals aiming at changing their government's regime.

That is not to say that business defection alone explains the coalition's difficulties, only that the coalition could have benefited from business unity when it inevitably suffered personality conflicts and disagreements over policy. In hindsight, Nidaa Tounes' failure appears the most likely conclusion, although it still came as a surprise to the many former regime elites and businesspeople who had invested significantly in the movement's success. As so many politicians discover, it can be quite difficult to convert shared preferences into a shared commitment to costly political action. Businesspeople never actively campaigned against Nidaa Tounes, they merely did not commit to the party in a way that could sustain its coalition over time.

3.5.3 Internal Rivals

The real test of these pro-authoritarian coalitions came not in their creation, as that could be subsidized by powerful businesspeople, but rather by the ability of these coalitions to endure over time. As has been discussed, Tunisia's pro-authoritarian coalition showed marks of fragility early on as firm collective action suffered from a prisoner's dilemma that the funding of Elloumi alone could not overcome. By contrast, the military-clientelist complex in Egypt affected the incentives of a much larger set of firms, creating a much broader and more cohesive initial coalition than Tunisia's. Ultimately, the crucial difference did not come down to the military's coup, but rather the point at which the Egyptian pro-authoritarian coalition became self-sustaining as firms began to coordinate around support to the new dictatorship. While internal rivals shattered Nidaa Tounes' forward momentum, Egypt's Tamarod successfully translated its initial strength into parties and candidates that produced a pliant legislature to implement pro-authoritarian policies.

Underneath the veneer of Nidaa Tounes' rising power, splits were already emerging in late 2015. The uneasy alliance between secular liberals and old regime elites erupted into wrenching policy debates before the 2014 elections had even occurred (Lefèvre 2015, 308). After barely a year in office, Nidaa Tounes officially split when a prominent secular liberal, Mohsen Marzouk, announced the formation of his own party in March 2016, the Tunisia Project. He managed to pull away twenty-two deputies from Nidaa Tounes, depriving them of the status of the legislature's largest party ("Tunisie: Lancement Officiel Du Parti de Mohsen Marzouk" 2016). While Tunisia Project remained nominally a part of the governing coalition, the public fracturing of Nidaa Tounes' power significantly undermined their ability to push legislation through the parliament. At the same time, personal feuds undermined party loyalty, most notably between factions for and against the leadership of President Essebsi's son, who was installed at the President's request as the vice president of Nidaa Tounes (Ryan 2015). Relations became so dismal that powerful businesspeople

3.5 Coalition Fracturing

who backed different parties in the governing coalition accused each other of attempting to bribe away MPs from each others' parties in a bid to increase their standing in the coalition, a phenomenon that appears to have plausibly occurred in a few cases ("Chafik Jarraya Revient Sur La Scène Avec Une Nouvelle Polémique" 2016).

Meanwhile, President Essebsi pursued a logical course of action as a resurgent executive, trying to heighten his public profile through international diplomacy and staying above the fray of mere party politics. However, the disputes over his son's role in the party apparently prevented him from acting as a unifying force, and Nidaa Tounes has more often than not seemed like a rudderless ship during its time as a governing party. President Essebsi took full advantage of a massive terrorist attack on a historic Tunis museum in July 2015 to impose a state of emergency that would give security forces wide latitude, a law that remained in place years after the attacks occurred ("Tunisia Extends State of Emergency Amid 'Terror Threats'" 2017). However, he was unable to parlay this increase in executive power into greater dominance over the other branches of government, possibly because his legislative allies could not or would not help him coerce powerfully autonomous agencies like the Ministry of the Interior.

The failure of Nidaa Tounes – especially in the eyes of some of its elite business backers – can be seen most clearly in the stalling of the economic reconciliation law. This euphemistically named law aimed to undercut Tunisia's truth and dignity commission by depriving it of the ability to examine any "financial crimes" committed by businesspeople or regime officials during Ben Ali's reign ("Tunisia: Amnesty Law Would Set Back Transition" 2016). However, the law was never allowed out of committee due to parliamentary opposition, despite multiple attempts by Nidaa Tounes to bring it to a vote (Lynch 2016). On the surface, the controversy over the economic reconciliation law is strange when the transitional justice commission was considering much more serious issues such as human rights abuses by security officials. Only when considering the support of businesspeople with strong connections to the Ben Ali regime does this legislation's importance make sense. However, even in this core interest that should have animated Nidaa Tounes, they ultimately failed to pass the law they wanted, and instead had to accept a watereddown version that only offered amnesty to bureaucrats, but not businesspeople (Yerkes and Muasher 2017).

For example, in one of the several attempts to push the law through parliament, which occurred in April 2017, the entire party developed a consistent messaging plan to create positive momentum for the bill, including media appearances and op-eds designed to re-frame the law around economic growth. To encapsulate their argument, I downloaded tweets from the Tunisian NGO Al-Bawsalah, which live-tweets Tunisian parliamentary sessions. I obtained 106 tweets each representing a condensed statement from an MP in an open plenary on the draft reconciliation bill. I then used the structural topic model (Roberts

3 Broad Rent-Seeking and Collapse

TABLE 3.3 *Representative tweets from parliamentary plenary on economic reconciliation law*

Topic	Party	Original	Translation
Topic 1	Nahda	Le réconciliation était dans le programme électoral de Beji Caied Essebsi, sa popularité est donc incontestable.	Reconciliation was part of Beji Caid Essebsi's electoral program, therefore its popularity is incontestable.
Topic 2	Nidaa Tounes	Il faut traiter ce projet de loi comme tout autre projet de loi. La com. lég. gén. ne peut pas l'abandonner.	We must treat this law the same way we would any law. The legislative committee should not just abandon it.
Topic 3	Front Populaire	L'article premier donne déjà le ton. Il nous parle d'instaurer un climat favorable a l'investissement. Hors sujet!	The first article already sets the tone. It speaks of making a favorable investment climate. Off-topic!

Source: Al-Bawsala Twitter (@AlBawsalah), April 26, 2017.

et al. 2014) to collapse these 106 tweets into three topics, and from each topic I pulled the tweet that the statistical model identified as the most typical. These tweets are shown in Table 3.3.

Table 3.3 shows how both Nahda and Nidaa Tounes were together pushing this law using a variety of discursive strategies. Interestingly, it is Nahda that referred to Beji Caid Essebsi's election victory as providing legitimacy to this law considering that Essebsi ran on a distinctly anti-Nahda platform. Nidaa Tounes, on the other hand, tried to push the law as just another part of ordinary legislative process, and also, as noticed by the Front Populaire (Topic 3), as a boon to economic growth. Nidaa Tounes' reasoning was that if prominent businesspeople who face corruption charges were given relatively lenient settlements, they would be more willing to invest in Tunisia. This argument was essentially a transparent threat to Tunisians to lay off their emphasis on corruption, or the economic elites would prevent the economy from pursuing a high-growth path.

However, even in this seemingly unified attempt, a prominent businessperson broke ranks. Bassem Loukil, CEO of the Loukil Group, currently one of the top ten largest conglomerates in terms of revenue, put out a public statement from his Facebook account condemning the law (Loukil 2017). In it he argued that not all businesspeople, by which he seems to imply himself, are connected with the old regime and need any help from dubious arrangements to save them from legal troubles:

3.6 *Plus Ça Change*

Those who are responsible for operating the economy are not all corrupt. Many still have integrity and resist the mafia and the predators of the old regime.

With this clever PR ploy, Loukil was able to set himself apart – and his conglomerate – from the costly effort to provide amnesty to businesspeople who could suffer under the transitional justice probe. This act of defection provides a concrete example of the troubles of Nidaa Tounes in unifying elites around policies which would seem to benefit them – even Loukil, who has been in business long enough to have had his own history with the Ben Ali regime. This self-serving statement is a concrete representation of the basic collective action dilemma: if Nidaa Tounes succeeds at its efforts, Loukil will only be helped by benefiting from the end of corruption probes. If Nidaa Tounes fails, Loukil will do better than the other businesspeople who supported the reconciliation law because he comes across looking as an anti-corruption reformer (one of the "good guys").

Again, these coalitional difficulties are not unique to Nidaa Tounes as a catch-all movement. Egypt's authoritarian coalition also had internal tensions and personality conflicts, but the coalition was successfully able to sideline rivals and bully powerful elites into submission. Nidaa Tounes had no such hidden weapon, and part of its weakness stemmed from business' willingness to work both sides of the aisle if it served their purpose. For example, with a considerable expenditure of resources, it might have been possible to keep the peace between Mohsen Marzouk and Caid Essebsi, preventing the early split that fractured Nidaa Tounes' legislative support. However, such extravagant measures were not in the interest of business as they did not prove to be necessary to achieve business' desire to avert democratic reforms and reestablish political influence. Cronyism and democracy, it turned out, were perfectly compatible with a bit of networking and quid pro quo.

While Tunisia does not have any lobbying disclosure requirements, and the press is generally unable to track interactions between businesspeople and the legislature, the Tunisian NGO Al-Bawsala maintained an active presence in the parliament during this time. During an interview with one of Al-Bawsala's parliamentary observers in July 2019, I learned that business leaders quite often visited MPs in their offices in Tunisia's parliamentary building throughout the tenure of the 2015 parliament. No record of the content of these conversations or their effect on policy, though, was ever reported.

3.6 PLUS ÇA CHANGE

By the end of Nidaa Tounes' tenure in 2019, Tunisia remained the democratic success story of the Arab Spring. That is not to say that there were not threats to civil and political liberties. As mentioned earlier, President Essebsi imposed an emergency law that has been used to imprison Islamists without trial and even to imprison some journalists for criticizing the security services. However, especially when compared to Egypt, Tunisia was a beacon of democratic freedom. The government successfully implemented its first-ever municipal elections in 2018, which continued the transformation, if slow and halting, of the state apparatus from the era of Ben Ali.

Yet, at the same time, the vacuum created by the weakness of Nidaa Tounes was never filled by a political reformulation that could push for reforms of the type that the country needs. Instead, the political failure of Nidaa Tounes resulted in a status quo democracy that avoided crises but has also proved inept at governing. For these reasons, by 2019, Tunisia had become an unstable democracy because it continued to be vulnerable to external challenges, such as foreign powers and Islamic terrorism, in addition to the potential for a second rural uprising given the dismal performance of democracy thus far. The best-case scenario for Tunisia's democratic future would have been for businesspeople to unite around implementing further democratization; given the near-impossibility of this outcome, it seemed the sticky status quo was the only feasible path for democracy to endure.

The primary effect of the disunity of the governing coalition, beyond its inability to undercut democratic institutions, was the policy gridlock that remained firmly in place. Roll-call voting data from the Tunisian Representative Assembly of the People reveals the dysfunction of the 2015–2019 parliament.[11] Of the 106 laws (not a very large number) that had been passed by the summer of 2016, nearly 32 percent of these bills were authorizations for the state to receive development aid or loans from international financial institutions (IFIs). None of the many other pressing issues, including security sector reform, investment regulation, and education, received only a handful of bills each. Furthermore, some of the substantive legislation that was passed, such as a financial reform act in early 2016, amounted to nothing more than a fine-tuning of regulations in order to meet IMF funding criteria for further loans ("ARP Approves Law on Banks and Financial Institutions, Again; Opposition Walks Out, Again" 2016). More scathing reports, such as the one issued by the World Bank in 2014 calling for a complete overhaul of the financial system, have been ignored despite lackluster economic growth and continued unemployment ("The Unfinished Revolution: Bringing Opportunity, Good Jobs and Greater Wealth to All Tunisians" 2014).

The stasis in parliament can be represented graphically through the use of item-response theory models, which put every legislator on a one-dimensional axis representing the dominant cleavage in the Tunisian parliament. I present a figure of the model here as it elucidates why this Tunisian parliament suffered from intractable stasis.

Figure 3.4 graphs the latent positions of MPs based on their roll-call voting data history from the Assemblee Representative du Peuple (ARP), the current

---

[11] Data provided by the NGO al-Bawsala.

3.6 Plus Ça Change

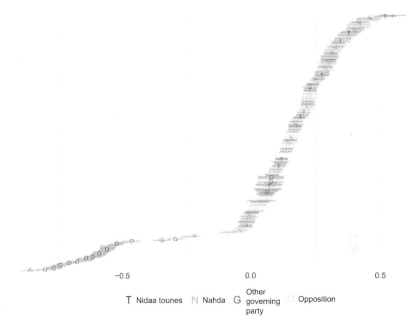

FIGURE 3.4 Similarity of voting records of Tunisian MPs, 2014–2016

session of which began following the elections in 2014. I label the points using four letters, "T" for Nidaa Tounes, "N" for Nahda, "G" for another member of the governing coalition, and "O" for opposition. G and O represent nearly a dozen smaller parties and blocs that comprise the fragmented Tunisian party landscape.

The main coalition – N, T, and G – comprise an outsize number of MPs in parliament, nearly 80 percent of the total number. Because some opposition MPs tend to vote with the government a fair amount of the time, less than 20 percent can be identified as true opposition based on roll-call votes (the long left tail in Figure 3.4). This outcome is surprising in Tunisia given the vitriol in the 2014 campaign, especially between Nidaa Tounes and Nahda. Nidaa Tounes MPs warned of a coming Islamist takeover in their campaign rhetoric, but on assuming power, they quickly reached a detente with Nahda. By 2017, only two years following the elections, the voting positions of Nahda and Nidaa Tounes members were statistically indistinguishable from each other.

This level of uniformity in the parliament is a direct violation of the minimum winning coalition principle (Riker 1980). Politicians should not band together to this great extent because it dilutes their ability to push for policies that match their ideological beliefs and constituent priorities. This discrepancy implies that there was some other factor than policy victories at play. At least the very least, it is clear that the legislative process was not being used by Nidaa Tounes and its allies in a conventional sense of implementing a policy platform that voters chose in an election. I argue that this policy stasis was a direct follow-on from the goals of Nidaa Tounes at undermining democratization combined with the internal weakness of the party due to broad rent-seeking by its business backers.

A strong authoritarian coalition should polarize the country, as occurred in Egypt. However, a weak authoritarian coalition is likely to need more partners in order to maintain power in the legislature. The Tunisian governing coalition can be thought of as primarily a defense structure aimed at avoiding a worst outcome, which would be the loss of privileges for Tunisia's economic elite. Absent an ability to realize the full return to dictatorship, businesspeople have retrenched themselves around protecting the privileges long held since the days of import substitution industrialization. While they will openly advocate for economic growth, they tend to view this outcome as happening primarily through government surplus from foreign donors (hence, the easy passage of development loans), not from any kind of fundamental restructuring of the Tunisian state.

While this outcome appeared beneficial from the perspective of businesspeople, it is at first odd that Nahda would be a willing partner in the coalition of "no change." However, as mentioned earlier from my interviews, it was readily apparent that businesspeople had been lobbying Nahda from as soon as the party came into power. It is difficult, of course, to track any actual campaign donations from businesspeople, but multiple sources confirmed that businesses were ready and even eager to reach out once Nahda gained the majority. In my own interviews with Nahda party officials, their positions seemed to be very much in favor of the economic elite. The party abandoned its early commitment to thoroughgoing economic reform, even though such initiatives would undoubtedly benefit its poorer rural base.

In one compelling example, I questioned a Nahda party official in February 2016 about the party's position on the controversial economic reconciliation law mentioned earlier. Supporting the law, for Nahda, implied supporting the cronies who benefited from the same dictatorship that repressed the movement for decades. However, this party official told me that there was no problem with the economic reconciliation law so long as there was a requirement that businesspeople invest some of their repatriated assets in businesses in the interior regions. Since then, this talking point became Nahda's official position and was echoed by their MPs in parliament. Opposition to the economic reconciliation law, and Nidaa Tounes' authoritarian tendencies, came from the socialist Front Populaire, which employed fiery rhetoric but held only a dozen seats in the parliament.

Thus, while it is not possible to obtain direct evidence that Nahda was in collusion with Nidaa, and that part of this collusion was brought about by businesspeople with significant interests involved, this theory best explains the available facts. Without Nahda's support, Nidaa Tounes would never have finally managed to pass a watered-down version of the economic reconciliation

3.6 Plus Ça Change

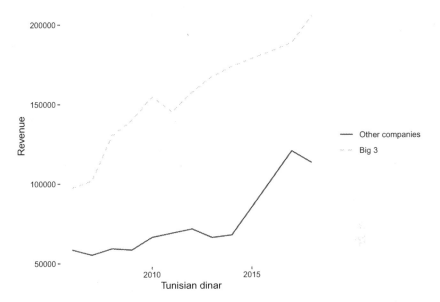

FIGURE 3.5 Comparison of top three Tunisian conglomerate revenue growth versus individual firms

law in the fall of 2017 that provided amnesty only to government officials, not businesspeople (Yerkes and Muasher 2017). Lacking the ability to undertake widespread institutional change, parties settled for a status quo in which economic reform efforts are slowed and anti-corruption initiatives obstructed, while virtually all major players are accepted into the governing coalition. As it turns out, businesspeople's openness to recruit allies across the spectrum proved to be an impediment to Nidaa Tounes' antidemocratic pursuits but perfectly capable of reestablishing business influence and protecting their access to valuable rents.

The success of business elites is most powerfully captured in Figure 3.5, which shows the yearly revenue average for the top three conglomerates in the country – Groupe Elloumi, Groupe Poulina and Groupe Mabrouk – alongside average revenue for other firms in the economy using data from the magazine L'Economiste Maghrebine. What is easily evident from the graph is that while revenue growth continued for most companies by 2016, the largest three conglomerates never saw as much of a slowdown in revenue growth and continued growing after the Arab Spring seemingly without much of a hindrance. While of course we do not know how much of this growth came from wise business decisions versus crony relations and politicking, it is clear that for the largest Tunisian firms, business has not been so bad despite the country's economic woes. Even for smaller established companies, growth has resumed even as unemployment remains high.

3.7 CONCLUSION: TUNISIA'S DEMOCRACY REMAINS UNDER THREAT

While this case study focuses on Tunisia's second parliament from 2015 to 2019, it is worth discussing the past few years of the country's politics as it directly connects to the same issues explored in this chapter. The 2019 elections at first signaled little change as Nahda reclaimed its plurality as the largest and best-organized political faction while Nidaa Tounes split into multiple factions competing for the support of the secular coastal cities. However, the presidential election witnessed something new as a law professor without strong political backing, Kais Saied, defeated the notoriously corrupt businessman Nabil Karaoui in a run-off election. Saied's ability to win the run-off depended in no small part on Karaoui's reputation, including a legal investigation into his movement of funds to illegal offshore accounts that led to Karaoui's imprisonment for part of the campaign season.[12] While the law professor's bizarre intellectual policy statements earned him a backing among some marginalized groups due to his outsider status, his election was primarily due to being less evil than the other candidate.

While initially it would seem that a law professor who specialized in constitutions would respect the rule of law, in July 2021 Saied staged a coup by suspending the parliament with an executive decree.[13] His antidemocratic action took place in the throes of the COVID-19 pandemic as Tunisians complained of a slow vaccine rollout, a problem Saied addressed immediately after shutting down the parliament.[14] The ensuing year witnessed ever increasing autocratic actions by Saied, including replacing members of Tunisia's independent elections authority[15] and the supreme judicial body.[16] As of the time of this writing, Tunisians will vote on a new constitution in late July 2022 which could affirm Saied's coup and grant him exceptional powers amounting to a new dictatorship.

In many ways, the corruption of democratic institutions by crony capitalists facilitated this outcome by blocking economic reforms that could have provided jobs and growth, as I have previously discussed. However, while the political equilibrium remained unstable and vulnerable to a potential strongman like Saied, the authoritarian president unfortunately faces the same conundrums that his pro-authoritarian predecessors did. Following his coup,

---

[12] For more information, see www.reuters.com/article/us-tunisia-election-karoui-explainer-idUSKBN1WO1WY.

[13] See www.france24.com/en/live-news/20210725-tunisian-president-saied-sacks-prime-minister-mechichi-suspends-parliament.

[14] See www.theguardian.com/world/2021/jul/28/what-is-going-on-in-tunisia-all-you-need-to-know.

[15] See www.usnews.com/news/world/articles/2022-04-26/u-s-state-dept-says-its-deeply-concerned-by-tunisias-move-to-restructure-the-election-authority.

[16] See www.reuters.com/world/africa/tunisian-president-dissolves-supreme-judicial-council-2022-02-06/.

3.7 Conclusion: Tunisia's Democracy Remains under Threat

Saied drew supporters from the secularist camp who appreciated his anti-Nahda bent.[17] Yet his inability to push through economic reforms to contain inflation and obtain needed foreign currency for food subsidies have undercut his support as of the spring of 2022.[18] Opposition figures have shown an increasing willingness to advance their own initiatives, including a national unity coalition bringing secularists and Islamists together for the first time since 2015.[19] Facing budget shortfalls, the Tunisian state has failed to keep bread on the shelves and salaries in government employees' pockets, threatening the country with mass unrest.[20] If Saied is unable to obtain additional funding from the IMF or a regional backer like the Gulf states, the government could lose its ability to fund basic social services like electricity and gas.

While there are many specific reasons why Saied is facing declining popularity and an uncertain future, at bottom his vulnerability comes from his lack of a strong political coalition. Again, comparison with Egypt's new dictatorship is instructive. Despite Egypt's economic woes, which easily match or exceed those of Tunisia's, the Fatah al-Sisi regime remains firmly in power as of 2022. Saied's popular appeal is unlikely to help him take on the extraordinary task of subduing the state bureaucracy and implementing major reforms to save the state's finances and win the approval of an IMF deal, a feat that the al-Sisi regime accomplished in 2016. To survive, Saied needs a cash infusion, but funders prefer to back strong leaders, and Saied has yet to show that he has any kind of monopoly on the political system despite his ambitions. Al-Sisi, by contrast, imprisoned thousands of Muslim Brotherhood and other political party members after his coup, effectively shutting down opposition to his rule through brute force.

Speculating about the future is always a risky endeavor, but it does seem safe to say that the underlying behaviors among political elites, including broad rent-seeking by Tunisian companies, do not offer an easy path for Saied to consolidate his political support. Democracy may return to the country solely because the elites are unwilling to come together and support a single person as the new dictator. The costs of toleration, in other words, are lower than the costs of building a new dictatorship that would grant someone the authority to use Tunisian institutions to reward friends and punish enemies. Businesspeople are far from being the only influential political faction in the country, but their deep pockets and control over employees would grant them considerable ability to support Saied's proposed dictatorship – but only if it was in their interest to do so.

---

[17] See www.theguardian.com/world/2021/oct/03/tunisia-police-arrest-mp-and-tv-host-who-called-president-kais-saied-a-traitor.

[18] See foreignpolicy.com/2022/01/04/tunisia-kais-saied-politics-protest-corruption/.

[19] See www.france24.com/en/live-news/20220515-2-000-attend-new-tunisia-opposition-alliance-demo.

[20] See www.mei.edu/publications/tunisias-food-shortages-shine-spotlight-its-core-economic-failings.

4

Experiments on Businesses and Political Connections

Up to this point, I have substantiated the main claims in this book with reference to the historical experience of two recent cases of regime transition, Egypt and Tunisia. In Chapters 5 and 6, I present a different kind of evidence through the use of online survey research. The aim in these chapters is to show how institutional changes following regime transitions affected business political engagement using a quantitative assessment of survey responses. The data I analyze in this chapter represent a new source of information about business political engagement in these countries, a topic about which relatively little is known on a quantitative level. Neither Egypt nor Tunisia collect data on the sources of finance in politics or lobbying activities, which makes it difficult to assess the level of business political engagement and especially to make comparisons across types of companies and over time.

To review, the main argument of this book is that I can explain business political engagement following democratic transitions as either driven by a company's particular needs (broad rent-seeking) or in terms of political coalitions (narrow rent-seeking). The differentiating factor is the control over rent disbursement networks. Maintaining control over rents following a transition is difficult for states with weak institutions due to competition between politicians, businesspeople, and rogue bureaucrats. These states tend to suffer from severe principal–agent problems in which bureaucrats are relatively unconstrained by legislation and regulation and may only be accountable through informal relationships. As these networks shift due to political changes and transitions, business political strategies likewise shift, but political action remains disbursed across the system. In the case when an institutional actor can gain control over rent networks, businesses may be forced for a period of time into narrow rent-seeking in which they must obtain the favor of the institutional gatekeeper. In this rarer case, businesses can be pulled much more closely into supporting a particular political coalition.

4 *Experiments on Businesses and Political Connections*

I employed primarily qualitative evidence in Chapters 2 and 3 to substantiate this argument. I showed how Tunisian and Egyptian businesspeople responded to political transitions with instrumental political logic that had serious ramifications for the health and survival of democracy in both countries. This chapter seeks to both build on and unify the research in Chapters 2 and 3 by combining the power of quantitative inference with specific, localized data on companies in the Middle East and, in Chapter 5, other regions.

In addition, this chapter will do what the previous chapters could not: attempt to manipulate the political preferences of businesspeople. Manipulation is an important element of causal inference that has been missing in this book up until now. While it is important to show how theories can explain observed data, and to see whether proposed mechanism are at work in influential cases, an even more important test is to whether the manipulation of firm-level factors can lead to changes in business political engagement. Of course, it is impossible to manipulate directly the institutional variables that are important to this study, such as the military's control over rent and resources in Egypt. Instead, I employ hypothetical experiments that permit me to vary the information I provide to companies. While the hypothetical nature of the experiments reduces their realism (i.e., external validity), the ability to control which companies receive which information provides an important test for the theory: Are companies more or less responsive to political opportunities as the theory might predict? This increase in validity due to having control over the causal factor is counterbalanced by the artificial nature of the experiment, and as such the results presented need to be interpreted in light of the historical and contextual information presented in the previous chapters.

It is important to note as well that experimental evidence in the study of crony capitalism and political connections of firms is quite slim. An important exception is Bhandari (2021), who implemented a field experiment by manipulating the political connections of door-to-door salespeople. Other studies are in the vein of what are known as quasi-experiments or natural experiments because the authors were able to determine when an intervention on business political connections took place and measure outcomes before and after the intervention. From this type of research, we have gained important findings, such as the pronounced ramifications of political transitions on firm earnings (Earle and Gehlbach 2015) and the way that elected office can assist businesses in obtaining rents from states (Szakonyi 2018). This chapter employs a different kind of experimental technique that brings with it new advantage, and, of course, limitations. As such, the results presented in Chapters 4 and 5 are best understood as an extension of the research already presented about how these processes affected political outcomes over time. When facing a difficult research problem, the best answers often come by employing diverse modes of inference (Kubinec 2022).

The data in this chapter come from online survey research in Tunisia, Egypt, while in Chapter 5, I examine similar data from Algeria, Jordan, Morocco,

Venezuela, and Ukraine. Some of the data that I analyze in this chapter, particularly from surveys performed in Tunisia and Egypt in 2017, was previously presented in article form in Kubinec (2019b). The methodology employed, which made use of social media to recruit respondents, is relatively novel for the field of business politics research. The great advantage of online survey research is in asking sensitive questions of the employees of companies without requiring them to disclose their identities; this enables me to probe crony capitalism in these countries in far greater scope than the case studies in Chapters 4 and 5. As such, this chapter both confirms the findings presented in the previous chapters and breaks new ground by exploring previously unobtainable data about how businesspeople in a diverse array of fields are influenced by rents and threats in their pursuit of political connections. I also collect data using the same techniques from Egyptian military personnel describing their role in economic enterprises in the country. Given the novelty of the data collection, I include a methodological appendix at the end of this chapter describing how I collected the data and validated it for the interested reader.

In Chapter 5, the inclusion of two non-Arab countries, Venezuela and Ukraine, along with three additional Arab countries, Jordan, Morocco, and Algeria, grants me an opportunity to apply the theory to countries beyond those from which it was developed. This step in testing theories is crucially important as it examines the applicability and generalizability of my ideas for business political participation across a subset of developing countries. Inevitably, this type of analysis raises new issues that the original theory cannot explain, but if the theory is externally valid, it should be able to provide empirical findings outside of its original domain.

The intent of this chapter is to empirically demonstrate what I have argued for in other parts of this book with more detailed, individual-level data on company employees and managers. In particular, I will show that Egyptian employees and managers compared to Tunisian employees and managers show an unusual attentiveness to the military as an institution, and that this attentiveness cannot be easily explained by variables which would predict the standard kind of back-door political engagement common in crony capitalism. Rather, crony capitalism in Egypt shows clear indications of narrow rent-seeking as a dominant strategy for companies. However, this trend appears to be decreasing over time, a possible sign that the military's hegemony in Egypt has weakened in the past few years.

To demonstrate this empirically, I will use online survey data to provide observational and experimental evidence. Observationally, Egyptian companies stand out for their strong linkages to military-owned companies compared to their Tunisian counterparts. As a result, prior to the Arab Spring, Egyptian businesspeople differed on this dimension before any institutional changes occurred. Egyptian companies also tend to have high involvement in relatively costly forms of political action, particularly vote coercion, that is, ordering their employees to vote for a particular candidate. In addition, it would appear

4.1 A New Way to Obtain Data on Business Political Engagement

that Egyptian companies would be much more involved in politics if they had more opportunities to be involved, while in Tunisia the demand for political engagement was much closer to the level of supply of opportunities for engagement.

Given the limitations of observational data, I analyze a conjoint survey experiment in which corporate employees were given hypothetical scenarios about their company being approached by parties for electoral support. This experiment allows me to estimate a wide variety of counterfactual scenarios in which any company could be exposed to the same level of political opportunity. I show with the experimental data that Egyptian companies are much more responsive to appeals for support that would bring them into the good graces of the military, an effect that is high both within the Egyptian sample and in cross-national comparison. This effect appears to be driven by the military's network in Egypt. Companies that lacked exposure to the military-linked network found themselves without allies and had to engage in politics to protect their access to valuable rents.

This chapter is divided into three parts. In the first, I present the experiment and the data collection strategy, which offers a helpful and original overview of political connections and activities of companies across these countries. In the second section, I use questions from the survey about businesses' historical experiences to discuss the nature of crony capitalism and the profound ramifications of the Arab Spring on companies. In the third section, I analyze the experiment on business political participation that was present in the online survey in each of the countries. In the final section, I provide a concise explanation of these findings and relate them to what was previously discussed in this book.

4.1 A NEW WAY TO OBTAIN DATA ON BUSINESS POLITICAL ENGAGEMENT

Before presenting results, I discuss in brief the unconventional methods used to collect the information analyzed, and I refer the reader for a more technical discussion in the appendix to this chapter. The nature of what I am studying in this book – political action by businesspeople in countries with high levels of corruption – necessitates a different approach than is often taken to studying businesses. Two main methods have been used to find data describing how businesses influence state institutions. The first and most common is to collect data that is reported to government institutions by companies, such as lobbying data in developed democracies or board membership from publicly traded firms (Faccio 2010; Kim and Kunisky 2017). These data sources have the advantage of being a sufficient indicator of political activity; if a company has given money to lobbyists or has recruited a politician to serve on its board, it is very likely that the company can be considered to be politically connected or at least politically influential. However, this form of analysis suffers from a high false negative rate: many companies exist that may not report this information, either because of a lack of lobbying/campaign finance disclosure laws in the country where they operate or because they are privately held and do not need to report board ownership.

These problems are compounded in developing countries where political finance regulations are nonexistent or poorly enforced (Hummel, Gerring, and Burt 2021). Furthermore, capital markets are under-developed, so relatively few companies need to disclose their board membership in order to maintain a stock market listing. In addition, political connections may involve relationships that are not as easy to quantify as an official position because they are based on unobservable transactions like bribes or other forms of quid pro quo. For all these reasons, existing research on political connections and companies tends to be limited by the availability of data documenting linkages between states and firms, which is something that crony capitalists have reason to obscure.

For example, Tunisia has campaign finance regulations which were supposed to both constrain the total level of financing available to political parties and entirely ban corporate political contributions. According to my interviews in 2016, the first objective was never met in the first two elections following the transition because of low capacity among the government agencies responsible for documenting and prosecuting campaign finance violations. The businesspeople easily circumvented the second restriction by giving in their "personal" capacity rather than via their company's bank accounts, as several businesspeople confirmed to in interviews. On the whole, the campaign finance laws produced almost no available data about the level or source of campaign expenditures. Officially, parties abided by campaign spending limits and refused donations from companies and foreign entities. In practice, both occurred quite often, but no data exist to document these transactions.

The second way to collect data on companies and political participation is traditional firm survey research. The best resource for this type of data in the developing world are the World Bank Enterprise surveys. Much can be learned from this data source, though it is very expensive to collect, and for that reason has generally been restricted to large research and financial institutions like the World Bank. Furthermore, the quasi-public nature of multilateral development banks means that they are hesitant to probe political connections too directly. As a result, analyses of this data has to use proxies of political connections instead of more direct questions. Furthermore, any information about partisanship and types of political activity (instructing employees to vote or donations to candidates and parties) is missing from large-scale firm surveys.

Given these limitations of existing data on business political engagement, I invested starting in 2017 in employing nascent online survey techniques targeted at companies. Online survey research has moved from a curiosity to a mainstay of sampling techniques (Boas, Christenson, and Glick 2020), particularly as some kinds of older sampling methods such as phone sampling have

4.1 *A New Way to Obtain Data on Business Political Engagement* 113

become much more difficult to impossible to implement. All of the data collected in these surveys was done through Facebook, widely considered to be the most popular social media network in the world and especially so in the Middle East (Radcliffe and Abuhmaid 2020). In fact, in the United States, the medium has become the dominant way for businesses to target each other for business-to-business marketing.[1]

Facebook has several advantages when it comes to collecting data on business managers and employees. First, the collection of information from social media profiles means that ads can be targeted at people who list some type of employment, and can even be further targeted to different kinds of industries. Managers can also be targeted separately from employees. Second, utilizing Facebook means that research can be done in authoritarian countries where social science research of any kind is difficult, such as in Venezuela and Egypt. Third, the medium has a relatively low cost (at most a few dollars per survey completion), particularly given that advertising markets in developing countries tend to be less saturated than those in more developed countries. Fourth, online sampling techniques can be combined with the provision of individualized incentives in the form of mobile credits that can encourage a more diverse group to complete the survey. Fifth, online sampling allows for more sophisticated kinds of experimental techniques, such as the conjoint design presented in this chapter.

At the same time, it is important to note that theoretically, Facebook only represents a "convenience" or opt-in sample due to the fact that respondents are not randomly selected from a population. Facebook's ad algorithms are not released to the public, and are generally designed to increase conversions or purchases for ad-buying companies. There is no guarantee that Facebook will show a set of ads to all members of a certain demographic equally, or that the members of this demographic are themselves a random or representative sample of the true population.

Despite these limitations, however, empirical evaluations of Facebook as a tool to recruit representative samples have shown very good results even when compared to traditional sampling strategies (Boas, Christenson, and Glick 2020; Zhang et al. 2020). Furthermore, while discrepancies exist between Facebook samples and the population of interest, these either do not matter very much when the aim is to capture a treatment effect or coefficient from a regression model (Coppock 2019), or they can be overcome by using statistical adjustment techniques like multiple regression and post-stratification (Wang et al. 2014). In this chapter, I do not employ further post-stratification as the aim is to provide explanatory inferences which can be adjusted by using control variables, and due to the fact that the population of companies is rarely

---

[1] According to a 2019 survey of 4,800 marketing executives by the research firm Social Media Examiner, Facebook has surpassed LinkedIn as the most important channel for B2B marketing. See www.socialmediaexaminer.com/.

4 Experiments on Businesses and Political Connections

TABLE 4.1 *List of online surveys*

Country	Date	N	% Managers
Algeria	2017	3552	32.2
Egypt I	2017	4008	51.1
Tunisia	2017	2424	48.0
Egypt Military	2018	5121	NA
Jordan	2018	917	44.5
Morocco	2018	704	34.7
Tunisia Military	2018	1311	NA
Egypt II	2020	1541	48.8
Ukraine	2020	2187	45.4
Venezuela	2020	1519	37.1

as precisely defined as the population of individuals via census data. Statistical adjustment is likely to do more harm than good if the data available to adjust inferences is less than certain.

The data presented in Chapters 5 and 6 represent the culmination of three years of survey research. The full list of surveys is shown in Table 4.1. As can be seen, there are samples of substantial size across a dozen countries, and managers generally represent between 30 and 60 percent of the sample. None of the analyses conducted in this section require respondents to be managers; however, it is helpful to point out that the sample far overweights managers relative to the general population, as would be expected from a targeted survey technique. To make analyses comparable, I re-weight descriptive statistics by sector using Egypt's distribution as the baseline. This re-weighting helps ensure that the surveys are comparable to each other, that is, there are approximately as many manufacturing or service-oriented firms when calculating relevant statistics. For statistical models, I include firm sector as a control to similarly account for differences across samples.

To evaluate the business surveys, I show the distribution of company sectors and number of employees in Figures 4.1 and 4.2. The distribution of company sectors is remarkably uniform across countries, and the distribution of company sizes shows more variability, though still is fairly similar. Larger countries, particularly Egypt, have larger companies on average, as can be expected given the size of economies. The similarity in the distribution of sectors is a reflection of the fact that these countries are at a similar level of economic development that are dominated by services. While there are certainly differences between countries, the apparently random nature of these distributions suggests that the sampling method was able to recruit broadly representative samples from all of the countries. If the sampling method had serious biases, we would observe pronounced imbalances in distributions, suggesting that only one type of company or firm was responding to the survey. However, that is clearly not the case.

4.1 *A New Way to Obtain Data on Business Political Engagement* 115

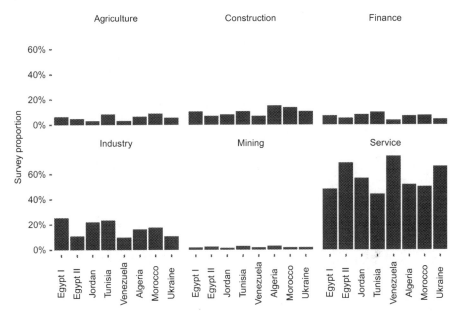

FIGURE 4.1 Proportion of respondents by firm sector and by country

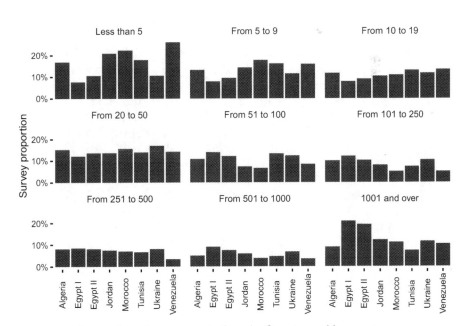

FIGURE 4.2 Proportion of survey respondents by firm size and by country

While most of the surveys in Table 4.1 were targeted at businesspeople, there are two exceptions, which are labeled as Military surveys. These two samples were taken to examine more closely links between businesspeople and the Egyptian and Tunisian militaries, and as such they explicitly targeted members of the militaries using Facebook ads. The data on companies is relatively limited by comparison, and these surveys did not contain the experiment defined in the previous section. These surveys targeted both businesspeople and military personnel, obtaining a fairly large sample to gain a more nuanced understanding of connections between the two groups. This survey, though it cannot be validated against population data about the military (which of course is not publicly available), pushes online sampling further to obtain difficult-to-find information about the military-clientelist complex. Obtaining data directly from members of the military provides a crucial method of verifying the scope and activity of military enterprises especially given that the data were collected anonymously.

Finally, it is important to emphasize one considerable improvement of online surveys over traditional surveys: anonymity. Conventional survey techniques cannot offer anonymity to respondents because the companies need to be identified ahead of time for sampling purposes. As such, the company has to trust that the survey firm will handle its data with care. When it comes to issues of corruption and political connections, as mentioned previously, there appears to be little reason for companies to trust third parties with this type of information. For these reasons, all of these surveys were implemented anonymously. While I am able to use the provision of mobile phone credit to identify individual respondents via mobile numbers, I do not know nor do I collect information about their companies names or other identifying information. While obtaining the identities of respondents and companies would of course be interesting information, the risks of biasing the survey results were too great.

The results of this anonymity can be seen by examining a question, the percentage of annual sales paid in bribes, that was included in some surveys and is identical to one employed by the World Bank in its Enterprise Surveys. Table 4.2 compares the rate of missing data for this survey question in the World Bank's surveys and in my online samples. As can be seen, missing data rates for this question are one-half to five times as low as missing data rates in the World Bank's survey data. These low missing data rates, which hold for other questions used in analysis in this section, suggest that anonymizing the questionnaire did result in lower missing data rates and consequently higher validity of the data. Ultimately, there is no perfect way to learn about company political connections in high-corruption countries, but online anonymous surveys are a powerful tool that can evade some of the long-standing barriers to data collection.

One final limitation in this data collection method is the need to make inferences at the level of company even though the data is collected from individual respondents. This sampling frame is different from conventional firm surveys

4.1 *A New Way to Obtain Data on Business Political Engagement* 117

TABLE 4.2 *Percentage of total annual sales as informal payment across survey types*

Country	Average % total sales	% Missing	Year	Sample
Algeria	2.64	7.54	2017	Online
Egypt	2.45	6.50	2017	Online
Tunisia	3.14	6.75	2017	Online
Algeria	7.97	54.00	2007	World Bank
Egypt	0.56	13.50	2013	World Bank
Egypt	1.45	12.40	2016	World Bank
Tunisia	0.28	30.07	2013	World Bank

Note: Ordinal scale converted to numeric scores by assigning midpoint of the ordinal category as a numeric value. For those who chose the top category, a value of 50 percent was assigned.

which usually have a sampling frame composed of businesses, and select these businesses (at least in theory) at random. By contrast, in this method, I first select individuals, and then learn about these individuals' companies. This distinction is not very important, however, for the use to which I put the data in this book. In any firm survey, there is always an actual person whose job it is to fill out the questionnaire (i.e., companies as such do not fill out surveys). There are always limitations between what the person filling out the questionnaire knows versus what the firm is in fact doing, but as I do not ask highly technical questions about the respondent's company, there is reason to believe that any employee with a general knowledge of his or her company would be able to answer.

The reason this sample is still useful is because of the type of inference that I am engaged in: learning about a company's political activities. In particular, I want to learn about companies where political connections are very important to their bottom line. As will be seen, I do not try to learn the actual amounts that companies provide to politicians as part of political action, but more about observable indicators such as the company holding rallies on behalf of candidates or instructing employees to vote for certain parties. While it is necessary to work at a company to obtain this information, it is not necessary or even preferable to be senior management, which may be uneasy providing this kind of information on a survey, anonymous or otherwise. If a company has powerful political patrons, it is quite likely that employees are going to have at least an inkling about the relationship due to the influence the patron will have on the company and vice versa. Quid pro quo arrangements usually have some kind of observable for each side, such as providing the patron a lucrative board member seat or some other business perk. If the company's livelihood does in fact depend on these relationships, it is likely that employees will have some idea that they are occurring. As I show later, employees are just as likely – and sometimes more likely – as their managers to know of and report political activity at their companies, possibly because they are less concerned about any reputational costs to their company.

4.2 EXPERIMENT ON BUSINESS POLITICAL ENGAGEMENT

In addition to a wide variety of questions about corporate performance and political connections, these surveys contained an embedded experiment. The aim of the experiment is to come up with a realistic scenario to test in what fashion businesses might respond to a new opportunity to participate in politics. To do so, I designed an experiment that focuses on transactions between companies and political parties in a hypothetical election. The idea for this experiment is a direct descendant of Figure 1.3 that specifies the causal process for politically connected companies following a regime transition. The experiment should permit me to vary the type of political engagement offered to companies and then see if companies are more or less likely to engage in broad vs. narrow rent-seeking.

Employing a hypothetical election is useful because it is well known that elections act as rent distribution mechanisms in authoritarian states (Magaloni and Kricheli 2010; Blaydes 2011; Boubekeur 2013), and of course are quite important for businesses in democratic regimes. In terms of my rent-seeking framework, political parties represent brokers that can facilitate exchanges of rents between bureaucrats and firms (Larreguy, Marshall, and Querubin 2016). The transaction happens in the time preceding an election when political parties are known to reach out to companies to ask for assistance. The use of elections is also helpful as it allows for a wide potential variety of rents to be exchanged in these transactions.

The manipulation in the experiment involves the type of offer that a party makes to a given company in exchange for the company's support in the election. By randomizing the offer that a party makes to the firm, I can see what kind of offers a company is more likely or less likely to respond to. The key advantage of the experiment design – despite its hypothetical nature – is that it equalizes political opportunities across companies. All observational methods suffer from the same bias in that the companies that choose to participate in politics are almost certainly different than companies that do not choose to participate politics. In other words, political opportunities are not random, and it is quite likely that crony capitalist companies also receive more opportunities for political action than companies that are less cronyist. This type of bias is difficult to address with statistical methods as we lack a clear understanding of why a particular firm may have decided to become more political relative to a different firm (especially without detailed over-time information).

Of course, I make an assumption that the party in question would be able to deliver on the offer of rent, which is always a difficult aspect of any transaction involving the exchange of services which are not entirely legal, or at least legally enforceable. However, the use of random assignment ensures that

4.2 Experiment on Business Political Engagement

all participants have an equal chance of receiving a credible offer. This limitation of real-world politics will not prevent me from learning about narrow and broad rent-seeking because I can still see which companies are at least hypothetically interested in the party's offer to the company even if the transaction might face obstacles in terms of execution.

To implement this experiment, I employed a form of what is known as a conjoint design. In a standard conjoint experiment, respondents often choose between two alternatives which have randomized attributes, such as picking between two political candidates in a hypothetical election. I modified this design so that the alternatives are instead requests for electoral support from two different political parties to the survey respondent's company. The respondent gives their opinion as to what kind of offer their CEO is more or less likely to respond to. The pairing of requests encourages respondents to think hard about the difference between the two offers, reducing survey satisficing (Hainmueller, Hangartner, and Yamamoto 2015). Because the types of offers made to a given company are randomized, the offers do not depend on a company's prior political connections, industry, or sectarian and ideological proclivity.

Each survey respondent sees the following vignette.

A member of a political party calls your CEO's office. The representative says that the party is in need of funding for their upcoming electoral campaign for the parliament. How likely do you think it is that your CEO would provide funding to each of these parties because of this appeal?

The party will ensure that INSTITUTION1 OFFER1.

The party will ensure that INSTITUTION2 OFFER2.

The INSTITUTION and OFFER texts represent different attributes of the messages that were independently randomized. Each of the possible treatments are shown in Table 4.3. The institutions are those government agencies that could provide crucial rents to the firm whether at the national or local levels. The various rents a firm might desire are represented by the different offers. By independently randomizing these parts of the party's message to the firm, I can estimate a broad range of hypotheticals in which a company receives offers that will be more or less relevant to the company's industry and allow me to test whether the company is interested in "broad" rent-seeking, or only those institutions/rents most relevant to its industry, or in "narrow" rent-seeking, in which companies must obtain relationships with a certain institution that acts as a gatekeeper.

The complication of a conjoint experiment is that it does not have a straightforward control group. Rather, the treatment effects for one attribute group are calculated relative to one of the attributes in that group. As a result, I need to select an attribute for both institutions and offers to use as baselines. For the institution treatment, I include a generic "government" actor that is used as a baseline because it does not signal any specific political institution. As a

TABLE 4.3 *Treatment profiles for conjoint survey experiment*

Number	Types of institutions	Types of offers
1	Military	Does not try to take control of your firm
2	Ministry of Interior	Does not try to take your firm's profits
3	President	Helps your company secure permits from regulators to do business
4	Ministry of Justice	Helps your company secure contracts to supply goods
5	Parliament	Helps your company export its goods & services
6	Municipality	Helps your company import necessary materials
7	Government	Will implement reforms that encourage economic growth and lower unemployment.

Note: Reproduced from survey preregistration.

consequence, the baseline here can be thought of as the default for companies of broad rent-seeking. For companies that simply want to obtain specific rents, it is relatively unimportant who provides those rents, and so providing those rents from "the government" as opposed to a different or more specific institution is a distinction without a difference. For companies who have to reach an arrangement with a gatekeeping institution, relationships with political actors without access to the gatekeeper will be much less valuable *regardless of the type of rent offered to the company.*

The baseline for the types of rents offered to companies, by comparison, is a macroeconomic reform message that would not provide any rents to the firm. Companies more responsive to this treatment would presumably be companies with little interest in obtaining rents as opposed to larger policy concessions. The utility of this baseline is that it provides an option for companies that are not rent-dependent and would rather opt for wholesale reform to promote transparency. It is important to note that even in countries where crony capitalism is a problem, many businesspeople still have little exposure to these types of rents and would rather live in a more transparent, less cronyist economy.

It is important to note that changing the baseline attribute only shifts the treatments by a constant (the baseline treatment effect), and as such does not define the strength of the treatments per se. But it is also important to keep in mind that the null hypothesis is defined by the baseline. In other words, an effect of 0 represents a treatment attribute that is statistically indistinguishable from the macroeconomic reform offer to a firm.

After the offer, each respondent is to answer three questions about their boss' reaction to each offer on a scale of 1 to 10:

How likely do you think it is that your CEO would instruct employees in your firm to vote for this party because of this appeal?

How likely do you think it is that your CEO would use your company's resources to hold rallies or distribute advertisements for this party because of their appeal?

4.3 *Observational Results on Business Political Engagement* 121

How likely do you think it is that your CEO would provide funding to each of these parties because of this appeal?

I use these 1 (least likely) to 10 (most likely) outcomes to evaluate my theoretical predictions. To test whether broad and narrow rent-seeking by firms varies across countries, I estimate an OLS model on each 1–10 outcome with country dummies as regressors along with the full range of treatments.[2]

What is particularly important about this design is that the effect of institutions is separate from the effect of the rents a company might obtain from those institutions. This separation will allow me to determine if an institution has a separate effect apart from rents, or whether the importance of a certain institution to a business is limited to particular rents the business requires. This diversity helps make the design more robust as a variety of rents will be offered to companies, ensuring that a broad array of possible rent-seeking relationships will be tested within the same framework. If my theory holds, Egyptian companies should be drawn to the military as an actor over other actors as a provider of rents, while in Tunisia I should not observe concentration around a specific political actor.

To summarize the experimental framework, I am using a hypothetical exchange between a company and a firm in which the types of rents and the types of actors providing rents are both manipulated. Based on my theory, I would expect that companies in political contexts requiring narrow rent-seeking will prefer specific institutions that act as gatekeepers while companies in more ordinary political environments will default to broad rent-seeking in which no particular institution is a priori preferred. Furthermore, my theory does not make any prediction about what type of rents will be preferred by companies in the aggregate. Instead, my theory infers that the gatekeeper institution should be preferred by companies in the aggregate with narrow rent-seeking, while no such institution will emerge if broad rent-seeking is the norm. If corporate political strategies are spread across the political spectrum, then when averages are taken, no single actor will emerge as dominant.

4.3 OBSERVATIONAL RESULTS ON BUSINESS POLITICAL ENGAGEMENT

Before turning to the results of the experiment, I examine data in the survey on the historical experiences of businesspeople in Egypt and Tunisia. This data can also help test the theories emphasized in this book concerning how, when and why businesses engage in politics. First, I look at general trends in the data. Figure 4.3 shows average values by country for responses to four questions about an employee's companies' political participation in the last electoral cycle: (1) did the company contribute funds to a campaign?, (2) did

---

[2] All of the conjoint estimations were done using the cjoint package in R (Hainmueller, Hopkins, and Yamamoto 2014).

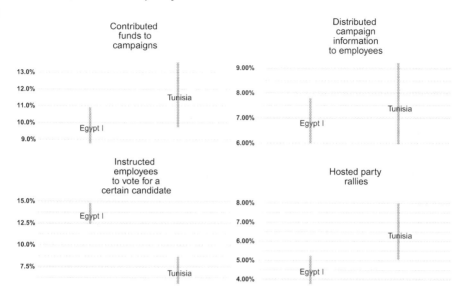

FIGURE 4.3 Reported firm political activity by country

the company distribute campaign information to employees?, (3) did the company instruct employees to vote for a particular candidate? and (4) did the company host party rallies? The responses in this figure are average values that take into account uncertainty in terms of missing data in responses and are re-weighted to match the relative proportions of managers and firm sizes in the Egypt I survey.[3]

Comparing Egypt and Tunisia shows that companies are broadly similar in terms of levels of reported political engagement with the notable exception of one category, employee vote coercion. In general, between 10 and 12 percent of companies in both countries provided some kind of monetary donation to political parties, while only half as many (approximately 5–7 percent) distributed campaign information or held a rally on behalf of a political party. In Egypt, by contrast, just as many companies ordered their employees to vote for a specific candidate as provided funds to candidates, while in Tunisia, only half as many companies took the step of ordering their employees to vote for a specific candidate. This difference is a revealing discrepancy as it suggests that Egyptian companies were more willing to take directly partisan actions involving pressuring their employees to vote for a specific candidate, while Tunisian companies were more hands-off with their employees even if their levels of political engagement were high in other areas.

---

[3] To be specific, the responses average over five multiple-imputed datasets.

4.3 Observational Results on Business Political Engagement

While it is important not to overinterpret a single descriptive finding, this difference does suggest that the type of political engagement undertaken by businesses is significantly different in Egypt in a way predicted by my theory. If narrow rent-seeking is more important in Egypt, then it is also important for companies to signal their partisan affiliation with the gatekeeper institution. As such, taking relatively heavy-handed measures like pressuring employees to vote for a certain candidate could signal that companies need to identify with the gatekeeper as opposed to other political actors. When such pressure is nonexistent, companies may find it more attractive to take the Tunisian path and provide funds to a variety of political parties while leaving their employees to vote their conscience. This latter strategy is clearly preferred from a human resources perspective as companies risk de-motivating or even losing employees if they make employment conditional on approved political behaviors.

I further explore this relationship in Figures 4.4 and 4.5. Figure 4.4 subsets the type of political activity a company could engage in by the answers to a question in the survey asking respondents whether "government officials' exploitation of regulations had increased since the Arab Spring." Figure 4.5 similarly subsets political activities by a question asked of respondents as to whether a company's payment in bribes to government officials increased since the Arab Spring. Both of these questions are ways of measuring one of the crucial variables discussed in this book, which is the loss of political connections

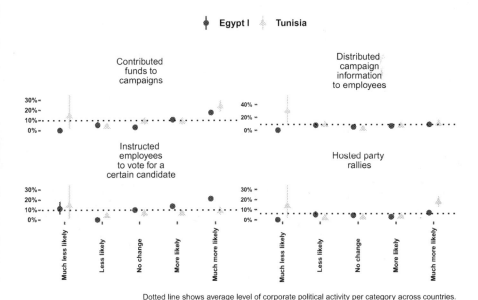

FIGURE 4.4 Political activities by answers to has government officials' exploitation of regulations increased since the Arab Spring?

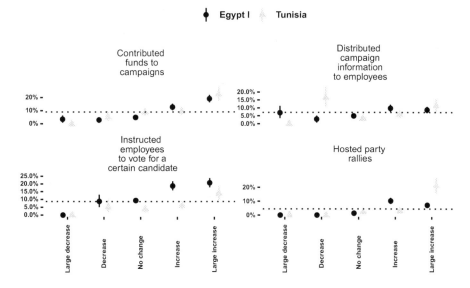

FIGURE 4.5 Reported political activities for companies who saw bribes increase post-Arab Spring

following a regime transition. I argue that it is the loss of these privileges which tends to motivate political action as companies must adjust to a new regime and a new set of rules.

These figures both show revealing patterns suggesting that a company's vulnerability to changing relationships with bureaucrats does indeed play a role in subsequent political activity. While the patterns are not without some noise, those who reported more exploitation of regulatory practices and bribes after the Arab Spring were more likely to report political activity above the dotted line in Figures 4.4 and 4.5, which represents the average value for that type of political activity. The pattern is more clearly evident in Egypt than in Tunisia for regulatory predation, while the trend is easy to see for both countries for increases in bribe payments. Those companies that lost some kind of access or favor with government officials are also those companies most likely to take costly steps to regain it.

Figure 4.6 shows a similar comparison but with a different question concerning the number of times a company was inspected in the previous year by regulators. The plot shows the average number of inspections subset by whether or not a company engaged in one of the four types of political activity. As can be seen, those companies which engaged in political activities were on the whole more likely to have above-average numbers of government

4.3 Observational Results on Business Political Engagement

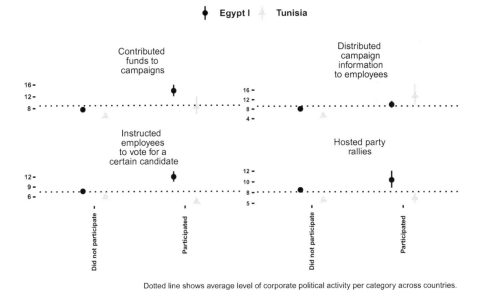

FIGURE 4.6 Number of inspections from regulators by whether company engaged in political activity

inspections in the previous year. Again, the pattern holds even more strongly in Egypt than in Tunisia. In Egypt, the average company which did not give funds to a party or order its employees to vote for a candidate was inspected only 7 to 8 times, while companies that did engage in these political behaviors were inspected around 12 to 14 times. This substantive difference suggests that changes in the vulnerability of companies to government provision of rents does indeed play a role in corporate political behavior following regime transitions.

The challenge, of course, in interpreting bivariate statistics is in knowing whether that relationship holds across different types of companies in the sample, such as large or small companies and different sectors. To test this association more robustly, I fit separate logistic regression model for three of the four types of political activities firms undertook: whether they gave funds to candidates, whether they ordered employees to vote for candidates, and whether they held rallies on behalf of candidates. I did not include the distribution of literature as an outcome because this type of action is relatively low-cost and may not be as relevant to the theory I am testing. I include a set of additional variables in the model that could plausibly explain political engagement, such as whether the respondent is a manager, whether bribe payments have increased in the last five years, firm profitability in the prior year, whether the firm belongs to a conglomerate, the percentage paid of firm income in bribes, firm sector and the number of inspections by government regulators.

126   4 *Experiments on Businesses and Political Connections*

I restrict the sample to domestic companies as introducing foreign-owned companies threatens to complicate the model's interpretation. I report the results of these models in Table 4.4. To compare the model results easily, each row in the table represents one of three reported types of political engagement.

TABLE 4.4 *Covariates predicting historical corporate political engagement*

Variable	Outcome	Egypt I	Tunisia
No. Times Inspected	Funds	0.001* (0.001, 0.002)	0 (−0.001, 0.002)
	Rallies	0 (−0.001, 0.001)	0 (0, 0.001)
	Votes	0.001* (0.001, 0.002)	0.001 (−0.001, 0.002)
Bribes Increase	Funds	0.034* (0.018, 0.053)	0.045* (0.014, 0.09)
	Rallies	0.046* (0.014, 0.101)	0.066* (0.033, 0.126)
	Votes	0.034* (0.019, 0.053)	0.044* (0.015, 0.086)
Conglomerate	Funds	0.023 (−0.015, 0.062)	−0.03 (−0.093, 0.029)
	Rallies	0.004 (−0.023, 0.031)	−0.015 (−0.06, 0.025)
	Votes	0.023 (−0.016, 0.061)	−0.03 (−0.094, 0.029)
Firm Performance	Funds	−0.001 (−0.003, 0)	0 (−0.001, 0.002)
	Rallies	0 (−0.001, 0.001)	0 (−0.002, 0.001)
	Votes	−0.001 (−0.003, 0)	0 (−0.002, 0.002)
No. Firm Employees	Funds	0.006 (−0.002, 0.015)	0.012* (0.002, 0.022)
	Rallies	0.005 (0, 0.01)	0.008* (0.001, 0.016)
	Votes	0.006 (−0.002, 0.014)	0.012* (0.002, 0.022)
Manager	Funds	0.034 (−0.003, 0.072)	−0.071* (−0.124, −0.019)
	Rallies	0.014 (−0.011, 0.041)	−0.045* (−0.082, −0.008)
	Votes	0.034 (−0.002, 0.072)	−0.071* (−0.122, −0.019)

4.3 Observational Results on Business Political Engagement 127

TABLE 4.4 *(continued)*

Variable	Outcome	Egypt I	Tunisia
Construction	Funds	0.113* (0.007, 0.247)	−0.164 (−0.392, 0.027)
	Rallies	3.935* (0.089, 15.568)	−0.106* (−0.219, −0.013)
	Votes	0.112* (0.002, 0.237)	−0.165 (−0.398, 0.021)
Finance	Funds	0.118 (0, 0.252)	0.124* (0.006, 0.251)
	Rallies	−2.115 (−17.664, 7.825)	−2.471* (−8.821, −0.184)
	Votes	0.118 (−0.002, 0.251)	0.123* (0.008, 0.244)
Manufacturing	Funds	0.122* (0.026, 0.245)	0.088 (−0.017, 0.206)
	Rallies	4.037* (0.195, 15.657)	−0.01 (−0.066, 0.048)
	Votes	0.121* (0.022, 0.246)	0.088 (−0.012, 0.197)
Mining	Funds	0.071 (−0.141, 0.263)	−0.037 (−0.277, 0.168)
	Rallies	4.032* (0.192, 15.621)	−0.08 (−0.215, 0.028)
	Votes	0.071 (−0.151, 0.269)	−0.035 (−0.252, 0.15)
Services	Funds	0.046 (−0.049, 0.169)	0.012 (−0.093, 0.131)
	Rallies	4.011* (0.171, 15.642)	−0.035 (−0.088, 0.023)
	Votes	0.046 (−0.056, 0.161)	0.011 (−0.092, 0.116)
Intercept	Funds	−0.441* (−0.583, −0.319)	−0.371* (−0.571, −0.221)
	Rallies	−4.326* (−15.957, −0.426)	−0.313* (−0.552, −0.169)
	Votes	−0.44* (−0.583, −0.314)	−0.367* (−0.552, −0.23)
R^2	Funds	0.117* (0.066, 0.17)	0.12* (0.069, 0.179)
	Rallies	0.085* (0.038, 0.145)	0.204* (0.105, 0.304)
	Votes	0.117* (0.067, 0.17)	0.12* (0.068, 0.18)

(continued)

128   4 Experiments on Businesses and Political Connections

TABLE 4.4 *(continued)*

Variable	Outcome	Egypt I	Tunisia
	Funds	699.2	413.8
		(688, 706)	(403, 424)
N Obs	Rallies	699.2	413.6
		(688, 706)	(403, 424)
	Votes	699.2	413.8
		(688, 706)	(403, 424)

Note: Estimation of Bayesian logistic regression using Markov chain Monte Carlo with Stan to handle issues of perfect separation. 5%–95% quantile intervals in parentheses. The coefficients are sample average marginal effects expressed as the increase in probability of the given outcome for a 1-unit change in the regressor. The number of observations has an uncertainty interval due to imputation uncertainty in the number of domestic firms. Estimates that are statistically significant are marked with an asterisk. (Because these are Bayesian regression models estimated via Markov Chain Monte Carlo, a coefficient is marked with an asterisk if the 5%–95% posterior interval did not include 0.)

The results of the model in Table 4.4, which is organized by the country in columns and variables and outcomes in the rows, show substantial heterogeneity between Egypt and Tunisia alongside very important similarities. As the coefficients are sample average marginal effects (Leeper 2021), I can interpret the coefficients as the increase in probability of the given type of political engagement.

One crucial pattern that emerges across both countries is that those companies who saw an *increase* in bribes since the Arab Spring have a much higher incidence of political activity across all three types of outcomes. This association parallels the bivariate and univariate patterns seen in the previous figures. Given that the question about increase in bribes had five possible Likert-scale answers (from very unlikely to very likely), the coefficients imply that moving from the bottom to the top of this scale would increase the probability of political engagement by approximately 15–30 percent. This relationship is strong in both countries, though even stronger in Tunisia. Importantly, compared to the previous figures, this relationship exists even when accounting for firm size, performance, and sector. In other words, the patterns holds when comparing companies of similar size, sector or recent performance.

This finding supports my contention that a major motivating factor of business political engagement post-transition comes from the rise in bribes faced by connected companies due to a loss of political influence. It is important to note that this association is quite strong despite controlling for firm sector, management, involvement in a conglomerate, firm performance, firm size, and vulnerability to regulatory predation. Even considering all of these other factors, an increase in bribe payments after the Arab Spring shows a strong relationship with increased business political engagement across three different types of political activity: directing employees to vote for a specific candidate,

4.3 *Observational Results on Business Political Engagement* 129

providing funds to political candidates, and holding rallies on behalf of candidates. Facing a loss of valuable relationships with bureaucrats and politicians, companies must increase their political activity to compensate, and this is true in both Egypt and Tunisia.

While this finding from the model is the most important for this book's theory, it is worth discussing some of the other relationships in Table 4.4. In Egypt, a company's number of inspections by tax officials is positively related to political activity, while this is not so in Tunisia. On the other hand, company size is strongly related to political activity in Tunisia, but not in Egypt. These differences again point to possible variations in the political context in both countries. Tunisia would seem to have company vulnerability defined more by payments for services from bureaucrats as opposed to direct predation by government officials, and political activity is a domain primarily of larger companies. In Egypt, by contrast, a worrisome association holds for government harassment and political activity with companies of all sizes equally willing to engage in politics.

There are also sector-based differences between the two countries. The baseline category for firm sector is agriculture, so in Egypt, construction, manufacturing and mining are all more politically active than agricultural companies and farmers. In Tunisia, by contrast, political activity among financial companies is much higher compared to others. Furthermore, Tunisian respondents who were managers were less likely to report political activity compared to employees, while in Egypt there was no relationship, suggesting that information about political activity in Egypt is not something that companies are as inhibited discussing.

In total, these models show that, as we might expect, there are important differences in the types of companies that engage in politics in Egypt and Tunisia. However, these differences are not as important for the theory put forward in this book as are the similarities. The most important similarity is the relationship involving companies that experienced an increase in bribe payments following the Arab Spring relative to companies that did not. Those companies that saw a subsequent increase in bribe payments, as predicted by my theory, show substantially higher levels of political engagement. While Egyptian and Tunisian companies do differ in important respects, both countries experienced transitions to democracy and companies that were most adversely affected by the loss of government relationships are also those that became the most politically active following the transition.

Of course, there remain limitations in this analysis. I cannot control for all factors that might cause a company to be involved in politics. Some companies may engage in politics regardless of any of the variables contained here, such as highly connected companies that were able to compensate for loss of patrons. Furthermore, some companies that did not engage in politics might have decided not to engage due to a lack of opportunity to do so rather than lack of a reason to do so. It is impossible to distinguish these comparisons using observational data alone, which is why I examine experimental evidence later in this chapter in which I have more control over the variables of interest.

However, first I will explore more observational evidence from these surveys about another crucial topic: the military as an economic gatekeeper in Egypt versus Tunisia.

4.4 DESCRIPTIVE EVIDENCE CONCERNING THE MILITARY-CLIENTELIST COMPLEX

These surveys also contain detailed information about the linkages between companies in these countries and the military-clientelist complex. This information is almost completely novel as neither country releases data about the economic activities of its military, and the Egyptian military is notorious for hiding and concealing even basic information about its holdings. Previous research on the military-clientelist complex has been limited to analyzing reported investments from news sources, which suggest that in Egypt the military's holdings have grown substantially since the 1980s (Sayigh 2019). In fact, military-affiliated enterprises have even formed joint ventures with foreign companies for domestic infrastructure projects (Marshall and Stacher 2012). While there is substantial reason based on the existing research that this complex is quite large, to date there has not been quantitative information available to understand how these economic activities vary by sector and types of companies in Egypt and Tunisia.

As a result, I collected information about linkages between military-affiliated and private companies by asking respondents to rank their dependence on six different potential suppliers and consumers of their products. In addition to military-affiliated companies, other options included domestic and foreign companies and markets, and individual producers and consumers. These rankings help establish the priority of the military-clientelist to a given firm without needing to collect detailed and likely unavailable data at the transaction level. As a result, these two questions provide useful aggregated information about the extent and scale of the military-clientelist complex across both countries without requiring respondents to disclose information about particular contracts or deals made.

Figure 4.7 shows the average ranks of the military as a supplier or customer to companies across Egypt and Tunisia. As can be seen, Egypt consistently has the highest penetration of military-affiliated economic activity across different sectors in the economy. For two sectors, agriculture and mining, Egyptian companies tend to rank the military as the third most important supplier and/or customer. While these ranks may seem relatively low, it is important to note that the other options included domestic companies, foreign companies, and individual purchasers. In other words, an increase in a single rank represents an

4.4 Descriptive Evidence Concerning the Military-Clientelist Complex

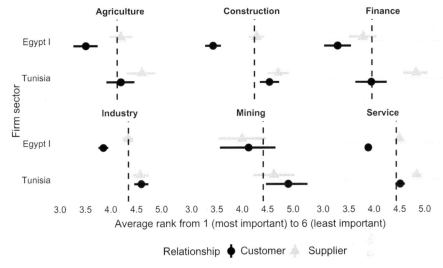

FIGURE 4.7 Ties between military-linked firms and companies in Egypt and Tunisia

enormous increase in economic influence. The dotted horizontal line in the figure shows the average per category, which is approximately between 4 and 5 for countries in the sample. What this figure shows is a quantification of macroeconomic impact of the military-clientelist complex in Egypt using data never previously available.

Another important relationship in Figure 4.7 is the fact that there are generally more companies in Egypt that report relying on the military as a consumer of their goods than on the military as a supplier of intermediate inputs. The relationship is most pronounced in agriculture, construction and industry, where a very large number of Egyptian companies report the military as their third-most valuable consumer of their products. As such, the economic effect of the military-clientelist complex is most strongly felt as a domestic purchaser of Egyptian products. This relationship is a crucial reason underpinning the military's economic influence in a country like Egypt in which economic growth and investment has long stagnated, leaving fewer alternatives for Egyptian companies to market their goods.

A different way of measuring military economic activity is by directly surveying Egyptian military personnel. I did so in a 2018 survey, also employing Facebook ads, which targeted both Egyptian businesspeople and the Egyptian military, ultimately recruiting a large and diverse sample of military personnel. While no particular claim is made for this sample's representativeness, the ability to ask the military direct questions about its economic operations proved

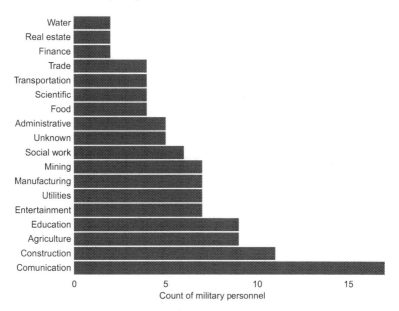

FIGURE 4.8 Count of Egyptian military personnel by sector

to be very informative. For all personnel who reported working for a military-affiliated company, I asked them which industry the company belonged to. The results are shown in Figure 4.8.

These results are not so different – agriculture is near the top – though communication is an unexpected category with a large number of personnel. This growing category appears to be a reflection of the military's diversification into media outlets. In 2017, the military set up a TV channel known as DMC TV Channels that was ostensibly private,[4] though it was clearly a part of its economic activities. Apparently, this new enterprise from the military attracted a fairly high number of its employees.

As Figure 4.9 shows, however, the total number of employees engaged in any kind of military commercial business is relatively low – only 14.2 percent reported spending any time working for a military-affiliated company. For military personnel who reported doing work for military-affiliated companies, the median percentage of their time in a given day devoted this type of work was

---

[4] See www.middleeastobserver.org/2017/03/09/egypt-new-private-tv-channel-funded-by-the-army-and-owned-by-generals/?__cf_chl_jschl_tk__=905c6b431e89d320aff53cd782e9f926f45712fa-1598793892-0-AUadPZ2HNl21PJDe47Gefdk32ieOrYvUU3ZhnUfmne_vJHYPBcLVr4N-rMnxKuyvWyDo2OfFLkX9tF2aITaTgraROhcSWGCCaLbKyFFkZhgYChELqo9mxhFKSaHJaNPQLK8FqtSSkFDOMMEgm9VVPSbIyld1pT7R2wfHT2iuFfltc1Vhr6Ubv1LDLZzFDo2jEonJ4JcDpDllTUGhmGqeX5j55Fi9o8TYy2QmI1doQ63CPYYJnnZpotDByB6W4OZdLby6ekjtYQAw6T53g_XbWRzePmmOHVh1moZQ_gyjI3jAumQMssjUhforog47EcXD5MetwjBxJof99nnTyfP67pi3sP3bSrJojDVVc4vDX1QawvpE8fpUG9Ey9xOdqO34OWw.

4.4 Descriptive Evidence Concerning the Military-Clientelist Complex 133

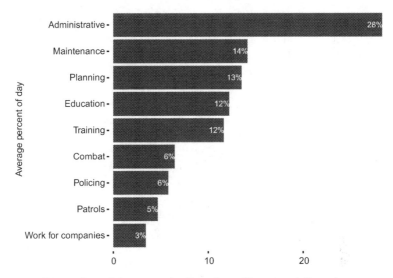

FIGURE 4.9 Proportion of time spent by Egyptian military on daily tasks

14 percent, with a standard deviation of 25 percent. In other words, while military business certainly is an important element of active-duty military work, it is by no means the dominant activity they are engaged in.

On the other hand, when we compare the proportion of time spent working for military-affiliated companies to other types of military activities in Figure 4.9, it is clear that the proportion of time spent working is not insignificant. Egyptian military personnel report spending a plurality of time doing administrative work while they spend only 6.5 percent of their time in active combat. In that context, Egyptian military personnel spend almost as much time working in military companies as they do in active combat. Indeed, some of their bureaucratic work may also be related to military-affiliated companies through state-owned enterprises or the quasi-corporate activities of the military-controlled National Service Projects Organization. As such, the reported amount of time in this survey is almost certainly a conservative estimate relative to the benefits that military-affiliated companies receive from the institution.

Given the size of these activities, it is also important to note what they are particularly important for. Based on this survey data, it is clear that military-affiliated companies are a way to offer employment to retiring officers; in essence, a form of coup-proofing. In the survey, 24.1 percent of military personnel reported a desire to work for military-affiliated companies upon retirement. For military officers (i.e., those with a rank of second lieutenant or higher), the percentage was even higher at 30.4 percent. As such, the military-clientelist complex also grants the military additional incentives they can use to maintain internal cohesion and reward loyalty (Sayigh 2019).

What is also clear from the data presented above is that while the military is concentrated in certain sectors whether expressed as manpower or macroeconomic impact, it is highly influential across virtually all sectors in Egypt. Figure 4.7 shows that the military is even dominant in the services sector relative to Tunisia, a sign of its ever-growing reach in the country. The diversity of the military's economic activities is why I term this institution the *military-clientelist complex*. These linkages extend far beyond the better-known military-industrial complex in which industries grow up around supplying the military's needs for equipment and material (Alptekin and Levine 2012). These economic activities have little to do with the military establishment's actual defense needs. In fact, in Egypt's case, much of their military hardware is exported from the United States under the very generous agreement stemming from the 1978 Camp David Accords. These economic activities are not only designed to enrich former and current officers in the military but also to extend the control of the military as an institution. It is this web of control which, I argue, pushed businesses toward involvement in the military-led political coalition starting with the coup that overthrew President Morsi in 2013. In other words, the military's growing economic clout pushed businesses away from broad rent-seeking and toward relatively difficult and expensive narrow rent-seeking in which they had to participate in a partisan coalition to ensure continued access to rents.

4.5 EXPERIMENTAL RESULTS

The observational results presented in the previous section show that Egyptian and Tunisian companies negatively affected by the Arab Spring are more likely to be politically active and that the military's economic linkages are far greater in Egypt relative to Tunisia. In addition, it would seem that Egyptian companies participate in some kinds of political activities, particularly employee vote coercion, at higher rates than their Tunisian counterparts.

However, it is difficult to tie together all the pieces of my argument from observational data alone. There is a well-known issue with data of reported activities where individuals are able to choose whether or not to participate, which is known as selection bias (Przeworski 2009b). In the case of politically connected companies, and those without such connections, decisions about whether to participate in politics have weighty consequences for the company and are rarely entered into lightly. For example, a correlation showing that companies that engage more in politics become more profitable could be confounded by companies only choosing to engage in politics because they first became more profitable.

The main concern with the observational analyses presented above has to do with the fact that not all companies are given equal opportunities to participate in politics. In other words, it is tempting to confuse demand and supply when studying business political engagement. Bureaucrats and party officials

4.5 Experimental Results
135

who are trying to secure support (or bribes) are more likely to contact those businesspeople who they expect to be amenable to their requests. As a consequence, the demand for political participation may be much higher than observed political activity because companies lack opportunities to participate. For this reason, univariate plots like Figure 4.3 need to be interpreted with caution. We cannot assume that the differences are solely due to company strategy as opposed to other factors like the availability of political opportunities to a given firm. Demand for political engagement could be high but supply of such opportunities could be low, and vice versa.

The experimental results in this section help ameliorate this problem by equalizing the political opportunities that companies experience. As described in the previous section, the results here show how companies reacted to randomly selected appeals from political parties. As a result, the respondents' companies' prior history of participation have nothing to do with which appeals for support they receive. This randomization allows me to better gauge what factors are driving company political participation because we can exclude prior history and access to politics as difficult-to-measure confounding factors.

As mentioned previously, there are three possible outcomes in this experiment: whether the respondent's boss gives a party funds in response to an appeal, orders employees to vote for a particular candidate in response to an appeal, or holds a rally in response to an appeal. Given the large number of treatments, in this section, I collapse the results across these three outcomes. To do so, I apply item response theory to produce a single measure from the three outcomes, which are coded on a 1 to 10 scale. Because the three outcomes are strongly correlated (approximately +0.5 to +0.7), collapsing them to a single scale improves the presentation of the results with minimal loss of nuance.

I first present the effects for the different treatments for Egypt and Tunisia, that is, for each possible type of rent offered to a company and each possible institution that could provide a rent. These results represent the average effects for the samples as a whole, and as such they necessarily obscure a lot of company-level differences. Figure 4.10 shows the results for all of the different types of offers that a party could make to a company. The results are measured on the scale shown to respondents asking them to rate how likely it would be for their company's CEO to respond positively to the offer, either by hosting a rally at the company's headquarters, ordering employees to vote for the party or offering funds to the party. This scale was standardized, so an effect of +1 would be equal to a one-standard deviation increase in the outcome.

What is immediately evident from Figure 4.10 is that offers that have to do with protecting the company from either government confiscation of income or the firm itself are less able to obtain the company's support compared to offers to help with government licenses or import and export permissions. The dotted line indicates the value for the control condition, which in this case is

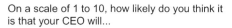
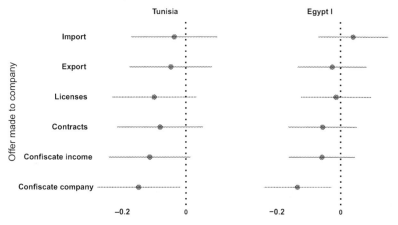

FIGURE 4.10 Estimates for rent treatments (appeal types) by dependent variable

the macroeconomic reform message. The fact that some estimates are approximately equal to the dotted line does not mean that they do not have any effect, but rather that they are about as equally effective as the control condition. In other words, the macroeconomic reform message is actually quite popular with companies, and only some of the other rents a party can offer are equally popular. Again, it is important to note that these findings average across all companies and across all countries, so it is quite possible given broad rent-seeking for certain companies to be very responsive to particular appeals while in the aggregate they are not as responsive.

However, it is still an important empirical fact that not all companies value rents when it comes to political action: anti-corruption and policy reforms are quite popular overall. Describing Egypt and Tunisia as "crony capitalist" countries obscures the fact that the majority of businesspeople likely engage in very few crony activities beyond having to provide small bribes to government officials. Cronyism is necessarily an exclusive enterprise only available to those with the necessary family background and political connections – if it were not the case, many more companies would take advantage of these kinds of relationships and ultimately prosper as a result.

It is also interesting to note that appeals having to do with protecting the company from threats are less popular across countries in the sample. This finding suggests that the predatory state hypothesis (Acemoglu, Johnson, and Robinson 2004) is less compelling as an explanation for company political engagement in crony capitalist states. The ability to obtain rents and access to markets is more important than whatever threats to expropriation exist.

4.5 Experimental Results

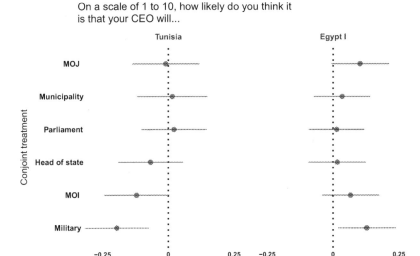

FIGURE 4.11 Estimates for political actor treatments by dependent variable

This result also suggests that the majority of company employees do not judge such threats against their firm as being very credible, at least in the present. Again, it is quite possible that such threats are credible to a subset of companies in the sample; it is just not very compelling in the aggregate. For example, threats to companies may be more likely to come from local-level actors like municipalities as opposed to national institutions like the ministry of interior (Markus 2015).

I now turn to Figure 4.11, which shows the pooled results for all of the different actors or institutions who could provide benefits to a company. These results show that in Tunisia no particular institution stands out as having more credibility or importance than the generic government actor, while in Egypt the military stands apart as a politically influential actor, with the ministries of justice and the interior somewhat less influential. In Tunisia, by contrast, the military and the ministry of interior are less likely to receive positive responses to appeals for support compared to the generic government actor.

It is immediately apparent that the macroeconomic impact of the military has a consequence on firm political behavior in Egypt relative to Tunisia. However, in addition it is intriguing to find less overall institutional differentiation in Tunisia. When pooling results across Tunisian companies, no one actor stands apart as having the most influence. This heterogeneity follows from the idea of broad rent-seeking because companies will want deals with whichever institution has some stake or influence in their field, and that will vary from company to company. By comparison, in Egypt the gatekeeping effect of the military tends to channel political influence toward itself.

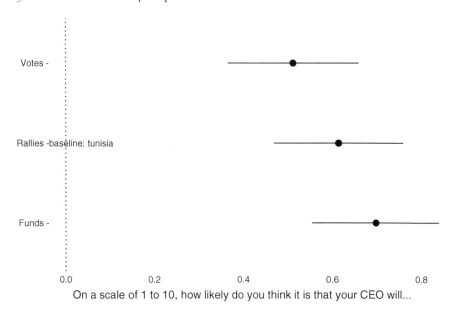

FIGURE 4.12 Egyptian country-level intercepts across all three experimental outcomes

Before I disaggregate the results, I also examine one other interesting result from the pooled model. Figure 4.12 shows Egyptian country intercepts, or average value of political activities, included in the pooled results. These intercepts can be thought of as representing the willingness of companies to engage in politics that is not explained by the types of appeals they saw. What is interesting to see in Figure 4.12 is that the Egypt sample shows unusually high responsiveness to appeals for support above and beyond the treatments. A different way of expressing this result is to say that Egyptian companies are much more likely to responding to political appeals for support regardless of the treatment offered. This finding reveals why randomized experiments can be so important. When examining the purely observational data about Egyptian business political engagement earlier in this chapter, Egyptian companies were more likely to engage in politics for only certain types of activity like employee vote coercion. By contrast, when political appeals are randomized, respondents reported that their businesses would engage in politics at much higher levels than past behavior would suggest.

In other words, it is quite possible that political interest of companies is higher than the present number of opportunities to engage in politics. It is difficult to gauge or measure this latent factor, that is, which businesses will parties target for support and why. If politicians have little interest in recruiting or receiving business support, then businesses will likewise have fewer opportunities to influence them regardless of the value of political connections.

4.5 Experimental Results

It is interesting to note too how these results mirror the descriptive analysis of military linkages in the economy shown in Figure 4.7. Tunisian companies interact with military-affiliated companies relatively infrequently, and it is thus not surprising that they are also less interested in political dalliance with the military. Egyptian companies are much more likely to rely on the military as an important consumer or supplier, and so they are also more responsive to appeals offering benefits from the military – even if these benefits are not traditionally the domain of the military, like import/export licenses.

The results just presented constitute core evidence in support of the theory advanced in this book. Political-economic differences affecting companies have profound consequences on their political behavior, although the outcomes are not always intuitive. One important additional question is to know whether companies with closer existing connections to the military tend to be more likely to obtain more support from the military. This test of the theory is important as it asks whether the strong effect of the military in the experiment is limited only to those companies who are already a part of the clientelist complex.

Figure 4.13 tests this hypothesis directly by interacting each type of institutional actor in the experiment with whether or not the company is already a core part of the military's network. To determine those companies which were highly connected to the military, I chose those companies that listed the military as a No. 1 or No. 2 supplier or consumer to the company. The results of this interaction in 4.13 reveal that the opposite is true: those companies who do not

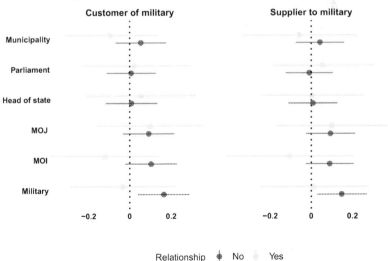

FIGURE 4.13 Appeal of institutions for companies with military connections

rank the military as a No. 1 or No. 2 consumer or supplier are in fact more likely to want political opportunities with the military. In other words, those companies who currently lack such connections with the military very much want to cultivate them, while already-connected companies see little need in working hard to maintain them.

This is a more nuanced way of addressing the question of this book as to the role of the military clientelist-complex in business political engagement. This comparison looks at relative differences between Egyptian companies rather than solely with Tunisia as a baseline. However, the evidence here is just as clear and compelling as that presented earlier. The military in Egypt plays a surprisingly powerful gatekeeping role to the point that companies that do not have the greatest reliance on the military as a consumer or supplier still need to curry favor with the military. As presented earlier in the chapter, the military's economic tentacles touch on a wide number of sectors in the Egyptian economy, and even if in aggregate terms the military is not the country's largest supplier or consumer, its importance is increasing and much larger relative to other countries.

Another way to examine the extent of the military's control over Egyptian companies is to see how the treatment affects their political enemies. While I did not directly ask for whether companies supported the Egyptian Muslim Brotherhood in the 2017 survey, I did ask a question that provides a proxy: whether or not the company took out Islamic loans. Islamic finance is a more expensive option for companies, and generally only those whose owners view themselves as more Islamist tend to take on the extra effort. Particularly in Egypt, both Islamic and "secular" financial products are available, which allows the choice of finance to be a reflection of the company's attitudes toward Islamism rather than structural conditions. Company owners who use Islamic financial products are much more likely to be sympathetic to the Muslim Brotherhood's Islamist project, though of course the correspondence will not be one to one.

In Figure 4.14, I interact the military treatment with a yes/no question for whether the company used Islamic financial products. Intriguingly, there is a large difference between these two groups. It turns out that companies with Islamic financial products are actually more likely to be responsive to the military as an institution. Those companies who would seem to be the most natural enemies of the military are actually even more likely to want to enter into some kind of arrangement with the military. I interpret this finding as providing very strong evidence of the need for Egyptian companies to engage in narrow rent-seeking and enter into a political coalition – even one that would lead to a betrayal of the company's owner's principles.

None of the results presented in this chapter emphasize this point as strongly as this finding. After the overthrow of President Muhammad Morsi, the Egyptian military launched into a bloody campaign targeting Brotherhood supporters, imprisoning and killing many. If it were not for the military's hegemonic position in the economy, it seems likely that Islamist company owners

4.6 Fading Influence Over Time

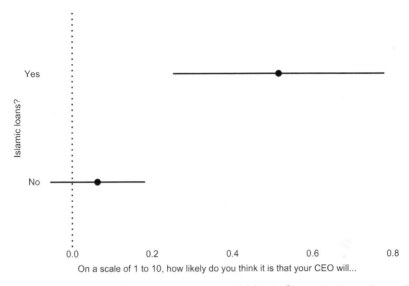

FIGURE 4.14 Interaction of military treatment and Islamic finance in Egypt Survey I

would avoid or disavow the military. Instead, even these companies seem to need to reach some kind of rapprochement with the military to secure their own survival.

4.6 FADING INFLUENCE OVER TIME

While the results so far presented show a hegemonic military-clientelist complex around which many Egyptian businesspeople must find a rapprochement, more recent data show that this may not remain the case in perpetuity. In 2020, I implemented an additional survey targeted at Egyptian businesspeople containing the same experiment. Figure 4.15, I examine how the treatments differ between the 2017 original sample versus three years later.

Figure 4.15 reveals that the increased support for the military has diminished somewhat, although support for the head of state, that is, the president, has increased. This finding is suggestive of a change in how Egyptian companies evaluate their political options because the president of Egypt, Fattah Abd El-Sisi, is well known for centralizing power in his office. His increasing authority has also allowed him to develop his own web of corruption. An Egyptian contractor who helped build President Sisi new extravagant dwellings exposed the president's corruption in YouTube videos in late 2019 that captured the country's attention and led to the first street protests in the country years.[5]

---

[5] See www.middleeastobserver.org/2019/09/08/contractor-and-actor-exposing-sisis-corruption-ignites-electronic-war-in-egypt/.

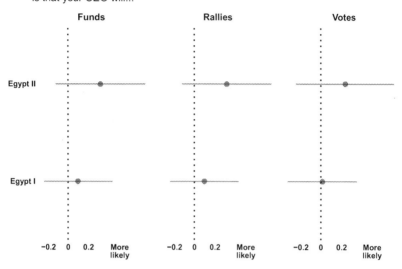

FIGURE 4.15 Estimates for head of state actor treatments by Egypt samples and dependent variable

Al-Sisi responded to these allegations obliquely at a youth conference when he said, "Are [the new palaces] for me? I am building a new state. ... No, I will keep building and building, but not for myself."[6] Al-Sisi's stranglehold on power gave him the ability to shrug off these accusations while admitting, quite publicly, to their veracity.

While it is important to avoid overinterpreting the differences between two surveys, the fact that the difference runs in this direction – decreasing emphasis on the military, more on the president – does suggest that Egyptian companies see the military as an institution is less important than personal ties to the president. If true, it could also suggest an undermining of the narrow rent-seeking which the military as an institution was able to produce during the country's transition to dictatorship.

Similarly, Figure 4.16, which has the same interaction between the military as a treatment and the use of Islamic financial products, shows that there is no longer a significant difference between the two groups in the Egypt II sample as in Figure 4.14. The very large effect in the Egypt I sample does not seem to have persisted up until 2020, suggesting that these companies no longer feel as compelled to be responsive to the military as a provider of rents. While on its own this finding does not provide conclusive interpretations, combined

---

[6] See www.reuters.com/article/us-egypt-politics/egypts-sisi-rebuffs-videos-alleging-corruption-idUSKBN1VZ0KO.

4.7 Conclusion

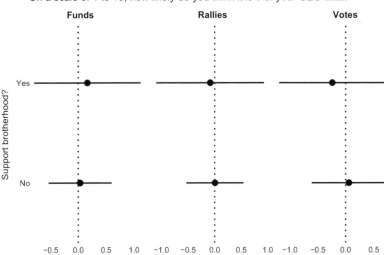

FIGURE 4.16 Interaction of military treatment and Brotherhood support in Egypt Survey II

with the other differences between the surveys, it would appear that Egyptian companies' previously united support for the military is shifting away from narrow rent-seeking and back toward traditional broad rent-seeking. However, it remains too early to know whether these signs are an indication of a true transformation in rent distribution networks.

4.7 CONCLUSION

In this chapter, I provided quantitative data drawn from several surveys in Egypt and Tunisia to substantiate the main contentions of this book. I was able to show that the Egyptian military-clientelist complex was far larger than other countries and also that it had a pronounced effect on the political behavior of Egyptian companies in 2017 and up until 2020. This kind of behavior follows from the distinction between narrow and broad rent-seeking. As the military increased its control over economic resources and state institutions, they were increasingly able to coerce Egyptian companies to work through themselves instead of seeking private arrangements with bureaucrats.

The result of this increasing control was the formation of a political coalition among Egyptian businesspeople which apparently extended to companies with Islamist sympathies. This near complete role reversal suggests that the military's hegemonic influence has decisively changed the behavior of companies from broad to narrow rent-seeking. As companies feel trapped by the military's growing economic clout, they must enter into some kind of agreement or risk losing everything.

Another conclusion to draw from this exercise is the importance of individual-level data from companies and the ability of online surveys to circumvent previously insurmountable challenges in surveying companies about political behavior. It is possible through online sampling to procure samples that provide much more detailed information about corporate political behavior, especially in states where such data collection is highly regulated or even forbidden. There is enormous possibility for this type of research to further clarify the inner workings of crony capitalism and provide more empirical data to evaluate our theories about its origins and consequences.

There is some reason, though, to think that quite recently the strength of the military coalition may be fading. The growing personalism and corruption of President Al-Sisi may be threatening the credibility and cohesiveness of the military's formidable clientelist complex that helps sustain its rule. However, how and to what extent these problems create room for challengers to the regime is an open question.

4.8 METHODOLOGICAL APPENDIX

In this section, I include more detail for the interested reader validating the demographics of the collected samples, as well as discuss the techniques for collecting the data. Collecting data on companies via social media methods, in particular Facebook, is not widely practiced in the literature to date, although social media recruitment as a means of obtaining public opinion data has become increasingly common. Many online panel service providers such as Qualtrics and YouGov recruit the panel members via Facebook and other social media ads. Online surveys have become a staple of public opinion reporting, including during presidential and legislative elections (Twyman 2008), where they have been found to be quite accurate even with the well-known limitations of reaching the entire population.

The reason that online polling can work even if the entire population is not accessible is because social media has spread to the point that most types of people are represented in the medium. Recent validation studies of Facebook surveys show that the online panels primarily fail to reach rural and lower-educated people in places like Kenya (Rosenzweig et al. 2020). These differences, though, can either be adjusted using weighting methods like multiple regression and post-stratification (Park, Gelman, and Bafumi 2004), or they can be directly controlled for in regression models by including covariates for potential factors that might be related to survey recruitment (Gelman 2007). Even unadjusted Facebook survey estimates, though, can be quite close to population totals (Boas, Christenson, and Glick 2020; Zhang et al. 2020).

The reason for this is that slight biases in survey recruitment may not result in differences in the target estimated, that is, what the analyst wants to learn about. For example, if the research question entails learning about ideological differences, and if both conservative and liberal respondents in rural and

4.8 Methodological Appendix 145

urban areas respond at similar rates, then lower numbers of rural people in the survey will not necessarily affect the overall conclusions. Especially with social-scientific analysis, the aim is not to know the population total, but rather to gain knowledge about the relationship between different variables. Even if the survey is somewhat unbalanced, these balances may matter little to the relationship being investigated.

For companies, these existing biases diminish. The survey frame is explicitly urban and well educated, and these respondents are in fact the most likely to be on Facebook. Because the population has employment, they likely have the means to browse the Internet, whether on desktop computers or on their phones. As a result, it is at least plausible to reach the majority of employed persons in many countries today using Facebook ads as a recruitment mechanism.

The exact methodology for recruiting the survey involved coming up with a compelling advertisement with images produced by a graphic designer. The survey advertisement was quite short, as mandated by Facebook, and essentially offered a mobile credit of USD 1 in exchange for completing a survey. The ads were targeted at employees and employers in the respective countries.

Facebook ad targeting involves selecting a set of criteria created by Facebook from users' profiles. The ad targets include both public and private user information, which is what renders them remarkably powerful at targeting. Even a business manager has a private profile, Facebook can still show them the ad based on their internal targeting database. At the same time, advertisers do not have control over the targeting algorithm, which is why it is difficult to state with certainty that a given survey is representative relative to a random sample. Based on my experience implementing these and other surveys, ad targeting with general demographics, such as age ranges and work categories, performs very well at recruiting a diverse sample. It is best to avoid over-targeting surveys as doing so can create a strong reliance on Facebook's ability to categorize users, which is far from foolproof. Generally speaking, even if a survey's ad targets are overly broad, it will still end up recruiting the correct demographic as those users will respond to the ad at higher rates.

After Facebook users clicked on the link, they were taken to a Qualtrics survey. A piece of HTML code known as a pixel tracked the users as they moved through the survey, information which was then returned to Facebook to improve ad targeting. On completion of the survey, I used research assistants to send the mobile credit to the respondent's numbers from within the respective countries. Other than these cell phone numbers, which were not necessary for the respondent to provide, no other identifying information was collected about the respondents.

The main issue with Facebook ad recruitment and company surveys is the concern whether the ads will reach all types of companies. There is no reason to expect that they would not – anyone at any company has an equal ability to use Facebook – but it is still important to check on these potential imbalances.

TABLE 4.5 *Proportion of respondents by age*

	25–29	30–34	35–44	45–54	55–64	65+
Algeria	0.26	0.32	0.28	0.09	0.04	0.01
Egypt	0.20	0.27	0.31	0.16	0.05	0.00
Tunisia	0.28	0.23	0.27	0.14	0.06	0.02

Note: Surveys are 2017 Facebook surveys of employees and business managers.

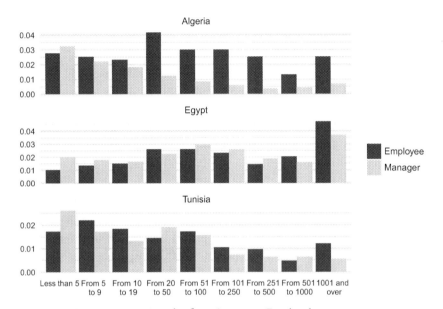

FIGURE 4.17 Survey proportions by firm size, 2017 Facebook surveys

Table 4.5 shows the distribution of respondents by age for the 2017 surveys, which is an important way to check for imbalance across countries. Algeria is included as it was a part of the 2017 data collection even though the survey was not presented in this chapter. As can be seen, the proportions are remarkably balanced across countries. The proportions are skewed younger, but this largely reflects the age demographics in these countries, where the median ages are in the mid-20s for the countries in the survey.

Similarly, Figure 4.17 shows the proportion of respondents by whether they are employees or managers and also by firm size. The plot is broken down as well by country to permit easy comparisons. As expected, Tunisia tends to have smaller firms on average than Egypt, which reflects the smaller size of the Tunisian economy. However, both countries have similar rates of managers and employees responding to the survey at roughly 50 percent. Algeria shows somewhat less involvement of managers at larger companies, which is in fact to be expected as the employee to manager ratio is normally higher in bigger

4.8 Methodological Appendix

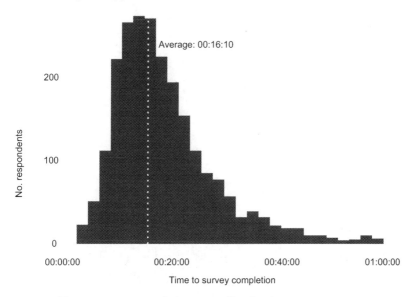

FIGURE 4.18 Time to survey completion, 2017 Facebook surveys

companies. What is clear is that there is ample representation across the countries and across all company sizes. It is not the case that the surveys are dominated by a single type of company, which permits more robust inferences about the distribution in the population.

The final plot in this section, Figure 4.18, shows the distribution of survey completion times across the three countries. As can be seen, the average user took 16 minutes to complete the survey, which represents a reasonable level of effort invested in the survey. These relatively high times reflect the incentives that were provided to respondents in mobile credit of approximately USD 1. While some respondents may have satisficed, answering questions too quickly, it is clear that the majority spent a considerable portion of their time working through the questions.

5

Crony Capitalism in International Comparison

In this chapter, I extend the analytic focus beyond Egypt and Tunisia to see how and to what extent the theory can explain similar situations in the Middle East and even outside of the region. As mentioned in Chapter 4, my survey research has implemented the same questionnaire in several other countries, permitting me to do intercountry and even interregional comparisons. While some of these comparisons can be difficult to pin down in terms of underlying differences, this chapter will nonetheless provide important context for the applicability of this book's argument outside of its original domain. There are certainly many issues with unstable regimes and crony capitalism outside of the Egyptian and Tunisian experience.

This chapter primarily offers the same analyses as the previous chapter, except with the addition of surveys in Morocco, Jordan, Algeria, Venezuela, and Ukraine. Given that quite similar questionnaires were used in the different surveys, it is possible to directly compare answers in most cases. Due to the fact that there are differences in sample composition, all of the plots are re-weighted to match the Egypt I survey's company sector distribution. When fitting statistical models, I include covariates to help adjust for these sample selection characteristics.

5.1 REGIONAL AND INTERNATIONAL PERSPECTIVE

While it is beyond the scope of this chapter to investigate the political economy of these additional countries in depth, I first discuss the salient differences between these countries to situate crony capitalism. Painting with a broad brush, all of these countries could be considered to have considerable obstacles with corruption. Using Transparency International's influential scale from 2021, the least corrupt country was Jordan, ranking 58th in the world, while Ukraine scored the worst with a ranking of 122nd. These high-level measures, though, need to be interpreted with caution as they rely on expert assessments

5.1 Regional and International Perspective

that can be difficult to compare across countries, and they do not involve only business corruption, but also low-level corruption involving bribes paid for government services. The conclusion that can be drawn, though, is that none of these countries is considered to be a paragon of transparency, accountability, and good governance.

If business–state relations were controlled by lobbying and campaign finance regulations, the game would be decidedly different and business political engagement would differ as well. At the same time, while corruption is an important scope condition, business political engagement will adjust to the varying institutional environments across these countries. As I have described in this book, corruption does not exist in a vacuum, but is rather a feature of institutions arising from the political balance of power. Even if corruption exists in some form in all these countries, the barriers to entry and consequences for the business climate will depend on how businesses maintain necessary relationships with office holders.

Figures 5.1 and 5.2 show relevant statistics concerning both economic performance from the World Bank and political institutions from the Varieties of Democracy project in these countries (Lindberg et al. 2014). Generally speaking, these are all middle-income countries with high unemployment rates (the dotted line shows 5% unemployment) and low levels of foreign direct investment (FDI). One caveat is that some economic data is missing for Ukraine

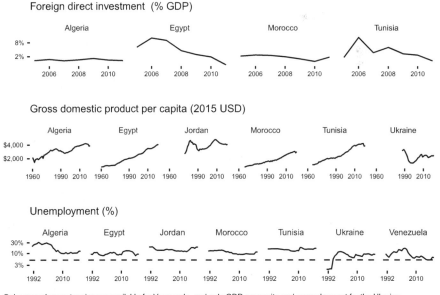

Only unemployment series are available for Venezuela, and only GDP per capita and unemployment for the Ukraine.

FIGURE 5.1 World Bank development indicator statistics

150   5 *Crony Capitalism in International Comparison*

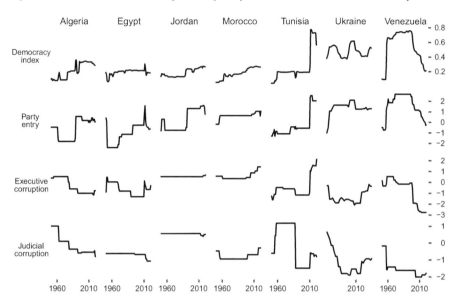

Index values derived from a statistical model of country expert ratings. Higher values indicate more democracy and more party entry for the top two indices and less corruption for the corruption indices.

FIGURE 5.2 Varieties of Democracy political indicators by country

and Venezuela in particular. Ukraine has a reasonably high level of FDI given its integration into European supply chains even if they do not report the total amount to the World Bank. For Venezuela, the missing data almost certainly masks declining economic output and virtually nonexistent FDI as the party in power has undermined economic stability in the country.[1]

The most relevant institutional difference to consider is regime type. Most of these countries are some form of dictatorship, though there are still significant differences. Morocco and Jordan are both monarchies with a substantial amount of electoral competition for parliament (Daadaoui 2010; Ryan 2011). These parliaments can be dismissed by the monarch, and sometimes are, but it is clear that they have considerable influence on policies and also act as a conduit for the regime to recruit elite allies (Lust-Okar 2006). Algeria is a presidential regime with strong military influence, not unlike Egypt, though the military does not quite have as strong a stranglehold on state institutions and the economy (Cook 2007). Venezuela is a former democracy that has fallen into a form of hybrid authoritarianism; it still has regular elections and there seems to be at least limited electoral contestation (Corrales 2020). Finally, Ukraine is

---

[1] See www.cfr.org/backgrounder/venezuela-crisis.

5.2 *Comparing Business Political Engagement across Regions* 151

the most fully democratic country, especially since popular movements pushed out pro-Russian leaders who had strong authoritarian tendencies (Chaisty and Whitefield 2018).

The best way of predicting how regime type will affect narrow and broad rent-seeking is to emphasize the channels through which businesspeople can obtain political influence. Companies in Ukraine are likely to have more options given the more open political system, potentially making broad rent-seeking a more plausible option for companies. Jordan and Morocco are likely to offer companies fewer political opportunities with their closed political systems and relatively tight controls over elections. Venezuela contrasts with many Arab countries because it is a democratic country that has become more authoritarian, leaving decreasing space for opposition representation though real contestation does still occur during elections. Algeria has a strongly authoritarian system, although it has seen some liberalization over the past few years due the declining health of its president.

The final and very important factor to note is the size and type of economies in these countries. Venezuela's economy is by far the poorest as the country's rapacious authoritarian regime has led to a near-total collapse in business activity. As such, the companies that exist in the country are only those who have managed to hold on during a period of deep recession. Jordan and Morocco have both seen GDP growth in the past decade, albeit with continued high unemployment among younger population, a common issue in Middle Eastern countries. Ukraine has seen economic growth undermined by the long-simmering conflict with Russia on its eastern border; this form of instability undermines investment and company creation and growth (Havlik 2014). Algerian economic activity is influenced strongly by oil prices; the relatively depressed climate for energy in the late 2010s has hurt both the government's fiscal capacity and output growth (Lefèvre 2017).

On the whole, the differences in these additional countries are similar to those between Egypt and Tunisia. Tunisia had a relatively more open democracy compared to Egypt's more vicious authoritarianism. On the other hand, it is not clear if any of these countries have a gatekeeper that can compare to the Egyptian military. There are of course powerful political actors in each of these countries, but whether they can monopolize power to the same extent is an important empirical question. For that reason, it is worth investigating to what extent these factors are related to differences in business political engagement as well.

5.2 COMPARING BUSINESS POLITICAL ENGAGEMENT ACROSS REGIONS

In this section, I compare rates of political activity across countries and regions to better understand how anomalous or similar the Egypt and Tunisian results are to other countries. Figure 5.3 shows average values by sample for responses to four questions about an employee's companies' political participation in the

152   5 *Crony Capitalism in International Comparison*

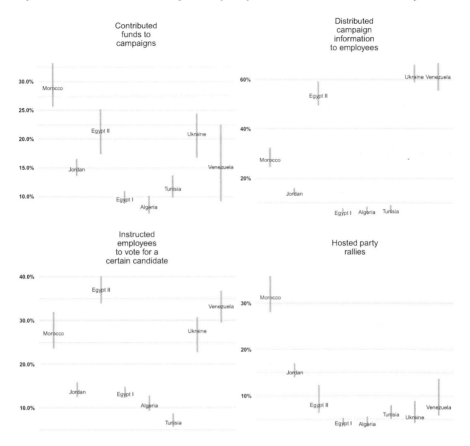

FIGURE 5.3 Reported firm political activity in regional comparison

last electoral cycle: (1) did the company contribute funds to a campaign?, (2) did the company distribute campaign information to employees?, (3) did the company instruct employees to vote for a particular candidate?, and (4) did the company host party rallies? The responses in this figure are average values that take into account uncertainty in terms of missing data in responses and are re-weighted to match the relative proportions of managers and firm sizes in the Egypt I survey.[2] As can be seen, average values for political activity vary considerably across countries, with Morocco and Jordan relatively high across all categories, and Tunisia and Algeria relatively low. Ukraine and Venezuela report very high rates of distributing campaign information to employees but are much lower on other types of activity.

[2] To be specific, the responses average over five multiple-imputed datasets.

5.2 *Comparing Business Political Engagement across Regions* 153

What is of interest is the high level of employee vote coercion in Egypt in regional comparison, particularly in the second sample taken in the spring of 2020. Even if the two samples are averaged together, Egypt has a quite high level of employee-voter coercion. This country-level difference suggests that this type of political activity is relatively common among Egyptian companies compared to others. By contrast, distributing campaign information is more common in Ukraine and Venezuela, and providing funding to campaigns is more common in Morocco and Jordan. It is quite clear that though all of these countries could be described as having serious issues with crony capitalism, reported political behavior among companies can vary quite dramatically. It is difficult to know from these types of plots what is the origin of these differences, especially as they may be affected by the relative knowledge or willingness of respondents to report on these issues. In the case of the Egypt samples, given that the recruitment methods were relatively similar, it would seem that trends would be toward increasing political participation among companies of a type that is associated with narrow rent-seeking: ordering employees to vote for a specific candidate rather than trying to remain neutral toward specific partisan actors. As an indicator of narrow rent-seeking, this association would suggest that rent-seeking networks are more centralized in Egypt than elsewhere.

In Figures 5.4 and 5.5, I look at how past bribe payments and inspections by regulators are associated with different types of political activity. Figure 5.4 shows a dark gray line for the proportion of respondents in a given country that said their company undertook a specific kind of political activity. The line connects across answers to the question about whether the respondent's company paid more in bribes now than it did five years ago – or for countries in the Middle East, whether bribes had increased since the Arab Spring.

The dark line shows the average value across countries for a given category. As can be seen, there is considerable country-level variation. For contributing funds to campaigns, country survey estimates range from a low of nearly 0 percent of respondents reporting such contributions if they saw a decrease in bribe payments up to a high of 30 percent reporting contributions for companies that witnessed a large increase in bribe payments. The dark average line shows a steady increase from approximately 10 percent of companies giving campaign funds to 20 percent of companies giving campaign funds if they had experienced a large increase in bribe payments. This general pattern holds across the other types of political activity except for distributing campaign information to employees. In that case, the average line shows little movement between companies that saw decreases or increases in bribe payments. On the whole, this figure suggests that one of the central patterns of this book – rising bribe payments can be a sign of a change in rent distribution networks which subsequently prompt political action – appears to be true across the various countries sampled, not only in Egypt and Tunisia. The relationship exhibits some noise, as we would expect, but the patterns nonetheless remain.

154   5 *Crony Capitalism in International Comparison*

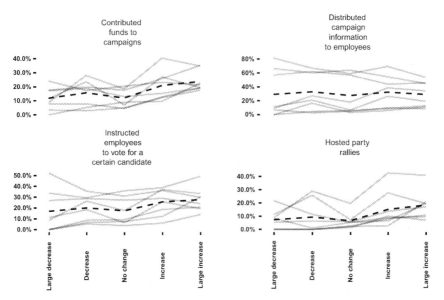

FIGURE 5.4 Political activities by answers to how much have bribes increased since the Arab Spring?

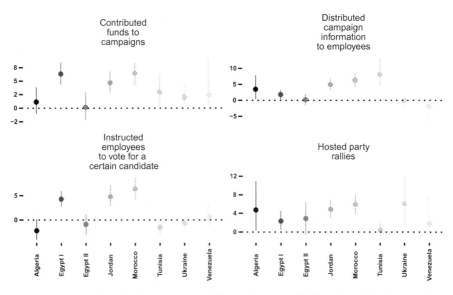

FIGURE 5.5 Difference in number of inspections from regulators for politically active versus politically inactive companies

5.2 Comparing Business Political Engagement across Regions

We can examine a similar association in Figure 5.5, except that in this case the plot shows the estimated increase in the prior year's number of regulatory inspections for the politically involved versus noninvolved companies. Again, this plot is broken out by the type of political activity undertaken. As can be seen, these estimates are almost uniformly positive, implying that companies that are more politically involved are also those that have been targeted by regulators more often in the past year. While regulatory inspections are not as clear an indicator as a specific increase in bribe payments, this result also suggests that political activity may be a way of averting negative attention with government officials. The finding appears to be the most consequential for contributing funds to campaigns and hosting party rallies, where politically involved companies received between two and eight more inspections in the prior year on average than noninvolved companies.

While these cross-country plots show intriguing evidence that these relationships hold across a wider swatch of countries, it is still important to consider adjusting these estimates to take into account other factors that may explain country-level differences in political participation among countries. In Table 5.1, I fit separate Bayesian logistic regression model for the same constructed outcome measure in the previous chapter that aggregates the four types of political activity using an item-response model. I include diverse set of variables in the model including whether the respondent is a manager, whether bribe payments have increased in the last five years, firm performance, whether the firm belongs to a conglomerate, the percentage paid of firm income in bribes, firm sector and the number of inspections by government regulators. The intention of including these variables is to look at general patterns that should hold based on my theory about why companies were interested in pursuing business political engagement. As in Chapter 4, I restrict the sample to domestic companies as introducing foreign-owned companies threatens to complicate the model's interpretation.

The results of the model are tabulated in Table 5.1, which is organized by the country in columns and variables in rows. One crucial pattern that emerges across both countries is that those companies who saw an *increase* in bribes since the Arab Spring, or for Ukraine and Venezuela in the past five years, have a much higher incidence of political activity across all four types of outcomes. The scale of the standardized outcome, which collapses across the four types of political activity, suggests that moving from a large decrease in bribes to a large increase in bribes increases political activity by about one-half of a standard deviation, though the effect varies by country. What is also important to note is that this effect is pronounced in all of the Arab countries in the sample, and for one non-Arab country, Venezuela, the effect is noticeable if smaller (the model assigns a very small probability of the effect being slightly negative for Venezuela). Only for Ukraine and Algeria does an increase in bribes have no apparent relationship with increased political activity.

TABLE 5.1 *Covariates predicting historical corporate political engagement*

Variable	Algeria	Egypt I	Egypt II	Jordan	Morocco	Tunisia	Ukraine	Venezuela
No. Times Inspected	0 (0, 0.001)	0.002* (0.001, 0.002)	−0.001 (−0.003, 0.001)	0.001 (0, 0.002)	0.002* (0.001, 0.003)	0 (−0.001, 0.001)	0.001 (0, 0.002)	0 (−0.001, 0.001)
Bribes Increase	0.005 (−0.022, 0.023)	0.043* (0.029, 0.06)	0.037* (0.016, 0.058)	0.046* (0.034, 0.062)	0.068* (0.045, 0.1)	0.038* (0.013, 0.085)	0.01 (−0.021, 0.034)	0.022* (0.001, 0.042)
Conglomerate	0.055* (0.026, 0.084)	0.011 (−0.019, 0.04)	0.073* (0.001, 0.138)	0.036 (−0.006, 0.08)	0.145* (0.093, 0.194)	−0.055* (−0.097, −0.014)	0.052* (0.009, 0.096)	−0.007 (−0.054, 0.036)
Firm Performance	−0.001 (−0.002, 0)	−0.001* (−0.002, −0.001)	0 (−0.002, 0.002)	−0.001 (−0.002, 0)	−0.003* (−0.005, −0.001)	0.001 (−0.001, 0.002)	−0.001 (−0.003, 0.001)	0.001 (−0.001, 0.003)
No. Firm Employees	0 (−0.005, 0.006)	0.012* (0.005, 0.018)	0.018* (0.008, 0.028)	0.009 (0, 0.018)	−0.002 (−0.013, 0.009)	0.009* (0.001, 0.016)	0.017* (0.008, 0.025)	0.011* (0.002, 0.02)
Manager	−0.052* (−0.087, −0.018)	0.018 (−0.009, 0.046)	0.023 (−0.025, 0.073)	−0.022 (−0.063, 0.019)	−0.006 (−0.06, 0.046)	−0.068* (−0.108, −0.03)	0.023 (−0.048, 0.099)	−0.026 (−0.073, 0.019)
Construction	0.013 (−0.059, 0.087)	0.071* (0.004, 0.141)	−0.103 (−0.238, 0.042)	0.083 (−0.071, 0.245)	0.026 (−0.085, 0.14)	−0.267* (−0.507, −0.099)	0.036 (−0.067, 0.154)	−0.043 (−0.222, 0.159)

Finance	−0.018	0.096*	0.039	0.133	0.1	0.116*	−0.1	0.053
	(−0.118, 0.074)	(0.016, 0.175)	(−0.137, 0.197)	(−0.004, 0.281)	(−0.023, 0.221)	(0.032, 0.202)	(−0.245, 0.106)	(−0.104, 0.261)
Manufacturing	0.057	0.074*	0.001	−0.071	0.035	0.051	−0.042	0.002
	(−0.006, 0.126)	(0.015, 0.138)	(−0.119, 0.11)	(−0.205, 0.078)	(−0.087, 0.154)	(−0.019, 0.127)	(−0.147, 0.079)	(−0.158, 0.203)
Mining	0.077	−0.095	−0.119	−0.204	0.045	0.002	0.061	0.138
	(−0.006, 0.16)	(−0.327, 0.088)	(−0.327, 0.066)	(−0.586, 0.103)	(−0.225, 0.303)	(−0.108, 0.113)	(−0.068, 0.193)	(−0.071, 0.393)
Services	0.061*	−0.009	−0.063	0.079	−0.033	−0.001	−0.031	−0.043
	(0.003, 0.123)	(−0.069, 0.057)	(−0.175, 0.045)	(−0.047, 0.221)	(−0.135, 0.077)	(−0.068, 0.07)	(−0.117, 0.086)	(−0.182, 0.147)
Intercept	−0.249*	−0.453*	−0.334*	−0.416*	−0.409*	−0.323*	−0.338*	−0.245*
	(−0.327, −0.16)	(−0.546, −0.368)	(−0.474, −0.202)	(−0.567, −0.278)	(−0.564, −0.265)	(−0.505, −0.204)	(−0.43, −0.244)	(−0.431, −0.094)
R^2	0.039*	0.111*	0.078*	0.084*	0.131*	0.087*	0.045*	0.053*
	(0.021, 0.062)	(0.077, 0.146)	(0.044, 0.113)	(0.06, 0.108)	(0.102, 0.159)	(0.053, 0.126)	(0.023, 0.076)	(0.028, 0.093)
N Obs	1209.4*	1327.8*	1101.8*	1220.4*	953*	812.8*	1670*	1297.4*
	(1193, 1225)	(1323, 1333)	(1051, 1141)	(1210, 1226)	(947, 963)	(802, 825)	(1573, 1729)	(1207, 1357)

Notes: Estimation of Bayesian logistic regression using Markov Chain Monte Carlo with Stan to handle issues of perfect separation. 5%–95% quantile intervals in parentheses. The coefficients are sample average marginal effects expressed as the increase in probability of the given outcome for a 1-unit change in the regressor. The number of observations has an uncertainty interval due to imputation uncertainty in the number of domestic firms. Estimates that can be considered statistically significant are marked with an asterisk. (Because these are Bayesian regression models estimated via Markov Chain Monte Carlo, a coefficient is marked with an asterisk if the 5%–95% posterior interval did not include 0.)

The weaker association in Ukraine and Venezuela does invite speculation about the role of the Arab Spring as a consequential scope condition for the theory. Of the Arab countries surveyed, only Egypt and Tunisia experienced either regime or leadership change as a result of the Arab Spring. Algeria subsequently experienced leadership change in 2019, but this occurred two years after the survey was fielded and seven years after the outbreak of the Arab Spring. Nonetheless, there are very similar patterns in terms of increase in bribe payments leading to increased political activity even in these countries that did not witness as large or as consequential political changes. While it would require follow-up research to examine the specific patterns of rent-seeking, it would appear that the Arab Spring's political consequences also mattered in countries that did not see as significant changes from popular mobilization for democracy. Relationships between elites still suffered ruptures that resulted in winners, losers and a subsequent scramble to regain political influence.

The fact that this pattern holds outside of Egypt and Tunisia provides crucial evidence that the mechanism has to do with political-economic incentives arising from regime machinations and not from factors distinct to these two countries. Prior work in the theory of authoritarian political economy suggests that whenever regime transitions occur, redistribution of rent-seeking privileges will follow as elites compete for the changing size of the pie (Albertus and Menaldo 2014; Martinez-Bravo, Mukherjee, and Stegmann 2017). Whenever consequential political changes disrupt relationships between businesspeople and regimes – assuming that such relationships are implicitly tolerated by weak state institutions – it stands to reason that the losers will attempt to reclaim their rent-seeking privileges through increased political activity.

While it is difficult to make statements about generalizability outside of the Arab world given the inclusion of only two non-Arab countries in the data presented, it is still nonetheless quite plausible that the explanation for the weaker or nonexistent associations in Ukraine and Venezuela is a consequence of relative stability in those regimes during the time period covered by the survey. Of course, there has been plenty of popular mobilization in both countries, but regime types have remained relatively constant between 2015 and 2020 – Ukraine a weak democracy and Venezuela an increasingly personalist dictatorship. If an event occurs which likewise fundamentally ruptures state-elite relations, it follows that bribe payments might increase for those who lose from the transition. There is strong evidence that this type of elite reconfiguration did in fact occur in Ukraine following its 2004 Orange revolution (Earle and Gehlbach 2015).

These results suggest that although weak state institutions may be a necessary condition for corrupt relations between states and firms, the nature of crony capitalism is more dynamic than we often envision. As companies compete for resources, alliances form and change, both affecting the political environment and morphing as a result of political transitions (Kang 2002). Mapping these consequential changes can help us understand the trajectory

5.3 Military-Clientelist Complex in Comparative Complex

of authoritarian states and so-called hybrid regimes and potential weaknesses arising from intra-elite struggles. It can also help us understand what drives corporate political participation and how this type of political activity can be quite consequential for the regimes themselves.

While the association between bribe payments and political activity is the most consequential finding from Table 5.1, it is worth considering some of the other patterns in the data.

5.3 MILITARY-CLIENTELIST COMPLEX IN COMPARATIVE COMPLEX

The surveys included the same question analyzed in Chapter 4 that asked respondents to rank military-affiliated companies as suppliers or consumers. As a result, I can examine how Egyptian and Tunisian military-clientelist complexes compare in regional and international perspective. Figure 4.7 reports average ranks for military-affiliated companies across all of the surveys broken out by sector. Important patterns quickly emerge. First, respondents in both of the Egyptian surveys report the highest linkages to military-affiliated companies of all countries surveyed. The military-clientelist complex is large in Egypt not only relative to Tunisia but to several other developing countries, suggesting that there are real political-economic differences arising from the military. There are some other discrepancies between the surveys, but it is difficult to know whether these are real changes or simply a reflection of sampling error. The contention of this book that rent-seeking behavior is likely to be influenced by the remarkable size and scope of Egypt's military-clientelist complex appears to be borne out both regionally and internationally. Only Algeria comes close, which indicates that Algeria's long-lived military dictatorship has likewise had the time and influence to build significant military economic enterprises.[3]

It is also interesting to note that Venezuelan and Ukrainian companies report fewer linkages to military-affiliated companies than Arab countries. This association is particularly interesting as it is well known that the Venezuelan regime favors the military and its dictators had previous military experience. Apparently, this military influence in the regime has not yet translated into the broad-based economic power of the Egyptian military, which could be due to the fact that the Egyptian military has stewarded its influence in the government for far longer than its Venezuelan counterpart. For Ukraine, it would seem its democratic institutions mitigate this kind of clientelist complex found in more authoritarian states.

It should also be noted that the Middle East is known as a highly militarized region where regimes receive an extraordinary amount of military aid and also have large numbers of active duty troops (Bellin 2004). As such, this could

---

[3] While it is well known that the Algerian military has powerful economic interests, relatively little of it has been either documented or quantified, leaving experts to guess at the size and scope of it (Springborg 2011).

be the reason why military-clientelist complexes are more likely to appear. It is entirely possible that the theory could operate with a different kind of actor monopolizing rent distribution and forcing companies into narrow rent-seeking in contexts where military power is not as important to regime survival. One possibility is that of state-owned banks which monopolize credit distribution, and consequently maintain a stranglehold over the political allegiance of businesspeople (Arriola 2013). It is difficult of course to speculate about which if any such institutions could be in a given country, but it is important to point out that the theory is not limited to countries with large military-clientelist complexes as occurs in the Middle East.

From these results, the country that appears to have a political economy closest to Egypt is that of Algeria. The military-clientelist complex is nearly as large, which is not surprising given that Algeria's military has had an intimate involvement, one might even say ruling by proxy, since Algeria's hard-fought independence from the French (Cook 2007). As previously mentioned, at the time of data collection, Algeria had not yet experienced sustained popular mobilization that could threaten the regime. Scholars cited Algeria's relatively recent experience with a bitter civil war combined with the flexibility of its petro-state to avoid regime-threatening mobilization as reasons for the lack of widespread mobilization (Volpi 2014).

Since then, however, Algeria has witnessed the outbreak of the Hirak movement, which became the longest lasting protest movement in the Arab world from 2019 to the outbreak of the COVID-19 pandemic in early 2020. The protests indicated a widespread rejection of the military as a ruling institution, and while protesters did show some fatigue as the months wore on, their demands were clearly for revolutionary change (Kubinec 2019b). It is still too early to know if this protest movement will meet its goals, which can only happen when the COVID-19 pandemic recedes and large gatherings are no longer a public health threat. If the movement proves successful, it is likely to be the case that businesspeople will face a similar environment to their counterparts in Egypt, navigating disruption in elite relations while facing the prospect of the military abusing its economic privileges to play for influence. Crucially, this may well depend on the extent to which the military can survive the transition and keep its economic influence intact.

5.4 EXPERIMENTAL RESULTS

I analyze the same experiment as in the previous chapter, except that I put the estimates in a broader comparative context. As with Chapter 4, to conserve space, I used the constructed scale for political engagement which was produced by collapsing outcomes across the three types of political activity. Figures 5.7 and 5.8 look at the main treatments of rent offer types and institutional actors across countries. These plots are averages across samples, and as such they are not necessarily as informative as they average across many

5.4 *Experimental Results* 161

different kinds of firms, including connected and unconnected firms. Nonetheless, some interesting patterns do emerge.

It is clear in Figure 5.7 that one rent type, that of protecting the company from expropriation by the government, is uniquely unpopular across countries, with the lone exception of the Egypt II sample. It is more difficult to derive conclusions from the Egypt II sample because it has less statistical power as a result of showing fewer experimental profiles to each respondent. Nonetheless, aside from Egypt II, taking control over a company is seen as a less desirable benefit than the baseline macroeconomic reform message. In Egypt II, two rents seem to emerge as more desirable, which are access to government contracts and export permissions. If anything, these results point to the continued and growing presence of corruption among government officials in the country.

It is of course interesting to note that in general the offered rents perform no worse nor better than the baseline macroeconomic reform message. This uniformity can have a few causes. First, as mentioned earlier, this result averages across a wide variety of companies, some of whom may either not depend on government rents for survival or assess that they stand little chance of winning rents from political parties. Second, different rents are often appealing to individual companies for reasons specific to their market. Only export-oriented companies, for example, would care about export permissions, while only companies with goods and services of interest to the government would want to compete for government contracts. For these reasons, it is perhaps exceptional that such a consistent pattern holds in companies preferring other types of rent or macroeconomic reform over protection from direct expropriation. It would appear that for the companies in these samples, this threat is not worth obtaining protection from politicians.

At the same time, it is an important empirical finding that not all companies in a country widely considered to suffer from crony capitalism are themselves willing to engage in politics. Anti-corruption messages are still very popular, suggesting that a credible reform alternative would do quite well. Of course, it is difficult for voters to evaluate reform messages as nearly all candidates in democratic elections proclaim their grandiose plans while decrying corruption and cronyism in others. Nonetheless, it is still important to note that many companies would prefer to operate in a system where political relationships confer fewer benefits.

The institutional actor treatments in Figure 5.8 show significantly more variation across countries. One result that particularly stands out is the very high support for the military in the Egypt I sample. In comparative perspective, that kind of willingness to appeal to the military as a provider of rents simply does not exist at the same scale. Furthermore, it is very interesting to note that the willingness to pursue the military as a rent provider tracks closely with reported linkages to the military in Figure 5.6. Both Tunisian and Venezuelan companies report very few linkages to military-affiliated companies, and they are also less responsive to the military as a provider of rents. In the Venezuelan case, this

162   5 *Crony Capitalism in International Comparison*

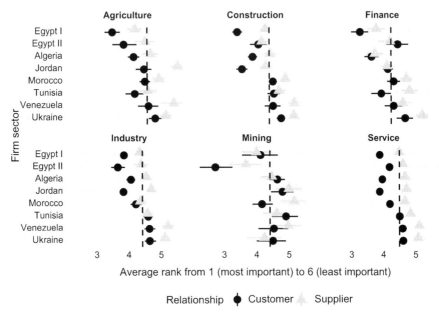

FIGURE 5.6 Ties between military-linked firms and companies by country

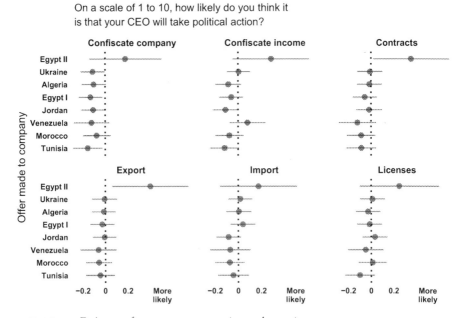

FIGURE 5.7 Estimates for rent treatments (appeal types)

5.4 Experimental Results

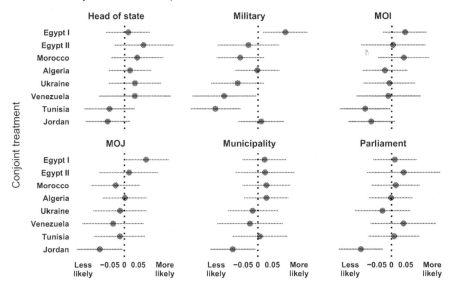

FIGURE 5.8 Estimates for political actor treatments

pattern is quite interesting as the military is a strong supporter of the dictator. The lack of an association may suggest that political proximity to the dictator is not enough to compel company interest; rather, control over rent disbursement networks is necessary as well.

The country with the second-highest level of support for the military is Jordan. In fact, compared to the other rent types, Jordanian companies showed the most responsiveness to the military as a provider of rent. While this level did not reach that of Egypt, it shows that the Jordanian military likely plays a significant role in the distribution of rent in the country. Figure 5.6 shows a sizable economic presence of the military in the country in terms of the relative rank as a consumer or supplier.

Finally, it would appear on the whole that the head of state has the highest interest from companies, though the effect does not exceed that of the baseline government actor. Again, it is important to note that there is a wide variety of companies in the sample and as a consequence it is not expected that strong patterns would emerge. As argued in this book, the native tendency of companies in countries with corrupt state institutions is toward broad rent-seeking and a willingness to engage with whatever actor is willing to provide the necessary rents. As a consequence, lacking a gatekeeper, companies are unlikely to target political patronage at one actor to the exclusion of others.

I further explore differences in the survey by looking at what factors tend to correlate with the success of appeals for political support. In Figure 5.9,

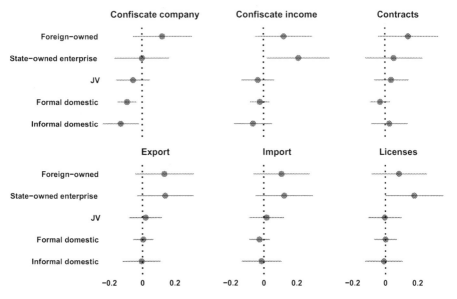

FIGURE 5.9 Rent treatments by firm type

I look at how different types of companies, such as state-owned firms, foreign companies, and formal and informal domestic companies evaluate different political appeals. The interesting pattern that emerges from this analysis is that foreign-owned companies and state-owned enterprises tend to be much more responsive to political appeals than domestic companies. Foreign-owned enterprises value virtually all types of benefits relative to the reform treatment, while state-owned enterprises are most interested in obtaining licenses from the state and to avoid confiscation of their income. This latter effect is particularly interesting as it is well known that political elites can use as cash cows for personal projects or even to funnel proceeds into personal accounts (Sukhtankar 2012).

The result for foreign-owned firms suggests that to invest into these countries, political relationships are very important. The fact that they are on average more responsive than domestic companies should not necessarily be surprising as they also tend to be larger and to have more resources to devote to political relationships. Nonetheless, this book's focus on domestic firms is still justified as domestic companies far outnumber foreign-owned firms. That is not say that foreign-owned companies do not play any role in the political system, but rather that explaining the political activities of domestic companies is likely to be more consequential. It is an open question as to whether the book's central logic concerning narrow versus broad rent-seeking also applies to foreign investors.

5.4 Experimental Results

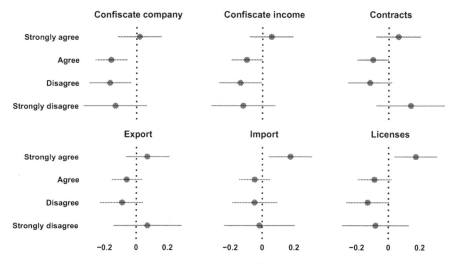

FIGURE 5.10 Estimates for rent treatments by beliefs about corruption

In Figure 5.10, I look at varying levels of responsiveness to appeals for support among answers to a question that asked respondents their level of agreement with the following question: "Government officials use compliance with local regulations to extract informal payments from businesses like ours." This figure shows strong differences between people who strongly agree with this statement versus those who only agree or disagree with the statement. Those with less agreement tend to be much less responsive to political appeals relative to those who strongly agree with the statement. For two categories, import permissions and licenses, those who strongly agree with the statement are much more responsive than the baseline treatment, the reform message.

These differences suggest that respondents' belief about how the government operates condition their political responsiveness. People who believe that government officials have a strong intention to extract payments from their company are also much more desirous of political benefits. It is not hard to make the interpretation that their political ambitions are driven by a desire to mitigate the risk that rogue bureaucrats pose to their firm.

It is important to note that for both Figure 5.9 and Figure 5.10 the combined samples were used. These patterns are clear even when combining results from different countries with different political-economic institutions, suggesting that these patterns apply to companies in similar settings within countries. While there is substantial diversity and still much we do not know about what drives corporate political participation in developing countries, it is also clear that access to political relationships to protect rents and the firm from government-sanctioned expropriation is a powerful motive for many companies.

Finally, we can also consider the country intercepts from these models. As mentioned in the previous chapter, a country intercept indicates the residual level of political interest above and beyond the particular type of rent or institution offered. In other words, this comparison allows us to say to what extent there appears to be heightened interest in political activities in a given country. As can be seen, Figure 5.11 shows that Egyptian companies in both the first and second samples show a significantly larger interest in any type of political action on behalf of their companies. Tunisia is the baseline signified by

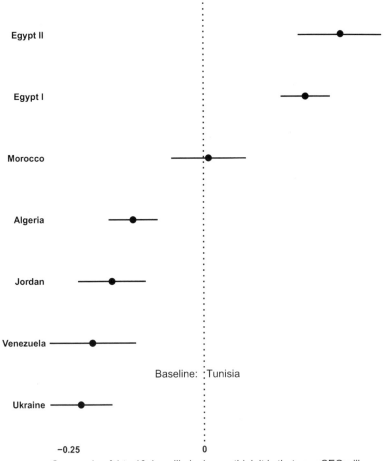

FIGURE 5.11 Country-level intercepts across all three experimental outcomes

5.5 Conclusion

a dotted line, so estimates above that line indicate interest in political action higher than Tunisian companies. The estimates indicate that Egyptian companies are about one-third of a standard deviation higher in their political interest than companies in Tunisia, and the difference grows larger from the Egypt I to Egypt II samples.

In international perspective, the level of political interest in Tunisia does not seem particularly low, only lower than in Egypt. Respondents in Venezuela and Ukraine are significantly less likely to be interested in political action of all types. Another way of framing this result would be to think about the difference between demand and supply of political opportunities. In Egypt, demand for corporate political activity probably exceeds supply, whereas in Venezuela and Ukraine, companies are much more accepting of the current level of political involvement. This could be because companies see less to gain from political action – which could be true in the relatively democratic Ukraine – or because they do not believe the government can provide any assistance, which could be true in dysfunctional Venezuela.

The result for Venezuela is fascinating in its own right given the importance of the military to Nicolas Maduro's coalition and the fact that the data were collected in the spring and summer of 2020. Companies in Venezuela would prefer to avoid connection to the military despite its prominence in the country. The inclusion of Venezuela shows that the presence of a ruling military is not necessarily a sufficient condition for companies to concentrate their political activities on the military as an actor. Unfortunately, given other factors which differ in the Venezuelan case such as state weakness and overall economic collapse, it is difficult to know whether this result is due to weaker political and economic control by the military in Venezuela or because the economy has worsened to the point that businesses see little value in playing along with the military when their own companies are facing devastation. At some point, control over rents may not matter if the rents lose their value.

5.5 CONCLUSION

The results in this chapter provide helpful context about the applicability of the theories outside of Egypt and Tunisia. While more research can always be done, it would appear that there are similar patterns in terms of how companies interact with states, particularly within the Arab Middle East. Arab countries tend to have a more pronounced presence of the military in the economy and tend to be more responsive to the military when presented as an option via experimental treatments. In addition, responsiveness to the military appears to correlate with the presence of the military within the economy. Algeria and Jordan are the two countries that stand out for the presence of a military-clientelist complex and political responsiveness to the military, though not to the same extent as Egypt.

168   *5 Crony Capitalism in International Comparison*

Another intriguing result is that increases in bribe payments over the past five years (or since the Arab Spring) appear to be strongly associated with increased political activity in the present. This finding is important as it does not simply measure an association in the present, such as between companies that are larger or more profitable. Rather, it measures a changing factor within individual companies – whether their access to government officials has improved or decreased over the past five years. It is clear that for many companies, political action is a way to substitute for a loss of access. As their political condition worsens, political action becomes more necessary to regain their political connections. Political connections are not a static feature of companies, but are rather a contested asset that is vulnerable to the winds of political change and the opportunities provided by the political system.

At the same time, there is still considerable ambiguity about the extent to which other institutions may play a gatekeeper role similar to the Egyptian military. There was no particular actor that stood out in the country surveys that all companies seemed to be interested in. This association suggests, as this book argues, that the success of a gatekeeper is likely to be ephemeral, especially in states with weak state institutions and control over bureaucrats. Corruption undermines incentives and norms that make bureaucrats follow a particular actor or leader, leading to decentralized rent distribution networks.

6

Conclusion

After reviewing the trajectories of emerging democracies in Egypt and Tunisia, it is tempting to conclude that democratization in crony capitalist regimes is virtually impossible. While this book has explored the many ways that corporations can hold significant influence during transitions, I do still believe that these challenges are surmountable. However, the window for democratization to result in lasting change to elite relationships must occur in the early years of the democratic transition, or risk entrenching business influence. Successful democratization requires not only sustaining popular belief in democracy, but also disrupting the elite relationships that underpinned the functioning of the prior autocracy.

These relationships may be difficult to unravel in part because democratization may take the form of a "pacted" transition that preserves the prerogatives of those elites willing to support democracy (O'Donnell and Schmitter 1986). Elements of this type of political thinking existed in both Egypt and Tunisia. On the Egyptian side, the military aggressively promoted itself as a neutral arbiter of the democratic transition, proclaiming its alliance with the protesters and pushing Mubarak out. Tunisia, by contrast, did not have a regime player with as much clout, but the cautious attitude adopted by Ennahda, the largest preexisting opposition party, helped preserve elite privileges at critical moments, such as their ill-fated sponsorship of the economic reconciliation law.

Companies and government institutions with corrupt ties rarely want these to be exposed, and it is difficult for relatively uninformed citizens to know who is corrupt and why, even if the system is clearly elite biased. Few Egyptians likely knew the full extent of the military's economic holdings and the way that the military would come to dominate government contracting and lucrative sectors. Similarly, Tunisians had relatively little objective information to know which of the country's economic elite were responsible for the anemic level of economic growth and corrupt government contracting. The explosion of the Tunisian civil society sector undoubtedly helped, but the best new NGOs

170   *6 Conclusion*

largely centered their work in the capital, Tunis, limiting their outreach to the country as a whole.

This information advantage accruing to companies is considerable. Politicians need funding in order to launch parties and reach the electorate; corporations are willing to foot the bill if they can preserve existing relationships. Even stalwart reformers may see some utility in doing a deal with the devil in exchange for the chance to gain power. Tunisia's Nahda calculated that appeasing elite actors would stabilize democracy in the short run, permitting them to push for further democratization in the long run. Problematically, their base did not see that trade-off as nearly as important, leading to Nahda's poor showing – approximately 20 percent of total votes – in the 2019 parliamentary and presidential elections. Corruption is easy to justify by political elites who have bigger problems on their agenda, such as preventing a reversion to autocracy.

For this reason, the key scope condition for crony capitalism to survive post-transition is for redistribution to have its limits. In both Egypt and Tunisia, legal accountability initiatives received widespread approval and notable prosecutions. In too many cases, though, accountability stopped with "brand-name" corruption rather than investigating the mechanisms through which businesspeople could obtain and build their influence. As a result, anti-corruption initiatives lost their power and instead became a tool to use to punish political opponents.

This dynamic helped undergird rising authoritarianism in both Egypt and Tunisia. Al-Sisi railed against corruption from the Muslim Brotherhood, while more recently, the populist Qais Saied has raised the same questions about the country's democratic politicians, most especially Nahda. If citizens believe that the regime is corrupt, but do not have a clear idea what reforms to adopt or who to blame for the corruption, then anti-corruption can become a grievance to be aired against any convenient political opponent.

In theory, civil society would serve its function by educating the population about how to hold the government accountable and see through the self-serving claims of politicians. In practice, the revival of NGOs in both countries held great promise but never materialized into reform movements with political heft. In Egypt, the military-backed regime moved quickly to cut off NGOs from foreign funds, imprisoning some well-known leaders of organizations for their ostensible ties to unsavory foreign elements.[1] As such, it could well be that civil society offers at least part of the answer, if it were widely mobilized and immunized from government interference, both relatively strong assumptions.

With the aim of encouraging a more robust framework for understanding how corrupt capitalism can affect regime transitions, I summarize my book's lessons into two main points:

---

[1] See www.movedemocracy.org/egypt-targets-civil-society-leader-esraa-abdelfattah-under-case-173.

6.1 *Corruption and Democracy*

1. Corruption survives regime transitions to democracy because businesspeople remain indispensable to nascent political parties.
2. Institutional actors who can maintain control over the provision of rents following a regime transition can very quickly build a coalition for or against regime change.

I detail these lessons below before returning to the main question of this chapter: how to encourage democratic transitions free from corrupt influence?

6.1 CORRUPTION AND DEMOCRACY

Research in corruption in developing and developed countries shows how difficult it can be to uproot despite the several decades of activism and institutional reform aimed at removing improper influence from government decision-making (Tanzi and Davoodi 1998; Svensson 2005; Olken 2007; Gingerich 2013). My research in this book shows some pathways through which corruption can survive a momentous political transition, even when that transition is founded on ending political corruption. In both Egypt and Tunisia, popular mobilization called out for the end of corrupt deals and an opening in political regimes that would reduce the role of cronyist business. As I show in this book, it is not quite as easy to remove business influence even when political transitions grant reformers considerable power to root out corruption in their countries.

A large part of the problem is that politicians have a multidimensional task in building a new regime following a previous one. If they could fully concentrate on deciphering the sticky web of relationships between prior elites and businesspeople, along with designing new measures to prevent undue influence of business over bureaucrats, then they might be able to live up their lofty goals of completely transforming state institutions. Instead, politicians need to develop parties which were often banned under previous regimes, as well as build coalitions which are able to govern. Reforming the state bureaucracy must wait while elections are contested, foundational constitutional documents are drafted, and control is re-exerted following the chaos of popular mobilization against authoritarianism. In both Egypt and Tunisia, efforts to corral corrupt businesspeople resulted in some high-profile cases against well-known business elites, but the underlying nature of relationships between business and bureaucrats remain unchanged. Indeed, as my survey data showed, businesspeople in both countries reported an increase rather than a decrease in bribe payments they had to make to bureaucrats in order to receive needed services in a timely manner. The players in charge of corruption changed, but the game itself did not.

Actually removing business influence would require considerable administrative capacity merely to document exactly how cronyism affected the decisions of bureaucrats from state contracts to simple regulatory procedures.

172   6 *Conclusion*

Tunisia's transitional reconciliation commission spent years investigating corruption, only to have its wings clipped once it finally moved toward releasing the details of the allegations. After the democratic transition, a clock began ticking as businesspeople worked to ingratiate themselves with incoming politicians, who as I mentioned previously, have a number of tasks which they must accomplish besides removing corruption. Alliances with those who benefited from the prior regime may be personally distasteful, but losing one's seat in the transitional parliament would be a far greater cost. Potential political leaders could gain the moral high ground yet lose in a chaotic election with poorly informed voters and a skewed media landscape.

As such, in Tunisia conditions for businesspeople returned to relative stability within the time frame they predicted during the immediate post-revolutionary period: about three to five years. By then, businesspeople had established themselves both as members of parliament and as crucial partners for parties seeking funds for the ever-increasing demands of open electoral competition. While we may never know exactly who benefited the most from the increased variety of political partners, it is clear that for the big conglomerates who survived Ben Ali's downfall, the democratic transition may have created as many new opportunities as it closed off long-standing relationships. While Egypt's democracy aborted early due to the military coup, we can theorize that its democracy would have taken a similar path as the Muslim Brotherhood likewise had to adjust to the rigors of governing, permitting relationships with businesspeople to undercut transparency and pro-competition initiatives.

6.2   RENTS ARE THE KEY TO POWER

It is very common to believe that a regime transition entails a complete change in the nature and character of a state – but quite usually, except in the case of revolutions that might decapitate the state (Skocpol 1979), it does not. As is well known, many democratic transitions today happen in countries that tend to be poorer and where particular patterns of development encourage crony capitalism, corruption and closed markets to endure (Levitsky and Way 2010). In these countries, access to rents, which are usually dispersed through informal client–patron relationships, are a powerful inducement for elites to support a given political side (Gehlbach and Keefer 2011; Marinov and Goemans 2014). As such, one of the key questions in any regime transition is who captures the provision of rents – if anyone at all. If an institutional actor can gain such a monopoly, as occurred in Egypt, then that actor is likely to be able to do what few other post-transition political groups can: compel support from businesspeople and any other elites whose livelihood depends on access to these state-sanctioned privileges.

Extrapolating from this theory requires further thought about what the conditions are for such institutions to emerge. It is not accidental, in my opinion, that the military came to be the dominant institution in Egypt. As analyzed in

6.3 A Perfect Transition Will Never Happen

this book, there are other countries that have powerful and economically entangled militaries (Izadi 2022). It seems quite natural that an institution with the de jure control over the use of force would also create increasingly large zones of economic privilege, employing the threat of violence as a way to secure its own property rights (North, Wallis, and Weingast 2009). Indeed, the history of economic development is closely tied to the growth of military technology and sophistication (Tilly 1992).

As such, it seems quite likely that the weaker a country's institutions, the more possible it is for the military to carve out a wider role for itself in economic production. What is more of an open question is why some militaries might be more predisposed to economic involvement relative to others even if their political influence is (supposedly) identical (Springborg 2011). In this book, I examine long-term determinants of the military's dominant economic and military position in Egypt, which stretch back to the country's early post-independence political climate. It would seem all but inevitable that once a military is given any type of rule over a state that it would inevitably start to build its own economic interests.

It could be, for that reason, that an intermediating variable in the presence and scope of the military's economic activities is war-making. Migdal (1988) classic work on post-independence Egypt describes how the threat of Israeli aggression led to increased military economic production, though it did not result in a functional defense establishment but rather increasing indebtedness to foreign lenders like the Soviet Union. It is quite possible that these external threats create opportunities for militaries to rationalize their economic expansion, which over time morphs into seemingly unassailable economic privileges.

However, I conclude this section by noting that this type of research is still in its infancy, if it exists at all. Understanding the institutions that will matter the most for the provision of rents at the time of a regime transition is important yet also a difficult measurement problem to resolve. Authoritarian countries do not often release the kind of data necessary to measure connections between business and the state, and the chaotic post-transition environment is not always conducive to exhaustive data collection. However, I believe that social science will progress in this area as we become both more thoughtful and more intentional in focusing on the provision of state-sanctioned subsidies to companies as a critical variable in the nature of regime politics following a transition.

6.3 A PERFECT TRANSITION WILL NEVER HAPPEN

While this book focuses on states where crony capitalism is an ever-present problem, the idea of a corrupt-free state is a Weberian ideal type, not a lived reality. Businesspeople maintain high levels of influence even in established democracies. Similarly, no democratic transition ever went according

174   6 Conclusion

to plan. With those caveats, I believe that the best opportunity to implement
democratization in these types of states is to focus on what rents exist and who
controls them. A political transition is incomplete if control over valuable rents
is not directly under the control of democratic government.

Classical liberal thinking has for a long time argued that rents must be
removed from a political system entirely, reducing any possible connection
between the government and business. However, as many have pointed out, the
"shrink the state" school has not performed well in regions like the Middle East
and North Africa (Sfakianakis 2004). Cutting down the size of government and
privatizing state-owned enterprises can result in a rapacious economic elite who
can capture rents for private interests that were previously used for public ends.
The "private sector" as a strictly separated world does not often exist, and
instead former or even current bureaucrats and politicians can create for-profit
companies to exploit liberalizing initiatives.

Instead, what should be more of a concern is who controls the distribution
of rents. As North, Wallis, and Weingast (2009) pointed out, an intermediate
condition for the rise of an open access society is for the rules underpinning elite
privileges to be stable and widely known. Knowing the contours of political
economy in many transitional democracies would greatly assist with identifying
the areas where institutional reforms could make a difference, even if elite bias
cannot be removed entirely. When a single actor has control over rents, any
kind of democratizing process will be conditional on that actor's support for
democratization.

Conversely, if the rent-seeking network is decentralized, then democratization might continue but only with the perpetuation of corrupt relationships.
As can be seen in Tunisia with the recent rise of Kais Saied, the illusion of
elite unity can allow crony capitalism to persist, resulting in popular disen-
chantment with democracy. The corrupt democracy will remain vulnerable to
authoritarian challengers who use its poor institutional condition to argue for
a fundamental change to the way that power is apportioned.

Making information available about the size, dispersion, and control over
important rents would not magically uncreate crony capitalism, but it could
help direct advocacy efforts and the scarce resources of civil society groups.
Increasing the quality and credibility of information about the role of special
interests, as well as effectively disseminating this information to the population, could help lower the informational advantage of influence-seeking businesspeople and encourage stronger voter responses to accountability drives.
Information on its own cannot result in political change, but when there
is substantial interest in achieving an outcome – ending corruption – then
insights can help direct political coalitions to focus on the most important
issues.

Finally, rent-seeking should not be ignored by international institutions and
governments who want to help stabilize a post-transition regime. It is tempting
to ignore rent-seeking relationships as part of status quo politics and instead

6.3 A Perfect Transition Will Never Happen

focus on the growth of parties or democratic activists. Strong parties require strong backers, and if crony businesspeople remain influential, they can undermine the independence and autonomy of the new political elite. Reforms that can change rent-seeking networks are difficult and costly, but as I argue in this book, necessary for democratization to reach its full potential.

References

"2012 Worker's Protests in Egypt." 2013. Egyptian Committee on Economic; Social Rights. http://ecesr.org/wp-content/uploads/2013/04/Protest-Movement-20122.pdf.

"32.5% Increase in Egypt's Foreign Debt: CBE." 2017. Egypt Independent. August 1, 2017. www.egyptindependent.com/cbe-32-5-increase-in-egypts-foreign-dept-in-march-2017/.

Abul-Magd, Zeinab. 2017. *Militarizing the Nation: The Army, Business, and Revolution in Egypt*. New York: Columbia University Press.

Acemoglu, Daron. 1995. "Reward Structures and the Allocation of Talent." *European Economic Review* 39 (1): 17–33. https://doi.org/10.1016/0014-2921(94)00014-Q.

Acemoglu, Daron, Tarek A. Hassan, and Ahmed Tahoun. 2017. "The Power of the Street: Evidence from Egypt's Arab Spring." *The Review of Financial Studies* 31 (1): 1–42.

Acemoglu, Daron, Simon Johnson, and James A. Robinson. 2004. "Institutions as the Fundamental Cause of Long-Run Growth." Working Paper. National Bureau of Economic Research. www.nber.org/papers/w10481.

Acemoglu, Daron, and James A. Robinson. 2006. *Economic Origins of Dictatorship and Democracy*. Cambridge, UK: Cambridge University Press.

Acemoglu, Daron, and James A. Robinson. 2008. "Persistence of Power, Elites, and Institutions." *American Economic Review* 98 (1): 267–93.

Adly, Amr. 2013. *State Reform and Development in the Middle East: Turkey and Egypt in the Post-Liberalization Era*. London, UK: Palgrave Macmillan.

2017. "Too Big to Fail: Egypt's Large Enterprises After the 2011 Uprising." Paper. Carnegie Middle East Center. http://carnegie-mec.org/2017/03/02/too-big-to-fail-egypt-s-large-enterprises-after-2011-uprising-pub-68154.

2020. *Cleft Capitalism: The Social Origins of Failed Market Making in Egypt*. Redwood City, CA: Stanford University Press.

Albertus, Michael, and Victor Menaldo. 2014. "Gaming Democracy: Elite Dominance During Transition and the Prospects for Redistribution." *British Journal of Political Science* 44 (3): 575–603.

2018. *Authoritarianism and the Elite Origins of Democracy.* Cambridge, UK: Cambridge University Press.

Albrecht, Holger, and Dina Bishara. 2011. "Back on Horseback: The Military and Political Transformation in Egypt." *Middle East Law and Governance* 3: 13–23.

Allani, Alaya. 2013. "The Post-Revolution Tunisian Constituent Assembly: Controversy over Powers and Prerogatives." *The Journal of North African Studies* 18 (1): 131–40.

Almond, Gabriel A. 1991. "Capitalism and Democracy." *PS: Political Science and Politics* 24 (3): 467–74.

Alptekin, Aynur, and Paul Levine. 2012. "Military Expenditure and Economic Growth: A Meta-Analysis." *European Journal of Political Economy* 28 (4): 636–50.

al-Sayyid, Mustafa Kamal. 2013. "What Went Wrong with Mubarak's Regime?" In *Egypt's Tahrir Revolution*, edited by Dan Tschirgi, Walid Kazziha, and Sean F. McMahon, 11–28. Boulder, CO: Lynne Rienner Publishers.

Amorós, José Ernesto, Luciano Ciravegna, Vesna Mandakovic, and Pekka Stenholm. 2019. "Necessity or Opportunity? The Effects of State Fragility and Economic Development on Entrepreneurial Efforts." *Entrepreneurship Theory and Practice* 43 (4): 725–50. https://doi.org/10.1177/1042258717736857.

Ansani, Andrea, and Vittorio Daniele. 2012. "About a Revolution: The Economic Motivations of the Arab Spring." *International Journal of Development and Conflict* 2 (3). www.worldscientific.com/doi/abs/10.1142/S2010269012500135.

Ansell, Ben W., and David J. Samuels. 2014. *Inequality and Democratization: An Elite-Competition Approach.* Cambridge, UK: Cambridge University Press.

"ARP Approves Law on Banks and Financial Institutions, Again; Opposition Walks Out, Again." 2016. Tunisia-TN. June 9, 2016. http://tunisia-tn.com/arp-approves-law-on-banks-and-financial-institutions-again-opposition-walks-out-again/.

Arriola, Leonardo. 2012. *Multiethnic Coalitions in Africa: Business Financing of Opposition Election Campaigns.* Cambridge, UK: Cambridge University Press.

2013. "Capital and Opposition in Africa: Coalition Building in Multiethnic Societies." *World Politics* 65 (2): 233–72. https://doi.org/10.1017/S0043887113000051.

"As Austerity Pummels Egypt's Importers, Dollar Resources Grow." 2017. *Reuters.* August 3, 2017. www.reuters.com/article/egypt-economy-idUSL4N1KO51X.

Ashford, Douglas E. 1965. "Neo-Destour Leadership and the 'Confiscated Revolution'." *World Politics* 17 (2): 215–31.

Aspinall, Edward. 2014. "When Brokers Betray: Clientelism, Social Networks, and Electoral Politics in Indonesia." *Critical Asian Studies* 46 (4): 545–70.

Attalah, Lina, and Mohamed Hamama. 2016. "The Armed Forces and Business: Economic Expansion in the Last 12 Months." Mada Masr. September 9, 2016. www.madamasr.com/en/2016/09/09/feature/economy/the-armed-forces-and-business-economic-expansion-in-the-last-12-months/.

Autio, Erkko, and Kun Fu. 2015. "Economic and Political Institutions and Entry into Formal and Informal Entrepreneurship." *Asia Pacific Journal of Management* 32 (1): 67–94. https://doi.org/10.1007/s10490-014-9381-0.

Aziz, Sahar F. 2017. "Military Electoral Authoritarianism in Egypt." *Election Law Journal* 16 (2): 280–95.

Barnett, Michael. 1992. *Confronting the Costs of War.* Princeton, NJ: Princeton University Press.

References

Başkan, Filiz. 2010. "The Rising Islamic Business Elite and Democratization in Turkey." *Journal of Balkan and Near Eastern Studies* 12 (4): 399–416. https://doi.org/10.1080/19448953.2010.531207.

Bates, Robert H. 1981. *Markets and States in Tropical Africa: The Political Basis of Agricultural Policies*. Oakland, CA: University of California Press.

Batjargal, Bat, Michael A. Hitt, Anne S. Tsui, Jean-Luc Arregle, Justin W. Webb, and Toyah L. Miller. 2012. "Institutional Polycentrism, Entrepreneurs' Social Networks, and New Venture Growth." *Academy of Management Journal* 56 (4): 1024–49. https://doi.org/10.5465/amj.2010.0095.

Bechri, Mohamed Z., and Sonia Naccache. 2006. "The Political Economy of Development Policy in Tunisia." In *Contributions to Economic Analysis*, edited by B. Baltagi and E. Sadka, 278:307–34. Bingley, UK: Emerald Publishing Ltd.

Bellin, Eva. 2002. *Stalled Democracy : Capital, Labor, and the Paradox of State-Sponsored Development*. Ithaca, NY: Cornell University Press.

2004. "The Robustness of Authoritarianism in the Middle East: Exceptionalism in Comparative Perspective." *Comparative Politics* 36 (2): 139–57.

Bennett, Andrew, and Jeffrey T. Checkel. 2014. "Introduction." In *Process Tracing: From Metaphor to Analytic Tool*, edited by Andrew Bennett and Jeffrey T. Checkel, 3–38. Cambridge, UK: Cambridge University Press.

Benoit-Lavelle, Mischa. 2016. "Tunisia's Celebrated Labor Union Is Holding the Country Back." *Foreign Policy*, July. http://foreignpolicy.com/2016/07/20/tunisias-celebrated-labor-union-is-holding-the-country-back/.

Besley, Timothy, and Torsten Persson. 2009. "The Origins of State Capacity:property Rights, Taxation, and Politics." *American Economic Review* 99 (4): 1218–44.

Bhandari, Abhit. 2021. "Political Determinants of Economic Exchange: Evidence from a Business Experiment in Senegal." *American Journal of Political Science* 66 (4): 835–52. https://doi.org/10.1111/ajps.12593.

Bhattacharya, Rina, and Hirut Wolde. 2010. "Constraints on Trade in the MENA Region." Rochester, NY. https://papers.ssrn.com/abstract=1555483.

Biezen, Ingrid van, and Petr Kopecký. 2001. "On the Predominance of State Money: Reassessing Party Financing in the New Democracies of Southern and Eastern Europe." *Perspectives on European Politics and Society* 2 (3): 401–29. https://doi.org/10.1080/1570585018458770.

Blackman, Alexandra. 2020. "The Politicization of Faith: Colonialism, Education, and Political Identity in Tunisia." PhD thesis, Stanford University.

Blau, Benjamin M., Tyley J. Brough, and Diana W. Thomas. 2013. "Corporate Lobbying, Political Connections, and the Bailout of Banks." *Journal of Banking & Finance* 37 (8): 3007–17.

Blaydes, Lisa. 2011. *Elections and Distributive Politics in Mubarak's Egypt*. Cambridge, UK: Cambridge University Press.

Boas, Taylor C., Dino P. Christenson, and David M. Glick. 2020. "Recruiting Large Online Samples in the United States and India: Facebook, Mechanical Turk, and Qualtrics." *Political Science Research and Methods* 8 (2).

Boix, Carles. 2003. *Democracy and Redistribution*. Cambridge, UK: Cambridge University Press.

Boix, Carles, M. Miller, and S. Rosato. 2013. "A Complete Data Set of Political Regimes, 1800-2007." *Comparative Political Studies* 46 (12): 1523–54.

Boix, Carles, and Susan Carol Stokes. 2003. "Endogenous Democratization." *World Politics* 55 (4): 517–49.

Boubekeur, Amel. 2013. "Rolling Either Way? Algerian Entrepreneurs as Both Agents of Change and Means of Preservation of the System." *Journal of North African Studies* 18 (3): 469–81.

Boudreaux, Christopher J., Boris N. Nikolaev, and Randall G. Holcombe. 2018. "Corruption and Destructive Entrepreneurship." *Small Business Economics* 51 (1): 181–202. https://doi.org/10.1007/s11187-017-9927-x.

Brooke, Steven. 2017. "Sectarianism and Social Conformity: Evidence from Egypt." *Political Research Quarterly* 70 (4).

Brownlee, Jason. 2002. "... and yet They Persist: Explaining Survival and Transition in Neopatrimonial Regimes." *Studies in Comparative International Development* 37 (3): 35–63.

——— 2007. *Authoritarianism in an Age of Democratization*. Cambridge, UK: Cambridge University Press.

Cammett, Melani. 2007. *Globalization and Business Politics in North Africa: A Comparative Perspective*. Cambridge, UK: Cambridge University Press.

Cammett, Melani, and Ishac Diwan. 2013. *The Political Economy of the Arab Uprisings*. Boulder, CO: Westview Press.

Cammett, Melani, Ishac Diwan, Alan Richards, and John Waterbury. 2015. *A Political Economy of the Middle East*. Oxfordshire, UK: Routledge.

Canen, Nathan, and Leonard Wantchekon. 2022. "Political Distortions, State Capture, and Economic Development in Africa." *Journal of Economic Perspectives* 36 (1). https://doi.org/10.1257/jep.36.1.101.

Cassarino, Jean-Pierre. 2004. "Participatory Development and Liberal Reforms in Tunisia: The Gradual Incorporation of Some Economic Networks." In *Networks of Privilege in the Middle East: The Politics of Economic Reform Revisited*, edited by Steven Heydemann, 223–42. New York: Palgrave Macmillan. https://doi.org/10.1057/9781403982148_8.

"Chafik Jarraya Revient Sur La Scène Avec Une Nouvelle Polémique." 2016. Huffington Post Maghreb. www.huffpostmaghreb.com/2016/05/10/chafik-jarraya-tunisie_n_9890182.html?ir=Maghreb&ncid=tweetlnkfrhpmg00000007.

Chaisty, Paul, and Stephen Whitefield. 2018. "Critical Election or Frozen Cleavages? How Voters Chose Parties in the 2014 Ukrainian Parliamentary Election." *Electoral Studies* 56 (December): 158–69. https://doi.org/10.1016/j.electstud.2018.08.009.

Chambers, Paul, and Napisa Waitoolkiat, eds. 2017. *Khaki Capital: The Political Economy of the Military in Southeast Asia*. Copenhagen, Denmark: Nordic Institute of Asian Studies.

Cheeseman, Nic. 2010. "Power-Sharing in Comparative Perspective: The Dynamics of Unity Government in Kenya and Zimbabwe." *Journal of Modern Africa Studies* 48 (2): 203–29.

Chomiak, Laryssa. 2011. "The Making of a Revolution in Tunisia." *Middle East Law and Governance* 3: 68–83.

——— 2014. "Architecture of Resistance in Tunisia." In *Taking to the Streets: The Transformatin of Arab Activism*, edited by Lina Khatib and Ellen Lust, 22–51. Baltimore, MD: John Hopkins University Press.

References 181

Claessens, Stijn, Erik Feijen, and Luc Laeven. 2008. "Political Connections and the Preferential Access to Finance: The Role of Campaign Contributions." *Journal of Financial Economics* 88: 554–80.

Cohen, Norma. 2011. "Egypt and Libya: Capital Takes Flight." *Financial Times*, September. http://blogs.ft.com/beyond-brics/2011/09/18/egypt-and-libya-capital-flight-up/.

"Constitution of the Tunisian Republic." 2014. Translation. Jasmine Foundation. www.jasmine-foundation.org/doc/unofficial_english_translation_of_tunisian_cons titution_final_ed.pdf.

Cook, Steven A. 2007. *Ruling but Not Governing: The Military and Political Development in Egypt, Algeria and Turkey*. Baltimore, MD: John Hopkins University Press.

Coppock, Alex. 2019. "Generalizing from Survey Experiments Conducted on Mechanical Turk: A Replication Approach." *Political Science Research and Methods* 7 (3): 61.

Corrales, Javier. 2020. "Democratic Backsliding through Electoral Irregularities: The Case of Venezuela." *European Review of Latin American and Caribbean Studies / Revista Europea de Estudios Latinoamericanos y Del Caribe*, no. 109: 41–65. www.jstor.org/stable/26936902.

"Crowds in Cairo Praise Morsi's Army Overhaul." 2012. *Aljazeera*, August. www.aljazeera.com/news/middleeast/2012/08/201281215511142445.html.

Daadaoui, Mohamed. 2010. "Rituals of Power and Political Parties in Morocco: Limited Elections as Positional Strategies." *Middle Eastern Studies* 46 (2): 195–219. https://doi.org/10.1080/00263201003612872.

Dahl, Robert A. 1971. *Polyarchy: Participation and Opposition*. Vol. 54. New Haven, CT: Yale University Press.

Dal Bó, Ernesto, Pedro Dal Bó, and Rafael Di Tella. 2006. "'Plata o Plomo?': Bribe and Punishment in a Theory of Political Influencea." *American Political Science Review* 100 (1): 41–53.

Dejoui, Nadia. 2017. "Imed Trabeli Comme Tèmoin." *L'Economiste Maghrébin*, May. www.leconomistemaghrebin.com/2017/05/20/imed-trabelsi-systeme-de-corruptionna-change-temps-de-ben-ali-aujourdhui/.

Diwan, Ishac, and Jamal Ibrahim Haidar. 2021. "Political Connections Reduce Job Creation: Firm-Level Evidence from Lebanon." *The Journal of Development Studies* 57 (8): 1373–96. https://doi.org/10.1080/00220388.2020.1849622.

Diwan, Ishac, Philip Keefer, and Marc Schiffbauer. 2015. "Pyramid Capitalism: Political Connections, Regulation, and Firm Productivity in Egypt." Policy Research Working Paper 7354. The World Bank. https://openknowledge.worldbank.org/handle/10986/22236.

Dixit, Avinash. 2002. "Incentives and Organizations in the Public Sector: An Interpretative Review." *The Journal of Human Resources* 37 (4): 696–727.

Djankov, Simeon, Rafael La Porta, Florencio Lopez-de-Silanes, and Andrei Shleifer. 2002. "The Regulation of Entry." *The Quarterly Journal of Economics* 117 (1): 1–37. https://doi.org/10.1162/003355302753399436.

Dunne, J. Paul, and Nan Tian. 2013. "Military Expenditure and Economic Growth: A Survey." *The Economics of Peace and Security* 8 (1): 5–11.

Dunne, Michelle, and Amr Hamzawy. 2008. "The Ups and Downs of Political Reform in Egypt." In *Beyond the Facade: Political Reform in the Arab World*, edited by

Marina Ottaway and Julia Chouair-Vizoso, 17–43. Washington, DC: Carnegie Endowment for International Peace.

Earle, John S., and Scott Gehlbach. 2015. "The Productivity Consequences of Political Turnover: Firm-Level Evidence from Ukraine's Orange Revolution." *American Journal of Political Science* 59 (3): 708–23.

Egorov, Georgy, and Konstantin Sonin. 2011. "Dictators and Their Viziers: Endogenizing the Loyalty-Competence Trade-Off." *Journal of the European Economic Association* 9 (5): 903–30.

"Egypt – Human Development Report 1995." 1995. United Nations Development Programme. www.arab-hdr.org/reports/nationalarab.aspx?cid=5.

"Egypt Reserves Reach Record High of over \$36 Billion." 2017. *The Washington Post.* August 1, 2017. www.washingtonpost.com/world/middle_east/egypt-reserves-reached-36-billion-highest-in-7-years/2017/08/01/61b293b0-76c5-11e7-8c17-533 c52b2f014_story.html?utm_term=.9f0636e210d8.

"Egypt Sees Value-Added Tax Revenue up by 8 Billion Pounds in 2017–2018." 2017. *Reuters.* March 28, 2017. http://af.reuters.com/article/commoditiesNews/idAFL5N1H5162.

"Egypt Sets \$18 Billion for Subsidies in FY 2017–2018 Budget." 2017. *Reuters.* June 5, 2017. www.reuters.com/article/us-egypt-economy-subsidies-idUSKBN18W2FX.

"Egypt Tightens Eligibility for Food Subsidy Cards." 2017. *Reuters.* August 8, 2017. www.reuters.com/article/us-egypt-economy-subsidies-idUSKBN1AO134.

"Egypt Unemployment Rate Eases to 12 Percent in Q1 2017." 2017. *Reuters.* May 17, 2017. http://af.reuters.com/article/africaTech/idAFKCN18B163-OZABS.

"Egypt: New Constitution Mixed on Support of Rights." 2012. *Human Rights Watch.* www.hrw.org/news/2012/11/30/egypt-new-constitution-mixed-support-rights.

Eibl, Ferdinand. 2020. *Social Dictatorships: The Political Economy of the Welfare State in the Middle East and North Africa.* Oxford, UK: Oxford University Press.

El-Khawas, Mohamed A. 2012. "Tunisia's Jasmine Revolution: Causes and Impact." *Mediterranean Quarterly* 23 (4): 1–23.

Elshami, Nancy. 2011. "Internal April 6 Dynamics, Egyptian Politics, and Outlooks for the Future: An Interview with Ahmed Maher." *Jadaliyya.* December 7, 2011. www.jadaliyya.com/pages/index/3429/internal-april-6-dynamics-egyptian-politics-and-ou.

Elster, Jon. 1994. "The Nature and Scope of Rational-Choice Explanation." In *Readings in the Philosophy of Social Science*, edited by Michael Martin and Lee C. McIntyre, 311–22. Boston, MA: Massachusetts Institute of Technology.

El-Tablawy, Tarek, and Abdel Latif Wahba. 2017. "Egypt Reels from Second Price Hike in a Week as Power Subsidy Cut." *Bloomberg Politics.* July 6, 2017. www.bloomberg.com/news/articles/2017-07-06/egypt-reels-from-second-price-hike-in-week-as-power-subsidy-cut.

Evans, Peter. 1995. *Embedded Autonomy: States and Industrial Transformation.* Princeton, NJ: Princeton University Press.

Evans, Peter B. 1989. "Predatory, Developmental, and Other Apparatuses: A Comparative Political Economy Perspective on the Third World State." *Sociological Forum* 4 (4): 561–87. http://link.springer.com/article/10.1007/BF01115064.

Evans, Peter, and James E. Rauch. 1999. "Bureaucracy and Growth: A Cross-National Analysis of the Effects of 'Weberian' State Structures on Economic Growth." *American Sociological Review* 64 (5): 748–65.

References

Faccio, Mara. 2006. "Politically Connected Firms." *American Economic Review* 96 (1): 369–86.

2010. "Differences between Politically Connected and Nonconnected Firms: A Cross-Country Analysis." *Financial Management* 39 (3): 905–27.

Fahmy, Omar, and Lin Noueihed. 2015. "Egypt Loyalists Take the Lead in Parliament Elections." *Reuters*. October 21, 2015. www.reuters.com/article/us-egypt-election-outcome-idUSKCN0SF2OS20151021.

Faiola, Anthony. 2011. "Egypt's Labor Movement Blooms in the Arab Spring." *The Washington Post*, September. www.washingtonpost.com/world/middle-east/egypts-labor-movement-blooms-in-arab-spring/2011/09/25/gIQAj6AfwK_story.html.

Fairfield, Tasha. 2015. *Private Wealth and Public Revenue in Latin America: Business Power and Tax Politics*. Cambridge, UK: Cambridge University Press.

Farah, Nadia Ramsis. 2013. "The Political Economy of Egypt's Revolution." In *Egypt's Tahrir Revolution*, edited by Dan Tschirgi, Walid Kazziha, and Sean F. McMahon, 47–66. Boulder, CO: Lynne Rienner Publishers.

Fisman, Raymond. 2001. "Estimating the Value of Political Connections." *The American Economic Review* 91 (4): 1095–1102.

Fox, Richard L., and Jennifer L. Lawless. 2005. "To Run or Not to Run for Office: Explaining Nascent Political Ambition." *American Journal of Political Science* 49 (3): 642–59.

Frye, Timothy. 2017. *Property Rights and Property Wrongs: How Power, Institutions, and Norms Shape Economic Conflict in Russia*. Cambridge, UK: Cambridge University Press.

Gailmard, Sean, and John W Patty. 2007. "Slackers and Zealots: Civil Service, Policy Discretion, and Bureaucratic Expertise." *American Journal of Political Science* 51 (4): 873–89.

Gandhi, Jennifer, and Ellen Lust-Okar. 2009. "Elections under Authoritarianism." *Annual Review of Political Science* 12 (1): 403–22. https://doi.org/10.1146/annurev.polisci.11.060106.095434.

Ge, Jianhua, Michael Carney, and Franz Kellermanns. 2019. "Who Fills Institutional Voids? Entrepreneurs' Utilization of Political and Family Ties in Emerging Markets." *Entrepreneurship Theory and Practice* 43 (6): 1124–47. https://doi.org/10.1177/1042258718773175.

Geddes, Barbara. 1999. "What Do We Know About Democratization after Twenty Years?" *Annual Review of Political Science* 2 (1): 115–44.

Geddes, Barbara, Joseph Wright, and Erica Frantz. 2014. "Autocratic Breakdown and Regime Transitions: A New Data Set." *Perspectives on Politics* 12 (2): 313–31.

Gehlbach, Scott, and Philip Keefer. 2011. "Investment without Democracy: Ruling-Party Institutionalization and Credible Commitment in Autocracies." *Journal of Comparative Economics* 39 (2): 123–39.

Gehlbach, Scott, and Alberto Simpser. 2014. "Electoral Manipulation as Bureaucratic Control." *American Journal of Political Science* 59 (1): 212–24.

Gehlbach, Scott, Konstantin Sonin, and Ekaterina Zhuravskaya. 2010. "Businessman Candidates." *American Journal of Political Science* 54 (3): 718–36.

Gelman, Andrew. 2007. "Struggles with Survey Weighting and Regression Modeling." *Statistical Science* 22 (2): 1.

Gerschenkron, Alexander. 1962. *Economic Backwardness in Historical Perspective: A Book of Essays*. Cambridge, MA: Belknap Press of Harvard University Press.

Gingerich, Daniel W. 2013. *Political Institutions and Party-Directed Corruption in South America: Stealing for the Team.* Cambridge, UK: Cambridge University Press.

Goel, Rajeev K., and James W. Saunoris. 2014. "Military versus Non-Military Government Spending and the Shadow Economy." *Economic Systems* 38 (3): 350–59.

Gohar, Nihad. 2008. "Mapping Participation in Egypt." In *Political Participation in the Middle East,* edited by Ellen Lust-Okar and Saloua Zerhouni, 171–91. Boulder, CO: Lynne Rienner Publishers.

Golkar, Saied. 2012. "The Paramilitarization of the Economy: The Case of Iran's Basij Militia." *Armed Forces and Society* 38 (4): 625–48.

Greenwood, Scott. 2008. "Bad for Business?: Entrepreneurs and Democracy in the Arab World." *Comparative Political Studies* 41 (6): 837–60. https://doi.org/10.1177/0010414007300123.

Grewal, Sharan. 2016. "A Quiet Revolution: The Tunisian Military after Ben Ali." *Carnegie Middle East Center.* http://carnegie-mec.org/2016/02/24/quiet-revolution-tunisian-military-after-ben-ali/iucy.

2020. "Tunisia's Foiled Coup of 1987: The November 8th Group." *The Middle East Journal* 74 (1): 53–71. https://doi.org/10.3751/74.1.13.

Grzymala-Busse, Anna. 2020. "Consequences of Authoritarian Party Exit and Reinvention for Democratic Competition." *Comparative Political Studies* 53 (10–11): 1704–37. https://doi.org/10.1177/0010414019897683.

Grzymala-Busse, Anna M. 2019. "Hoist on Their Own Petards? The Reinvention and Collapse of Authoritarian Successor Parties." *Party Politics* 25 (4).

Haber, Stephen, Armando Razo, and Noel Maurer. 2003. *The Politics of Property Rights: Political Instability, Credible Commitments, and Economic Growth in Mexico, 1876–1929.* Cambridge, UK: Cambridge University Press.

Haddad, Bassam. 2011. *Business Networks in Syria: The Political Economy of Authoritarian Resilience.* Redwood City, CA: Stanford University Press.

Haggard, Stephan, Sylvia Maxfield, and Ben Ross Schneider. 1997. "Theories of Business and Business-State Relations." In *Business and the State in Developing Countries,* edited by Sylvia Maxfield and Ben Ross Schneider, 36–60. Ithaca, NY: Cornell University Press.

Hagopian, Frances. 2007. "Parties and Voters in Emerging Democracies." In *The Oxford Handbook of Comparative Politics,* edited by Carles Boix and Susan Carol Stokes, 582–603. New York, NY: Oxford University Press.

Hainmueller, Jens, Dominik Hangartner, and Teppei Yamamoto. 2015. "Validating Vignette and Conjoint Survey Experiments against Real-World Behavior." *Proceedings of the National Academy of Sciences of the United States of America* 112 (8): 2395–400.

Hainmueller, Jens, Daniel J. Hopkins, and Teppei Yamamoto. 2014. "Causal Inference in Conjoint Analysis: Understanding Multidimensional Choices via Stated Preference Experiments." *Political Analysis* 22 (1): 1–30.

Hajji, Noureddine, and Sami Zaoui. 2012. "Barometre 2012 Des Enterprises En Tunisie."

Halime, Farah. 2013. "Egypt's Big Businesses Feel Neglected amid Turmoil." *The New York Times.* www.nytimes.com/2013/01/31/world/middleeast/egypts-big-businesses-feel-neglected-amid-turmoil.html?_r=0.

Hammami, Mohammed Dhia. 2020. "The Historical Origins of Networked Capitalism in Tunisia." *PolNet Conference 2020.*

References

Havlik, Peter. 2014. "Economic Consequences of the Ukraine Conflict." www.econstor.eu/handle/10419/204257.

Hearst, David. 2013. "Why Saudi Arabia Is Taking a Risk by Backing the Egyptian Coup." *The Guardian.* August 20, 2013. www.theguardian.com/commentisfree/2013/aug/20/saudi-arabia-coup-egypt.

Henry, Clement M. 1996. *The Mediterranean Debt Crescent: Money and Power in Algeria, Egypt, Morocco, Tunisia and Turkey.* Gainesville, FL: University Press of Florida.

Henry, Clement Moore, and Robert Springborg. 2010. *Globalization and the Politics of Development in the Middle East.* Cambridge, UK: Cambridge University Press.

Herb, Michael. 1999. *All in the Family: Absolutism, Revolution, and Democracy in Middle Eastern Monarchies.* Albany, NY: SUNY Press.

Hertog, Steffen. 2016. "Late Populism: State Distributional Regimes and Economic Conflict After the Arab Uprisings." Memo. Project on Middle East Political Science. May 3, 2016. http://pomeps.org/2016/06/02/late-populism-state-distributional-regimes-and-economic-conflict-after-the-arab-uprisings/.

Heydemann, Steven. 2007. "Upgrading Authoritarianism in the Arab World." The Brookings Institution. www.brookings.edu/~/media/research/files/papers/2007/10/arabworld/10arabworld.pdf.

Hibou, Béatrice. 2011. *The Force of Obedience: The Political Economy of Repression in Tunisia.* Translated by Andrew Brown. Cambridge, UK: Polity Press.

Hinnebusch, Raymond. 2006. "Authoritarian Persistence, Democratization Theory and the Middle East: An Overview and Critique." *Democratization* 13 (3).

Hummel, Calla, John Gerring, and Thomas Burt. 2021. "Do Political Finance Reforms Reduce Corruption?" *British Journal of Political Science* 51 (2): 869–89.

Huntington, Samuel P. 1957. *The Soldier and the State: The Theory and Politics of Civil-Military Relations.* Cambridge, MA: Harvard University Press.

Hussein, Walaa. 2015. "Egypt's Tamarod Outlives Its Purpose." *Al-Monitor.* May 29, 2015. www.al-monitor.com/pulse/originals/2015/05/egypt-tamarod-movement-political-campaign-mubarak-sisi.html.

Husted, Bryan W. 1994. "Honor Among Thieves: A Transaction-Cost Interpretation of Corruption in Third World Countries." *Business Ethics Quarterly* 4 (1): 17–27. https://doi.org/10.2307/3857556.

Izadi, Roya. 2022. "State Security or Exploitation: A Theory of Military Involvement in the Economy." *Journal of Conflict Resolution* 66 (4): 729–54. https://doi.org/10.1177/00220027211070574.

Jamal, Amaney, and Mark Tessler. 2008. "The Democracy Barometers (Part II): Attitudes in the Arab World." *Journal of Democracy* 19 (1): 97–111. https://doi.org/10.1353/jod.2008.0004.

Johnstone, Sarah, and Jeffrey Mazo. 2011. "Global Warming and the Arab Spring." *Survival* 53 (2): 11–17. https://doi.org/10.1080/00396338.2011.571006.

Kang, David C. 2002. *Crony Capitalism: Corruption and Development in South Korea and the Philippines.* Cambridge Studies in Comparative Politics. Cambridge: Cambridge University Press. https://doi.org/10.1017/CBO9780511606175.

Ketchley, Neil. 2017. "How Egypt's Generals Used Street Protests to Stage a Coup." *Washington Post: The Monkey Cage.* July 3, 2017. www.washingtonpost.com/

news/monkey-cage/wp/2017/07/03/how-egypts-generals-used-street-protests-to-st age-a-coup/?utm_term=.co4cd44b3718.

Khalaf, Roula. 2013. "Morsi Adviser Blames IMF for Delaying Egypt $4.8b Loan Agreement." *The Financial Times.* June 9, 2013. www.ft.com/content/f2376bea-dofc-11e2-a3ea-00144feab7de.

Kim, In Song, and Dmitriy Kunisky. 2017. "Mapping Political Communities: A Statistical Analysis of Lobbying Networks in Legislative Politics." http://web.mit.edu/insong/www/pdf/network.pdf.

Kim, Nam Kyu. 2021. "Previous Military Rule and Democratic Survival." *Journal of Conflict Resolution* 65 (2–3): 534–62. https://doi.org/10.1177/0022002720957064.

Kinda, Tidiane, Patrick Plane, and Marie-Ange Véganzonès-Varoudakis. 2011. "Firm Productivity and Investment Climate in Developing Countries: How Does Middle East and North Africa Manufacturing Perform?" *The Developing Economies* 49 (4): 429–62. https://doi.org/10.1111/j.1746-1049.2011.00146.x.

King, Stephen J. 2003. *Liberalization against Democracy: The Local Politics of Economic Reform in Tunisia.* Bloomington, IN: Indiana University Press.

Kirkpatrick, David. 2012a. "Egyptian Is Counting on Worries of Elites." *The New York Times.* www.nytimes.com/2012/05/28/world/middleeast/ahmed-shafik-counting-on-egyptian-elites-fears.html.

2012b. "Named Egypt's Winner, Islamist Makes History." *The New York Times,* June. www.nytimes.com/2012/06/25/world/middleeast/mohamed-morsi-of-muslim-brotherhood-declared-as-egypts-president.html.

2013. "Army Ousts Egypt's President; Morsi Is Taken into Military Custody." *The New York Times,* July. www.nytimes.com/2013/07/04/world/middleeast/egypt .html.

Kohli, Atul. 2004. *State-Directed Development: Political Power and Industrialization in the Global Periphery.* Cambridge, UK: Cambridge University Press.

Krueger, Anne O. 1974. "The Political Economy of the Rent-Seeking Society." *The American Economic Review* 64 (3): 291–303.

Kubinec, Robert. 2019a. "Patrons or Clients? Measuring and Experimentally Evaluating Political Connections of Firms in Morocco and Jordan." Working Paper.

2019b. "Politically-Connected Firms and the Military-Clientelist Complex in North Africa." Working Paper. Socarchiv.

2022. "Getting Off the Gold Standard: A Holistic Approach to Causal Inference with Entropic Causal Graphs." https://doi.org/10.31235/osf.io/a492b.

Kuran, Timur. 1991. "The East European Revolution of 1989: Is It Surprising That We Were Surprised?" *The American Economic Review* 81 (2): 121–25.

1995. "The Inevitability of Future Revolutionary Surprises." *American Journal of Sociology* 100 (6): 1528–51.

Kuran, Timur, and Cass R Sunstein. 1999. "Availability Cascades and Risk Regulation." *Stanford Law Review,* 683–768.

Larreguy, Horacio, John Marshall, and Pablo Querubin. 2016. "Parties, Brokers, and Voter Mobilization: How Turnout Buying Depends Upon the Party's Capacity to Monitor Brokers." *American Political Science Review* 110 (1): 160–79.

Leeper, Thomas J. 2021. "An Introduction to 'Margins'." CRAN. https://cran.r-project .org/web/packages/margins/vignettes/Introduction.html.

References

Lefèvre, Raphaël. 2015. "Tunisia: A Fragile Political Transition." *The Journal of North African Studies* 20 (2): 307–11.

2017. "The Algerian Economy from 'Oil Curse' to 'Diversification'?" *The Journal of North African Studies* 22 (2): 177–81. https://doi.org/10.1080/13629387.2017.1281561.

Lesch, Ann M. 2012. "Arab Spring in Egypt." In *Arab Spring in Egypt: Revolution and Beyond*, edited by Bahgat Korany and Rabab el-Mahdi, 17–42. Cairo, Egypt: American University in Cairo Press.

Levi, Margaret. 1989. *Of Rule and Revenue*. Berkely, CA: University of California Press.

Levitsky, Steven, and Mara Victoria Murillo. 2009. "Variation in Institutional Strength." *Annual Review of Political Science* 12: 115–33.

Levitsky, Steven, and Lucan A. Way. 2010. *Competitive Authoritarianism: Hybrid Regimes After the Cold War*. Cambridge, UK: Cambridge University Press.

Li, Hongbin, Lingsheng Meng, Qian Wang, and Li-An Zhou. 2008. "Political Connections, Financing and Firm Performance: Evidence from Chinese Private Firms." *Journal of Development Economics* 87 (2): 283–99.

Li, Hongbin, Lingsheng Meng, and Juhsen Zhang. 2007. "Why Do Entrepreneurs Enter Politics? Evidence from China." *Economic Inquiry* 44 (3): 559–78.

Lindberg, Staffan I., Michael Coppedge, John Gerring, and Jan Teorell. 2014. "V-Dem: A New Way to Measure Democracy." *Journal of Democracy* 25 (3): 159–69.

Lindblom, Charles Edward. 1977. *Politics and Markets: The World's Political-Economic Systems*. New York, NY: Basic Books.

Linn, Emily Crane. 2016. "The Army and Its President." Democracy Lab. *Foreign Policy Magazine*, January. http://foreignpolicy.com/2016/01/28/the-army-and-its-president-egypt-sisi/.

Lipset, Seymour M. 1959. "Some Social Requisites of Democracy: Economic Development and Political Legitimacy." *The American Political Science Review* 53 (1): 69–105.

Lohmann, Susanne. 1994. "The Dynamics of Informational Cascades." *World Politics* 47 (1): 42–101.

Loukil, Bassem. 2017. "Non à La Loi de l'impunité." Facebook. April 27, 2017. www.facebook.com/notes/bassem-loukil/non-%C3%Ao-la-loi-de-limpunit%C3%A9/420197818342133/.

Loxton, James. 2015. "Authoritarian Successor Parties." *Journal of Democracy* 26 (3): 157–70.

Lust, Ellen, and David Waldner. 2017. "Authoritarian Legacies and Post-Authoritarian Challenges in the Middle East and North Africa." In *Parties, Movements and Democracy in the Developing World*, edited by Nancy Bermeo and Deborah J. Yashar. Cambridge, UK: Cambridge University Press.

Lust-Okar, Ellen. 2005. *Structuring Conflict in the Arab World: Incumbents, Opponents, and Institutions*. Cambridge, UK: Cambridge University Press.

2006. "Elections under Authoritarianism: Preliminary Lessons from Jordan." *Democratization* 13 (3): 456–71. https://doi.org/10.1080/13510340600579359.

Lynch, Marc. 2013. *The Arab Uprising: The Unfinished Revolutions of the New Middle East*. New York, NY: PublicAffairs Store.

2016. "Tunisia May Be Lost in Transition." *Carnegie Middle East Center*. http://carnegie-mec.org/diwan/64510.

Ma, Debin, and Jared Rubin. 2018. "The Paradox of Power: Principal-Agent Problems and Fiscal Capacity in Absolutist Regimes." *LSE Latin America and Caribbean Centre Working Paper*. www.lse.ac.uk/lacc/publications/PDFs/Ma-Rubin-ParadoxOfPower.pdf.

Magaloni, Beatrice. 2006. *Voting for Autocracy: Hegemonic Party Survival and Its Demise in Mexico*. Cambridge, UK: Cambridge University Press.

Magaloni, Beatriz, and Ruth Kricheli. 2010. "Political Order and One-Party Rule." *Annual Review of Political Science* 13 (1): 123–43. https://doi.org/10.1146/annurev.polisci.031908.220529.

Magnusson, Bruce A. 2001. "Democratization and Domestic Insecurity: Navigating the Transition in Benin." *Comparative Politics* 33 (2): 211–30. https://doi.org/10.2307/422379.

Mahoney, James. 2012. "The Logic of Process Tracing Tests in the Social Sciences." *Sociological Methods & Research* 41 (4): 570–97.

Malesky, Edmund J., and Markus Taussig. 2009. "Where Is Credit Due? Legal Institutions, Connections, and the Efficiency of Bank Lending in Vietnam." *The Journal of Law, Economics and Organization* 25 (2): 535–78.

Malik, Adeel, Izak Atiyas, and Ishac Diwan. 2020. "Introduction." In *Crony Capitalism in the Middle East: Business and Politics from Liberalization to the Arab Spring*. Oxford, UK: Oxford University Press.

Malki, Fatim-Zohra El. 2017. "Tunisia's Partisan Path to Transitional Justice." Report. Carnegie Endowment for International Peace. http://carnegieendowment.org/sada/68206.

Mani, Kristina. 2011. "Military Entrepreneurs: Patterns in Latin America." *Latin American Politics and Society* 53 (3): 25–55.

Marcus, Gary, and Ernest Davis. 2014. "Eight (No, Nine!) Problems with Big Data." *The New York Times*, June.

Marinov, Nikolay, and Hein Goemans. 2014. "Coups and Democracy." *British Journal of Political Science* 44 (4): 799–825.

Markus, Stanislav. 2015. *Property, Predation and Protection: Piranha Capitalism in Russia and Ukraine*. Cambridge, UK: Cambridge University Press.

Markus, Stanislav, and Volha Charnysh. 2017. "The Flexible Few: Oligarchs and Wealth Defense in Developing Democracies." *Comparative Political Studies* 50 (12): 1632–65.

Marsh, David, Sadiya Akram, and Holly Birkett. 2015. "The Structural Power of Business: Taking Structure, Agency and Ideas Seriously." *Business and Politics* 17 (3): 577–601. https://doi.org/10.1515/bap-2015-0001.

Marshall, Shana. 2015. "The Egyptian Armed Forces and the Remaking of an Economic Empire." *Carnegie Middle East Center*. https://carnegieendowment.org/files/egyptian_armed_forces.pdf.

Marshall, Shana, and Joshua Stacher. 2012. "Egypt's Generals and Transnational Capital." *Middle East Research and Information Project* 42. www.merip.org/mer/mer262/egypts-generals-transnational-capital.

Martinez-Bravo, Monica, Priya Mukherjee, and Andreas Stegmann. 2017. "The Non-Democratic Roots of Elite Capture: Evidence from Soeharto Mayors in Indonesia." *Econometrica*, 6th series, no. 85: 1991–2010.

Masoud, Tarek. 2014. *Counting Islam: Religion, Class and Elections in Egypt*. New York: Cambridge University Press.

References 189

Mazaheri, Nimah, and Steve L. Monroe. 2018. "No Arab Bourgeoisie, No Democracy? The Entrepreneurial Middle Class and Democratic Attitudes Since the Arab Spring." *Comparative Politics* 50 (4): 523–43. www.jstor.org/stable/26532702.

McCarthy, Rory. 2016. "The Tunisian Uprising, Ennahda and the Revival of an Arab-Islamic Identity." In *Political Identities and Popular Uprisings in the Middle East*, edited by Shabnam J. Holliday and Philip Leech, 157–76. Lanham, MD: Rowman & Littlefield.

McCubbins, Matthew D., Roger G. Noll, and Barry R. Weingast. 1987. "Administrative Procedures as Instruments of Political Control." *Journal of Law, Economics and Organization* 3 (2): 243–77.

Meky, Shounaz. 2015. "Two Years on, Where Is Egypt's Tamarod Movement Today?" Al-Arabiya. June 30, 2015. http://english.alarabiya.net/en/perspective/analysis/2015/06/30/Two-years-on-where-is-Egypt-s-Tamarod-movement-today-.html.

Meng, Anne. 2020. *Constraining Dictatorship: From Personalized Rule to Institutionalized Regimes*. Cambridge, UK: Cambridge University Press. https://doi.org/10.1017/9781108877497.

Méon, Pierre-Guillaume, and Khalid Sekkat. 2005. "Does Corruption Grease or Sand the Wheels of Growth?" *Public Choice* 122 (1): 69–97. https://doi.org/10.1007/s11127-005-3988-0.

Messieh, Nancy, and Ali Mohamed. 2015. "Who Is Participating in Egypt's Parliamentary Elections?" MENASource. Atlantic Council. www.atlanticcouncil.org/blogs/menasource/who-is-participating-in-egypt-s-parliamentary-elections.

Migdal, Joel S. 1988. *Strong Societies and Weak States: State-Society Relations and State Capabilities in the Third World*. Princeton: Princeton University Press.

Monroe, Steve L. 2019. "Varieties of Protectionism: Ethnic Politics and Business Politics in Jordan." In *Crony Capitalism in the Middle East*, edited by Ishac Diwan, Adeel Malik, and Izak Atiyas. Oxford, UK: Oxford University Press.

Moore, Barrington. 1966. *Social Origins of Dictatorship and Democracy: Lord and Peasant in the Making of the Modern World*. Beacon Press: Boston.

Moore, Clement Henry. 1965. *Tunisia Since Independence*. Oakland, CA: University of California Press.

Moore, Pete W. 2009. *Doing Business in the Middle East: Politics and Economic Crisis in Jordan and Kuwait*. Cambridge, UK: Cambridge University Press.

Morgan, Stephen L., and Christopher Winship. 2007. *Counterfactuals and Causal Inference: Methods and Principles for Social Research*. New York: Cambridge University Press.

Morsy, Ahmed. 2014. "The Military Crowds Out Civilian Business in Egypt." Carnegie Endowment for International Peace. http://carnegieendowment.org/2014/06/24/military-crowds-out-civilian-business-in-egypt-pub-55996.

Mossallam, Alia. 2013. "'These Are Liberated Territories': Everyday Resistance in Egypt." In *Democratic Transition in the Middle East*, edited by Larbi Sadiki, Heiko Wimmen, and Layla al-Zubaidi. New York: Routledge.

Moyo, Gorden. 2016. "The Curse of Military Commercialism in State Enterprises and Parastatals in Zimbabwe." *Journal of Southern African Studies* 42 (2): 351–64.

Murphy, Emma C. 1999. *Political and Economic Change in Tunisia: From Bourguiba to Ben Ali*. New York: St. Martin's Press.

2006. "The Tunisian Mise à Nouveau Programme and the Political Economy of Reform." *New Political Economy* 11 (4): 519–40.

Myoe, Maung Aung. 2014. "The Soldier and the State: The Tatmadaw and Political Liberalization in Myanmar Since 2011." *South East Asia Research* 22 (2): 233–49. www.jstor.org/stable/43818522.

North, Douglass C. 1990. *Institutions, Institutional Change and Economic Performance*. New York: Cambridge University Press.

North, Douglass C., John Joseph Wallis, and Barry R. Weingast. 2009. *Violence and Social Orders: A Conceptual Framework for Interpreting Recorded Human History*. Cambridge, UK: Cambridge University Press.

Noueihed, Lin, and Alex Warren. 2013. *The Battle for the Arab Spring: Revolution, Counter-Revolution and the Making of a New Era*. New Haven, CT: Yale University Press.

Nugent, Elizabeth. 2020. *After Repression*. Princeton, NJ: Princeton University Press. https://press.princeton.edu/books/hardcover/9780691203065/after-repression.

O'Donnell, Guillermo, and Philippe C. Schmitter. 1986. *Transitions from Authoritarian Rule: Tentative Conclusions about Uncertain Democracies*. Baltimore: Johns Hopkins University Press.

Oliva, Maria-Angels. 2000. "Estimation of Trade Protection in Middle East and North African Countries." IMF Working Paper. International Monetary Fund. www.imf.org/en/Publications/WP/Issues/2016/12/30/Estimation-of-Trade-Protection-in-Middle-East-and-North-African-Countries-3464.

Olken, Benjamin. 2007. "Monitoring Corruption: Evidence from a Field Experiment in Indonesia." *Journal of Political Economy* 115 (2): 200–249.

Olson, Mancur. 1993. "Dictatorship, Democracy, and Development." *The American Political Science Review* 87 (3): 567–76.

Park, David K., Andrew Gelman, and Joseph Bafumi. 2004. "Bayesian Multilevel Estimation with Poststratification: State-Level Estimates from National Polls." *Political Analysis* 12: 375–85.

Pearl, Judea. 2000. *Causality: Models, Reasoning, and Inference*. Cambridge, UK: Cambridge University Press.

Pearlman, Wendy. 2013. "Emotions and the Microfoundations of the Arab Uprisings." *Perspectives on Politics* 11 (02): 387–409.

Pepinsky, Thomas. 2009. *Economic Crises and the Breakdown of Authoritarian Regimes: Indonesia and Malaysia in Comparative Perspective*. New York: Cambridge University Press.

2014. "The Institutional Turn in Comparative Authoritarianism." *The British Journal of Political Science* 44 (3): 631–53.

Pepinsky, Thomas B., Jan H. Pierskalla, and Audrey Sacks. 2017. "Bureaucracy and Service Delivery." *Annual Reviews of Political Science* 20: 249–68.

Pond, Amy, and Christina Zafeiridou. 2020. "The Political Importance of Financial Performance." *American Journal of Political Science* 64 (1): 152–68. https://doi.org/10.1111/ajps.12480.

Przeworski, Adam. 2009a. "Conquered or Granted? A History of Suffrage Extensions." *British Journal of Political Science* 39: 291–321.

2009b. "Is the Science of Comparative Politics Possible?" In *The Oxford Handbook of Comparative Politics*, edited by Carles Boix and Susan C. Stokes, 147–71. Oxford, UK: Oxford University Press.

Radcliffe, Damian, and Hadil Abuhmaid. 2020. "Social Media in the Middle East: 2019 in Review." Rochester, NY. https://doi.org/10.2139/ssrn.3517916.

References

Rashidi, Yasmine El. 2013. "Cairo, City in Waiting." In *Diaries of an Unfinished Revolution: Voices from Tunis to Damascus*, edited by Layla al-Zubaidi, Matthew Cassel, and Nemonie Craven Roderick, 48–65. New York: Penguin Books.

Reuter, Ora, and Jennifer Gandhi. 2010. "Economic Performance and Elite Defection from Hegemonic Parties." *British Journal of Political Science*, no. 41: 83–110.

Rijkers, Bob, Caroline Freund, and Antonio Nucifora. 2014. "All in the Family: State Capture in Tunisia." Policy Research Working Paper 6810. The World Bank. https://openknowledge.worldbank.org/bitstream/handle/10986/17726/WPS6810.pdf?sequence=1&isAllowed=y.

Rijkers, Bob, Leila Baghdadi, and Gael Raballand. 2015. "Political Connections and Tariff Evasion Evidence from Tunisia." *World Bank Economic Review* 31 (2): 459–82.

Riker, William. 1980. "Implications from the Disequilibrium of Majority Rule for the Study of Institutions." *The American Political Science Review* 74 (2): 432–46.

Roberts, Margaret E., Brandon M. Stewart, Dustin Tingley, Christopher Lucas, Jetson Leder-Luis, Shana Kushner Gadarian, Bethany Albertson, and David G. Rand. 2014. "Structural Topic Models for Open-Ended Survey Responses." *American Journal of Political Science* 58 (4): 1064–82.

Rosenzweig, Leah, Parrish Bergquist, Katherine Hoffmann Pham, Francesco Rampazzo, and Matto Mildenberger. 2020. "Survey Sampling in the Global South Using Facebook Advertisements," October. https://doi.org/10.31235/osf.io/dka8f.

Rueschemeyer, Dietrich, Evelyne Huber Stephens, and John D. Stephens. 1992. *Capitalist Development and Democracy*. Cambridge: Cambridge University Press.

Ryan, Curtis R. 2011. "Political Opposition and Reform Coalitions in Jordan." *British Journal of Middle Eastern Studies* 38 (3): 367–90. https://doi.org/10.1080/13530194.2011.621699.

Ryan, Yasmine. 2015. "Tunisia's Ruling Party Implodes as President Beji Caid Essebsi Stands Accused of Trying to Build a Political Dynasty." *The Independent*. www.independent.co.uk/news/world/africa/tunisia-s-ruling-party-implodes-as-president-beji-caid-essebsi-stands-accused-of-trying-to-build-a-a6718626.html.

Sallam, Hesham. 2014. "Egypt: Transition in the Midst of Revolution." In *Elections and Democratization: The Tenacious Search for Freedom, Justice and Dignity*, 35–66. New York: Palgrave Macmillan.

Sances, Michael W. 2021. "Missing the Target? Using Surveys to Validate Social Media Ad Targeting." *Political Science Research and Methods* 9 (1): 215–22. https://doi.org/10.1017/psrm.2018.68.

Sayan, Serdar. 2009. *Economic Performance in the Middle East and North Africa: Institutions, Corruption and Reform*. Abingdon, UK: Routledge.

Sayigh, Yezid. 2019. "Owners of the Republic: An Anatomy of Egypt's Military Economy." Carnegie Middle East Center. https://carnegie-mec.org/2019/11/18/owners-of-republic-anatomy-of-egypt-s-military-economy-pub-80325.

Scheve, Kenneth, and David Stasavage. 2017. "Wealth Inequality and Democracy." *Annual Review of Political Science* 20: 451–68.

Schneider, Ben Ross. 2004. *Business Politics and the State in Twentieth-Century Latin America*. Cambridge, UK: Cambridge University Press.

Schumpeter, Joseph. 1976. *Capitalism, Socialism and Democracy*. Abingdon, UK: Routledge.

Sein, Gamal M. 2015. "Egypt under SCAF and the Muslim Brotherhood: The Triangle of Counter-Revolution." *Arab Studies Quarterly* 27 (2): 177–99.

Sfakianakis, John. 2004. "The Whales of the Nile: Networks, Businessmen, and Bureaucrats during the Era of Privatization in Egypt." In *Networks of Privilege in the Middle East: The Politics of Economic Reform Revisited*, edited by Steven Heydemann, 77–100. Camden, UK: Palgrave Macmillan.

Shepsle, Kenneth A. 2008. "Rational Choice Institutionalism." In *The Oxford Handbook of Political Institutions*, edited by Sarah A. Binder, R. A. W. Rhodes, and Bert A. Rockman, 23–38. New York: Oxford University Press.

Shleifer, Andrei, and Robert W. Vishny. 1993. "Corruption." *The Quarterly Journal of Economics* 108 (3): 599–617. https://doi.org/10.2307/2118402.

Sirgany, Sarah El. 2015. "The 24 Year Old Party Leader Who Seeks to Rule Egypt." MENASource. Atlantic Council. www.atlanticcouncil.org/blogs/menasource/the-24-year-old-party-leader-who-seeks-to-rule-egypt.

Skocpol, Theda. 1979. *States and Social Revolutions*. Vol. 29. Cambridge, UK: Cambridge University Press.

Slater, Daniel. 2012. *Ordering Power: Contentious Politics and Authoritarian Leviathans in Southeast Asia*. Cambridge, UK: Cambridge University Press.

Soifer, Hillel David. 2013. "State Power and the Economic Origins of Democracy." *Studies in Comparative International Development* 48 (1): 1–22.

Soliman, Samer. 2011. *The Autumn of Dictatorship: Fiscal Crisis and Political Change in Egypt under Mubarak*. Redwood, CA: Stanford University Press.

Springborg, Robert. 2011. "Economic Involvements of Militaries." *International Journal of Middle East Studies* 43 (3): 397–99. www.jstor.org/stable/23017306.

Stacher, Joshua. 2012. *Adaptable Autocrats: Regime Power in Egypt and Syria*. Redwood, CA: Stanford University Press.

Staniland, Paul, Adnan Naseemullah, and Ahsan Butt. 2020. "Pakistan's Military Elite." *Journal of Strategic Studies* 43 (1): 74–103. https://doi.org/10.1080/01402390.2018.1497487.

Stepan, Alfred. 2012. "Tunisia's Transition and the Twin Tolerations." *Journal of Democracy* 23 (2): 89–103. https://doi.org/10.1353/jod.2012.0034.

Stokes, Susan. 2011. "Political Clientelism." In *The Oxford Handbook of Political Science*. Oxford, UK: Oxford University Press.

Storm, Lise. 2014. *Party Politics and Prospects for Democracy in North Africa*. Boulder: Lynne Rienner Publishers.

Sukhtankar, Sandip. 2012. "Sweetening the Deal? Political Connections and Sugar Mills in India." *American Economic Journal: Applied Economics* 4 (3): 43–63.

Svensson, Jakob. 2005. "Eight Questions about Corruption." *Journal of Economic Perspectives* 19 (3): 19–42.

Svolik, Milan. 2012. *The Politics of Authoritarian Rule*. Cambridge, UK: Cambridge University Press.

Svolik, Milan W. 2015. "Which Democracies Will Last? Coups, Incumbent Takeovers, and the Dynamic of Democratic Consolidation." *British Journal of Political Science* 45 (4), 715–38.

Szakonyi, David. 2018. "Businesspeople in Elected Office: Identifying Private Benefits from Firm-Level Returns." *American Political Science Review* 112 (2): 322–38.

References

193

Tadros, Samuel. 2014. *Reflections on the Revolution in Egypt*. Stanford, CA: Hoover Institution Press.

Tanzi, Vito, and Hamid Davoodi. 1998. "Corruption, Public Investment, and Growth." In *The Welfare State, Public Investment, and Growth*, edited by Hirofumi Shibata and Toshihiro Ihori, 41–60. Tokyo: Springer Japan. https://doi.org/10.1007/978-4-431-67939-4_4.

Tarouty, Safinaz El. 2015. *Businessmen, Clientelism, and Authoritarianism in Egypt*. Camden, UK: Palgrave Macmillan.

"The Mega National Projects ... A Locomotive of Development." 2017. State Information Service of Egypt. www.sis.gov.eg/section/337/4683?lang=.

"The Unfinished Revolution: Bringing Opportunity, Good Jobs and Greater Wealth to All Tunisians." 2014. The World Bank. http://documents.worldbank.org/curated/en/658461468312323813/pdf/861790DPR0P12800Box385314B00PUBLIC0.pdf.

Tilly, Charles. 1992. *Coercion, Capital and European States, AD 990–1992*. Cambridge, MA: Blackwell.

"Timeline: Egypt's Revolution." 2011. Al-Jazeera. February 14, 2011. www.aljazeera.com/news/middleeast/2011/01/201112515334871490.html.

"Tunisia Extends State of Emergency Amid 'Terror Threats'." 2017. *Middle East Monitor*. www.middleeastmonitor.com/20170217-tunisia-extends-state-of-emergency-amid-terror-threats/.

"Tunisia: Amnesty Law Would Set Back Transition." 2016. *Human Rights Watch*. www.hrw.org/news/2016/07/14/tunisia-amnesty-bill-would-set-back-transition.

"Tunisia: Majlis Nawwab Ash-Sha'ab." 2017. *Inter-Parliamentary Union*. www.ipu.org/parline-e/reports/2392_E.htm.

"Tunisie: Lancement Officiel Du Parti de Mohsen Marzouk." 2016. *Huffington Post Maghreb*. www.huffpostmaghreb.com/2016/03/20/mohsen-marzouk_n_9512798.html.

Twyman, Joe. 2008. "Getting It Right: YouGov and Online Survey Research in Britain." *Journal of Elections, Public Opinion and Parties* 18 (4): 343–54. https://doi.org/10.1080/17457280802305169.

Urbano, David, Sebastian Aparicio, and David Audretsch. 2019. "Twenty-Five Years of Research on Institutions, Entrepreneurship, and Economic Growth: What Has Been Learned?" *Small Business Economics* 53 (1): 21–49. https://doi.org/10.1007/s11187-018-0038-0.

Vatikiotis, P. J. 1961. *The Egyptian Army in Politics: Pattern for New Nations?* Bloomington: Indiana University Press.

Volpi, Frédéric. 2014. "Algeria versus the Arab Spring." In *Democratization and Authoritarianism in the Arab World*, edited by Larry Diamond and Marc F. Plattner, 326–37. John Hopkins University Press.

Waldner, David. 1999. *State Building and Late Development*. Ithaca, NY: Cornell University Press.

2007. *Transforming Inferences into Explanations: Lessons from the Study of Mass Extinctions*. New York: Palgrave Macmillan.

2015. "Process Tracing and Qualitative Causal Inference." *Security Studies* 24: 239–50.

Waldner, David, Brenton Peterson, and Jon Shoup. 2017. "Against the Grain of Urban Bias: Elite Conflict and the Logic of Coalition Formation in Colonial and Post-Colonial Africa." *Studies in Comparative and International Development.*

Wang, Wei, David Rothschild, Sharad Goel, and Andrew Gelman. 2014. "Forecasting Elections with Non-Representative Polls." *International Journal of Forecasting* 31 (3): 980–91.

Ware, Lewis. 1986. *Tunisia in the Post-Bourguiba Era: The Role of the Military in a Civil Arab Republic.* Maxwell Air Force Base, AL: Air University Press.

Waterbury, John. 1983. *The Egypt of Nasser and Sadat: The Political Economy of Two Regimes.* Princeton, NJ: Princeton University Press.

1999. "The Long Gestation and Brief Triumph of Import-Substituting Industrialization." *World Development* 27 (2).

Weyland, Kurt. 2012. "The Arab Spring: Why the Surprising Similarities with the Revolutionary Wave of 1848?" *Perspectives on Politics* 10 (4): 917–34.

Woodward, James. 2003. *Making Things Happen: A Theory of Causal Explanation.* Oxford, UK: Oxford University Press.

Yerkes, Sarah, and Marwan Muasher. 2017. "Tunisia's Corruption Contagion: A Transition at Risk." *Carnegie Endowment for International Peace.* http://carnegieendowment.org/2017/10/25/tunisia-s-corruption-contagion-transition-at-risk-pub-73522.

Youssef, Adham. 2017. "Supply Ministry Re-Crafts Subsidies Cut Law Deals after Angry Protests." March 8, 2017. https://dailynewsegypt.com/2017/03/08/617735/.

Zhang, Baobao, Matto Mildenberger, Peter D. Howe, and Jennifer Marlon. 2020. "Quota Sampling Using Facebook Advertisements." *Political Science Research and Methods* 8: 558–64.

Index

Al-Bawsalah, 100, 102
al-Nahda, 3, 86, 96, 100
al-Sisi, Abdel Fattah, 3, 5, 65, 107, 170
Algeria, 110, 155
Ali, Mohamed, 2, 76
Arab Spring, 153, 158, 168, 171
  Egypt, 55, 124, 128
  Tunisia, 83, 124, 128
authoritarian durability, 9, 83, 85, 95, 98, 104,
  107, 141, 158, 169

Badr, Mohamed, 69
Bel Hadj, Ridha, 92
Ben Ali, Zine Abedine, 1, 80, 91, 172
Bouazizi, Mohamed, 57, 83
Bourguiba, Habib, 79, 80, 93
bribery, 16, 24, 26, 28, 61, 90, 116, 124, 128,
  153, 155, 165, 168
broker, 25, 27, 36, 88, 89, 98, 118, 164, 174
business associations, 15
business political engagement, 5, 7, 8, 14, 29,
  37, 40, 68, 88, 90, 94, 95, 97, 111, 118,
  120, 122, 126, 135, 149, 152, 155, 172

campaign finance, 14, 32, 33, 94, 97, 112,
  122, 149, 152, 164
capital flight, 61
causal graphs, 9, 11, 18, 46, 78, 109, 163
civil society, 170, 174
collective action, 6, 7, 31, 33, 68, 76, 85, 95,
  98, 137, 170
conjoint experiment, 111, 119,
  135, 161

corruption, 9, 11, 17, 25, 76, 87, 116, 142,
  170, 171
coup
  Egypt, 66
  proofing, 55
  Tunisia, 80, 83, 95, 106
COVID-19 pandemic, 106
crony capitalism, 2, 15, 86, 110, 158, 161,
  167, 169
  Egypt, 52, 53

Day of Rage, 58
deals
  back room, 17, 33, 35, 37
  front room, 17, 18, 35, 37
debt crisis
  Egypt, 51
  Tunisia, 80
Democratic Constitutional Rally (RCD), 91,
  93, 94
democratic preferences, 30, 62, 75,
  89, 96
democratic transitions, 9, 22, 30, 58, 84, 85,
  95, 99, 102, 107, 159, 169, 171

economic reform, 6, 102, 104, 107
elections, 60, 63, 67, 85, 94, 102, 172
Elloumi, Fawzi, 92, 105
employer vote coercion, 14, 68, 97, 122, 126,
  135, 138, 152, 153
Essebsi, Beji Caid, 93, 96, 99–102
event map, 46, 78
exogeneity, 84

expropriation, 26, 87, 125, 129, 137, 153, 161
Ezz, Ahmed, 2, 61

Facebook, 110, 113
financial industry, 80
food subsidies, 75
foreign firms, 164
Front Populaire, 97

gatekeeper, 5, 8, 10, 18, 20, 28, 36, 37, 62, 67, 95, 98, 123, 130, 137, 159, 163, 168

historical political economy
  Egypt, 49

ideology, 38, 75
import substitution industrialization, 13, 50, 79, 83
inequality, 53
infitahiyeen, 53
institutions
  bureaucrats, 12, 16, 23, 24, 60, 61, 86, 88, 89, 121, 124, 155, 165
  developing countries, 13, 14, 19, 170
  economic, 11, 159, 161
interviews, 68
  number, 48, 93
  type, 96
Islamic finance, 140
Islamism, 91, 93, 140, 170

Jarraya, Chafik, 92
Jordan, 19, 110, 150, 155

Karaoui, Nabil, 92, 106
Kefaya movement, 56

land reform
  Egypt, 50
liberalization
  Egypt, 51
  Tunisia, 82
lobbying, 14, 101, 112, 149
Loukil, Bassem, 100

Maduro, Nicolas, 167
Malhalla demonstration, 57
Marxism, 19
Marzouk, Mohsen, 99, 101
mechanisms, 11, 23
Middle East and North Africa, 12
military

Algerian, 159, 160
clientelist complex, 5, 20, 21, 48, 67, 70, 98, 130, 132, 134, 137, 141, 159, 160
  origins, 54, 70, 71, 73, 173
  Egyptian, 4, 5, 130, 132, 137, 163
  Jordanian, 159, 163
  Moroccan, 159
  Tunisian, 82, 130, 137
  Ukrainian, 159
  Venezuelan, 159
minimum winning coalition, 104
Mise à Nouveau, 81
monarchy, 19
Morocco, 110, 150, 155
Morsi, Mohammed, 63
Mostafa, Sahar Talaat, 69
Mubarak, Gamal, 53, 61
Mubarak, Hosni, 2, 53, 56, 58
Muslim Brotherhood, 59, 63, 64, 140, 170

Nasser, Gamal Abd El, 49
National Democratic Party, 56, 61, 63, 70
nationalization
  Egypt, 50
Nazif, Ahmed, 53
Neo-Doustour, 79
Nidaa Tounes, 3, 92, 96, 97, 100

online surveys, 108, 110, 113, 116

political connections, 13, 15, 27, 30, 35, 81, 86, 149
principal agent, 23, 36, 60, 88, 124
property rights, 21
protests, 170, 171
  Algeria, 160
  Egypt, 56, 58
  Tunisia, 83, 92

reconciliation law, Tunisian, 2, 99, 104
redistribution, 32, 87, 170, 171
regime change, 2, 13, 19, 22, 58, 84, 86, 88, 98, 124, 140, 153, 158, 168, 171
rent networks, 163, 174
rent seeking, 10, 11, 13, 15, 17, 89, 108, 120, 158, 172
  broad, 4, 8, 9, 16, 17, 29, 33, 63, 91, 95, 97, 104, 107, 119, 143, 163, 172
  narrow, 4, 8, 9, 16–18, 28, 29, 73, 91, 119, 122, 143, 153, 172
  networks, 18, 20

Index

research design, 39, 46, 78, 108, 114, 118, 130, 135
rural incorporation, 50, 54, 57, 80, 82, 83

Sadat, Anwar El, 51
Saied, Kais, 2, 106, 174
Salah, Ben Ahmed, 79
Sawiris, Naguib, 64, 69, 72
sectoral differences, 129, 131, 159, 161, 164
secularism, 39, 87, 91, 93
Shafik, Ahmed, 63
Sidi Bouzid, 83
state capture, 27
structural adjustment, 65, 74, 83, 102, 174
  Egypt, 52
  Tunisia, 82
Supreme Council of the Armed Forces, 58, 59

Tamarod, 3, 64, 65
taxation

direct, 7
inspections, 125
value-added, 6, 74
Thabet, Safwan, 63
Trabelsi, Imed, 1, 3, 87
transaction costs, 27, 86
transitional justice committee, 87
Transparency International, 2
Tunisia Project, 99
Tunisian Association of Industry, Trade, and Handicrafts (UTICA), 92
Tunisian General Labor Union (UGTT), 79, 92
Turkey, 31

Ukraine, 110, 150, 155, 159, 167
  regime change, 158
union activism, 56, 61

Venezuela, 110, 150, 155, 158, 159, 167

Wikileaks cables, 85

Printed in the United States
by Baker & Taylor Publisher Services